Theodore Spandounes
On the origin of the Ottoman Emperors

Theodore Spandounes (or Spandugnino) belonged to a Byzantine refugee family who had settled in Venice after the Ottoman conquest of Constantinople in 1453. He wrote an account of the origins of the Turkish rulers and of their phenomenal rise to power. It was partly a plea to the Popes and princes of western Christendom to unite against the infidel, and one of the earliest works of its kind.

The first version of the book, written in Italian, appeared in 1509 and was translated into French in 1519. The final version was made in 1538, and a full Italian text was published in 1890, though without any historical commentary. This book presents an English translation of the full text with a preface, commentary and notes; a discussion of the sources which Spandounes might have consulted; and an assessment of the value and interest of this hitherto neglected and undervalued treatise.

Theodore Spandounes

———

On the origin
of the
Ottoman Emperors

———

Translated and edited by

DONALD M. NICOL

Translated from the Italian text of 1538 as edited by
C. N. Sathas, *Documents inédits relatifs à l'histoire de la Grèce
au moyen âge*, IX (Paris, 1890), pp. 133–261: *Theodoro
Spandugnino, Patritio Constantinopolitano, De la origine deli
Imperatori Ottomani, ordini de la corte, forma del guerregiare
loro, religione, rito, et costumi de la natione.*

CAMBRIDGE
UNIVERSITY PRESS

CAMBRIDGE UNIVERSITY PRESS
Cambridge, New York, Melbourne, Madrid, Cape Town, Singapore, São Paulo, Delhi

Cambridge University Press
The Edinburgh Building, Cambridge CB2 8RU, UK

Published in the United States of America by Cambridge University Press, New York

www.cambridge.org
Information on this title: www.cambridge.org/9780521102629

Translated from the Italian text of 1538 as edited by
C. N. Sathas, *Documents inédits relatifs à l'histoire de la Grèce au moyen âge,*
IX (Paris, 1890), pp. 133–261.

First published in English by Cambridge University Press 1997 as
Theodore Spandounes: *On the origin of the Ottoman Emperors*

This digitally printed version 2009

A catalogue record for this publication is available from the British Library

Library of Congress Cataloguing in Publication data

Spandouginos, Theodōros.
[*Discorso di Teodoro Spandugino Cantacusino Gentil'homo
Costantinopolitano Dall'origine de'principi Turchi*. English]
Theodore Spandounes: *On the origins of the Ottoman Emperors* /
translated and edited by Donald M. Nicol.
p.   cm.
'Translated from the Italian text of 1538 as edited by C. N. Sathas,
Documents inédits relatifs à l'histoire de la Grèce au moyen âge,
IX (Paris, 1890), pp. 133–261 . . . '
Includes bibliographical references and index.
ISBN 0 521 58510 4 hardback
1. Turkey – History – 1288–1453. 2. Turkey – History – 1453–1683.
3. Sultans, Turkey. I. Nicol, Donald M.
DR485.S63 1997
956.1'01 – dc21   96–47661 CIP

ISBN 978-0-521-58510-1 hardback
ISBN 978-0-521-10262-9 paperback

Contents

———

v

———

Introduction

In the early sixteenth century in western Europe there was a ready market for works about the origins and history of the Ottoman Turks. Many of them were collected and reprinted with greater or lesser accuracy in the celebrated compendium of Francesco Sansovino entitled *Historia Universale dell' origine, guerre, et imperio de Turchi,* which went through seven editions between 1565 and 1654. The texts which Sansovino collected and reissued were all in the Italian language. Among them is a substantial part of the present treatise, under the title of: *Discorso di Teodoro Spandugino Cantacusino Gentil'homo Costantinopolitano Dall' origine de' principi Turchi,* divided into three parts.[1] It was not the first work of its kind. But it was the first to be presented by an author who was of Byzantine Greek extraction, for all that he wrote in Italian. He knew his market in the west, and it was to western readers that he directed his observations on the emergence of a world power which was neither Greek nor Latin, which had already engulfed all of the Greek-speaking east and which, in his day, seemed capable of conquering the rest of the Christian world in western Europe.

Theodore Spandounes or Spandugnino was proud to boast descent from the imperial Byzantine family of Cantacuzene which had once produced Emperors of Constantinople and Despots or princes in the Peloponnese. He had lived in Constantinople under Ottoman rule. He had relatives in Thessalonica and in eastern Macedonia; and he had family connections in Serbia and Bosnia. He knew the Turks and

---

[1] Francesco Sansovino, *Historia Universale* (Venice, 1654), pp. 107–31, 132–40, 182–207.

their language. He was not unduly bigoted against them. He found some things to admire in Turkish culture. Yet, as a second-generation Greek-speaking refugee from Constantinople and the lost world of Byzantium, he felt bound to alert his Christian friends in the west to the danger that threatened them from the east. From time to time they were jolted into an awareness of the danger. The Popes, the Holy Roman Emperors, the Kings of France and Spain, of Hungary and Poland, the Doges of Venice expressed pious horror and dread of impending doom. Momentous events like the fall of Constantinople in 1453, the Ottoman conquests of Smederevo in 1459, of Negroponte (Euboia) in 1470, of Belgrade in 1521, of Rhodes in 1522, or the battle of Mohacs in 1526, concentrated their minds on the idea of a united counter-attack or a crusade against the infidel warriors of the Muslim faith. Spandounes repeatedly deplores the inability of the western Christian powers to sink their own petty squabbles and collaborate in this nobler and more vital cause.

He was a devout Christian, though not given to the obsessive Orthodoxy which so many of his fellow Byzantine expatriates found comforting after the loss of their material world. He condemns the ignorance of the Orthodox Christians. He was half in love with the humanist culture of Italy. He numbered Popes and prelates of the Roman church among his acquaintances and indeed served as a confidant and adviser to Popes Leo X (1513–21), Clement VII (1523–34) and Paul III (1534–49). In them he saw the champions and promoters of a just war which might drive the Turks at least out of Europe. He was particularly disappointed by Pope Hadrian VI (1522–3) who showed little enthusiasm for this project. Spandounes accuses Hadrian, not without justice, of failing to support the Knights of St John in Rhodes and so contributing to their defeat. There was also some personal ill-will. For it was Hadrian who cut short the pension which his predecessors had been paying to the Spandounes family. It was to the Republic of Venice, however, that Spandounes owed his special allegiance; for it was in Venice that his forebears had been accepted as refugees from Byzantium; and it was in Venice that he most probably was born. His mother, Eudokia, was a Cantacuzene, which entitled him to use that name. She had moved to Italy before the fall of Constantinople in 1453; and about 1460 she had married another Byzantine refugee called Matthew Spandounes or Spandugnino.[2] Matthew is said to have distinguished himself as one of the Greek cavalrymen in the service of Venice known as the *stradioti*. Theodore has nothing to say about his father's military exploits; but for one reason or another Matthew was honoured by the Habsburg Emperor Frederick III in 1454 with the titles of a Count and Knight of the Holy Roman Empire. He was also granted a fief in Greece on the northern side of the Gulf of Corinth not far from Naupaktos or Lepanto. It included the town of Loidoriki and the offshore island of Trizonia or Tridonia. It was *in partibus infidelium* and hardly in the Emperor's gift at the time; but the deed may indicate the fact that this part of Greece was the earlier home of the Spandounes family, for the island of Trizonia was also called Spandonisi and the district had been given the name of Cantacuzinopolis after the heroic deeds done there in 1446 by one Constantine Cantacuzene.[3]

Matthew Spandounes and Eudokia Cantacuzene had at least three children: a daughter who married Michael Trevisan of Venice; a son called Alexander who served the interest of Venice and his own family as a merchant; and Theodore. Matthew was dead by 1511; but long before that date, perhaps when Eudokia died (before 1490), he sent the still young Theodore to be a ward of his great-aunt Mara or

---

[2] Eudokia was a daughter of Theodore, son of George Cantacuzene Palaiologos whom Spandounes names as the grandfather of his mother ('mio avo materno'). Her name as wife of the 'egregius vir Matthaeus Spandoninus' is attested by a Venetian document of June 1475, ed. C. N. Sathas, *Documents inédits relatifs à l'histoire de la Grèce au moyen âge*, IX (Paris, 1890), p. xxxviii; D. M. Nicol, *The Byzantine Family of Kantakouzenos (Cantacuzenus) ca. 1100–1460* (Washington, DC, 1968), no. 102, pp. 230–3.
[3] Document of 1454, Spandounes, ed. Sathas, pp. xl–xli; Nicol, *Byzantine Family*, p. 231.

Introduction

Maria who was living in some style as a wealthy widow in eastern Macedonia. Maria-Mara was a Serbian princess who had been given in marriage to the Ottoman Sultan Murad II. When he died in 1451 she had been granted her freedom as the favoured stepmother of his son and successor, the Sultan Mehmed II, soon to be known as the Conqueror. He was very attached to her as a mother-figure, for all that she remained a Christian; and it was he who in the end settled her on her estate at Ježevo in Macedonia not far from the city of Serres in 1459. She was well provided for and maintained a privileged and protected enclave of Christian faith and charity in what had become a Muslim world. Her stepson allowed her to be joined at Ježevo by her elder sister Catherine who had become a widow in 1456; and the two widowed ladies for many years thereafter held court in Macedonia. Though they did not venture far afield their influence was well known and respected not only in Turkish Constantinople but also in Christian Venice. Ambassadors from Venice and elsewhere in the west would often make a detour on their missions to the Sultan Mehmed to seek the advice and support of the great man's step-mother.[4]

It was in this exalted and privileged atmosphere that Theodore Spandounes spent some of his boyhood; and it was no doubt under the care of his great-aunts Mara and Catherine that he learnt some Turkish and acquired his interest in the history and customs of the Ottoman people and their rulers. In later life he was to put his knowledge to good use. For he had relatives, friends and acquaintances in many quarters of the Christian and Muslim worlds of the late fifteenth century, in Venice, in Constantinople, in the great city of Thessalonica which the Turks had taken from the Venetians in 1430, in Greece and the Aegean islands, and in Serbia. He seems to have visited Constantinople in 1503, after peace, or at least a truce, had been

---

[4] On Maria-Mara: D. M. Nicol, *The Byzantine Lady* (Cambridge, 1994), pp. 110–19.

made between Venice and the Ottoman Porte following three years of warfare. His purpose was partly to try to disentangle the business affairs of his brother Alexander who, like many other Venetian merchants in the Ottoman Empire, had been financially ruined by the terms of the peace treaty, for it had allowed the Turks to retain all the Venetian goods that they had seized during the hostilities. He was too late to make any representations, for he found that his brother had died. Nothing of his fortune was ever restored. It was, as he admits, to recover from the shock of this affair that he undertook the laborious task of composing his account of the rise of the Ottoman Empire.

The patriotic Greek scholar and statesman of the nineteenth century, Constantine Sathas, who produced the first proper text of Spandounes, eagerly seized upon any scraps of evidence in that text to show that its author had been one of the glorious *stradioti*, heroically serving Venice and his Greek fatherland in warfare against the Turks. The evidence is meagre. Theodore's patriotism is not in doubt; but it was a patriotism for the whole Christian world, east and west alike, Roman as well as Greek. It was not directed, as Sathas would have liked to prove, simply to a war of Greek independence from the Turks. To Spandounes the word Greece or Grecia meant Europe, not merely the peninsula of the Hellenes. Taking his cue from the Ottomans, he divided the world into Grecia or Rumelia and Asia or Anatolia, the European and the Asiatic territories. By the time that he was writing Anatolia had been Turkish for many generations. It was probably irredeemable. His concern was to ensure that Greece, or Christian Europe, should not suffer the same fate. There is, however, little in his work to suggest that he ever took up arms in the cause himself. What influence or wealth he enjoyed derived more probably from business, merchandise or property. On the other hand he knew where and in what quarters he could best exert his influence.

His religious persuasion inclined him more to the Roman church than to the Orthodoxy which was his ancestral faith; and it was to the

Popes and princes of that church that he addressed himself. It was to Pope Leo X that he sent the second draft of his treatise in 1519.[5] He emphasised the moral that the victories of the Turks in Europe were signs of God's punishment of the princes of Christendom for their greed and selfishness. Disaster upon disaster could be attributed to the sins of the Christians. This was music to the ears of the leaders of the church. In truth, however, Spandounes was more excited by the new humanism in Renaissance Italy than by Christianity whether Greek or Roman, sympathetic though he was to the plight of Christians condemned to live under Turkish rule. He goes out of his way to record how Sigismondo Malatesta exhumed the mortal remains of the neoplatonist philosopher George Gemistos Plethon from Mistra and brought them to Rimini.[6] He cultivated the friendship of the humanist scholar Janus Lascaris who, like himself, claimed Byzantine ancestry. It was a friendship that cost him dear, for Lascaris had been acting as ambassador of the French King Louis XII in Venice and was obliged to leave when the League of Cambrai was formed in December 1508. Spandounes, as a suspected Francophile, was exiled by the Venetian government. He was later to be found in France; and it was to Louis XII that he presented another early version of his treatise on the Ottomans. He was back in Venice in 1516, actively pressing his claim to possession of the castle of Belgrado in Friuli, which rightly belonged to his father Matthew and which the Venetians had appropriated.[7]

He had interests of his own and perhaps property in the city of Thessalonica, where Venetian merchants had settled again after its conquest by the Turks in 1430. In 1458 the Sultan Mehmed II had granted Theodore's great-aunt Maria-Mara full possession of and rights over the monastery of St Sophia in the city; and one of the most

---

[5] Spandounes, ed. Sathas, p. xviii.
[6] Spandounes, ed. Sathas, p. 160.   [7] Spandounes, ed. Sathas, pp. xxi–ii.

---

prosperous and successful of the business men there was a member of Theodore's own family, Loukas Spandounes.[8] He died in 1481 and advertised his own success and claim to immortal fame by a huge and lavish marble tomb which still, somewhat incongruously, occupies a wall of the great and ancient Byzantine church of St Demetrios in Thessalonica. It seems incongruous because it is a blatantly Italian monument of the Venetian Renaissance style. Yet the inscription on it recording the many virtues of the deceased is carved in elegant classical Greek lettering in the form of iambic metre. It is strange that almost nothing is known about Loukas Spandounes. The record of his talents and achievements before his death in January 1481 is so rhetorically generalised that the elegant inscription reveals no historical facts. He was 'an exile from his country', in other words a refugee from Constantinople; and at the end he is described as 'a scion of Byzantium and of the Hellenes'. Yet it is obvious that the style and sculptural adornment of his monument is neither Byzantine nor Hellene. It is undeniably Venetian in form and fashion; and it was probably produced in the workshop of Pietro Lombardo in Venice. Theodore Spandounes commented on and admired the great tomb of the Doge Pietro Mocenigo in Venice which was created in the same workshop only a few years before that of his own relative Loukas Spandounes.[9] Whoever Loukas may have been, and Theodore makes no mention of him, his tomb remains as testimony to the wealth of the Spandounes family; for the cost of its construction and of shipping the stones from Venice to Thessalonica must have been very considerable.

Theodore writes about his own connections with Thessalonica

---

[8] Nicol, *Byzantine Family*, p. 212. On Loukas Spandounes and his tomb in Thessaloniki: Ch. Bouras, Τὸ ἐπιτύμβιο τοῦ Λουκᾶ Σπανδούνη στὴ βασιλικὴ τοῦ Ἁγίου Δημητρίου Θεσσαλονίκης, Ἐπιστημονικὴ Ἐπετηρὶς τῆς Πολυτεχνικῆς Σχολῆς, VI (Thessaloniki, 1973), pp. 1–63.

[9] Spandounes, ed. Sathas, p. 162. Mocenigo died in 1476.

only to record his memory of having known of the presence there of
Ishak Pasha, who was Ottoman governor of the city from 1482 to
1487. It was he who built the Alatzà mosque which still stands in the
upper town of Thessalonica. The same Ishak Pasha had helped
Bayezid II to become Sultan in Constantinople in 1481.[10] It is strange
that Theodore has nothing to say about his illustrious older contemporary and relative Loukas Spandounes, who was evidently a very
wealthy and influential citizen of Turkish Thessalonica. Several other
members of the Spandounes family are recorded between the fourteenth and sixteenth centuries, all of whom could no doubt trace their
origins back to Byzantine Constantinople. Theodore was not alone in
describing himself as 'Constantinopolitanus'. Some, however, were
living in Venice as early as the 1370s and their names, in the Italian
forms of Spandolino or Spandino appear in Venetian documents of
the time.[11]

Theodore's great-grandfather on his mother's side was one
George Palaiologos Cantacuzene who first distinguished himself in
the service of Constantine Palaiologos, Despot of the Peloponnese,
who was to become the last Byzantine Emperor. George was a scholar
as well as a soldier. He left the Peloponnese about 1437 and, after a
while in Constantinople, he settled in Serbia where his sister Eirene
had married the Serbian Despot George Branković. It was he who
built the great fortress of Smederevo on the Danube; and Theodore
records with pride how his ancestor helped to defend it against the
Hungarians in 1456. He died about four years later.[12] The other sister

---

[10] On Ishak Pasha: Spandounes, ed. Sathas, p. 236. Bouras, Τὸ ἐπιτύμβιο, p. 18; F. Babinger,
Mehmed the Conqueror and his Time (Princeton, NJ, 1978), p. 406; A. E. Vakalopoulos, Ἱστορία
τῆς Θεσσαλονίκης (Thessaloniki, 1983), p. 209.

[11] Lists of the names of recorded members of the Spandounes family (from 1316 to 1581) are
provided in Spandounes, ed. pp. iv–vi; Bouras, Τὸ 'ἐπιτύμβιο, pp. 14–21; *PLP*, I, no. 1568; XI,
nos. 26448, 26483.

[12] Spandounes, ed. Sathas, pp. 151, 158–9. On George Palaiologos Cantacuzene: Nicol, *Byzantine
Family*, no. 67.

of George Palaiologos was Helena, who became the wife of David Komnenos, the last Greek Emperor of Trebizond. Theodore's account of Helena's tragic death in 1463, which is recorded in no other source, must have been an often-told anecdote in his family. He was also naturally well informed about the Serbian family of his other great-aunt Eirene, the wife of George Branković; for the elder of Eirene's two daughters was that Maria-Mara who, as the widow of Sultan Murad II, lived at Ježevo in Macedonia under the protection of her devoted stepson Mehmed II. It was with her that Theodore Spandounes, her great-nephew, stayed as a child. He also knew her sister Catherine, who had married Ulrich II, Count of Cilly, in 1434. Ulrich was assassinated in 1456 and Catherine, after some stormy years, joined her widowed sister in her estate in Macedonia. All that she had managed to save from the wreck of her family fortunes was a castle in Friuli; and in 1488 she made this over to Theodore's father Matthew Spandounes.[13] Theodore therefore knew much of the local history of Friuli and Gorizia through Catherine of Cilly when she was living with her sister Mara in Macedonia. He recalls that Catherine's daughter married Matthew I Corvinus Hunyadi of Hungary, who died in 1490. He also recalls that, when he was a lad and in the care of his great-aunts, he saw a crowd of Christian prisoners-of-war at Gallipoli.[14]

Another branch of the post-Byzantine ruling families in the Balkans with whom Theodore Spandounes could claim a connection was that of the Duchy of St Sava in Bosnia. For Anna, another of the five daughters of Theodore's great-grandfather George, had married Ladislas or Vladislav, Duke of St Sava, about 1454. When the Sultan Mehmed II invaded Bosnia in 1463 Anna fled with her husband to Hungary, where Ladislas seems to have died in 1489. Theodore

---

[13] Spandounes, ed. Sathas, p. 160. On Catherine of Cilly: Nicol, *Byzantine Family*, no. 94.
[14] Spandounes, ed. Sathas, pp. 158, 161.

recalls that the unhappy couple stayed with his family in Venice when they were on their way to Hungary.[15]

Among Theodore's more distant relatives trapped in the ruins of the Byzantine Empire in the Balkans and the east were some who despaired and went over to the enemy by becoming or being made Muslims. One was the younger brother of Ladislas, Duke of St Sava, who had been given as a hostage to Mehmed II. Later in his life he came to be known as Sinan (or Ahmed?) Pasha Herzegoglou, or son of the Duke (Herzeg), and rose to the high office of *Beylerbey* of Anatolia.[16] Another was Mesih (or Mesit) Pasha (Palaiologos), who participated in Mehmed II's abortive attack on Rhodes in 1480. He was evidently a brother of Theodore's grandmother. Later in his life he redeemed his reputation in the military service of the Sultan Bayezid II who made him *Beylerbey* of Rumelia and Grand Vizir. He had a brother called Hass Murad Pasha (Palaiologos) who became a favourite of the Sultan Mehmed II.[17]

There are two independent sources for the family background and ancestry of Theodore Spandounes, although both are more directly concerned with the genealogy of the family of Cantacuzene, to which Theodore's mother belonged. Neither mentions the name of Spandounes; but both provide much information about persons whom Theodore names as his forebears. One is the short dossier of documents relating to the Cantacuzene family drawn up by Hugues Busac early in the sixteenth century. Busac was a member of the French ascendancy in Cyprus. He had married Carola Cantacuzène de Flory, daughter of James II de Flory, Count of Jaffa. Her mother, Zoe Cantacuzene, was one of the five daughters of George Palaiologos Cantacuzene whom Spandounes claimed as his mother's

---

[15] Spandounes, ed. Sathas, pp. 162, 170. On Anna of St Sava: Nicol, *Byzantine Family*, no. 89.
[16] Spandounes, ed. Sathas, pp. 161, 170. [17] Spandounes, ed. Sathas, pp. 164, 176.

grandfather ('avo materno'). Carola died in Rome in 1515. Busac's documents, written in a form of Greek transcribed in Roman characters, were published in 1952.[18]

The other source remains unpublished. It is contained in a manuscript in the Vatican (Codex Vaticanus Latinus 12127, fols. 349ᵛ–53), among some of the minor works of Angelus Massarellus. It is entitled: 'Dell'Imperadori Constantinopolitani'. Massarellus was papal secretary and diarist of the Council of Trent and died in 1566. No doubt he had access to documents in the Vatican which are otherwise unknown; but there is no knowing his reasons for compiling what amounts to a work of genealogy detailing the ramifications of the families of Palaiologos and Cantacuzene in the fourteenth and fifteenth centuries. Some of his information is fanciful; but much of it is extraordinarily accurate and can serve to correct, control or amplify the facts offered by Spandounes and by Busac about members of these families.

The text and its sources

Theodore Spandounes produced several versions of his treatise, revising, rewriting and adding new passages to it over a number of years. All were written in Italian. His first version was dedicated to King Louis XII of France (1498–1515), in whose kingdom he was living in exile from Venice from 1509. This was translated into French by Balarin de Raconis in 1519 and formed the basis of the

---

[18] Hugues Busac, 'Informations sur la très illustre lignée des Cantacuzènes, de Carola Cantacuzène de Flory, fille de l'illustre Conte de Jaffa, et de ses enfants', ed. V. Laurent, in E. Brayer, P. Lemerle and V. Laurent, 'Le Vaticanus Latinus 4789: histoire et alliances des Cantacuzènes au XIVᵉ–XVᵉ siècles', *Revue des études byzantines*, 9 (1952), 64–105.

[19] On Massarellus (Angelo Massarelli): K. M. Setton in *Enciclopedia Italiana*, XXII, p. 513. His genealogical work is recorded in S. Merkle, *Concilii Tridentini Diariorum pars prima: Herculis Severoli Commentarius. Angeli Massarelli Diaria*, I–IV (Freiburg in Breslau, 1901), Prolegomena, p. CI: 'Angelus Massarellus de Sancto Severino agri Piceni scripture diverse visu lectuque digne.' I am deeply indebted to Mr Lindsay L. Brook for lending me photographs of the manuscript.

French edition by C. H. A. Schéfer which was published in 1896 under the title: *Petit traicté de l'origine des Turcq̧ par Théodore Spandouyn Cantacasin* (Paris, 1896). This, with all its deficiencies, was for long the only published version of the text.

A few years later Spandounes prepared a revised version. This he presented to Pope Leo X, with a copy to Giovanni Giberti, who had been the private secretary of Pope Clement VII and papal legate to Venice in 1531 as Bishop of Verona. His final version, made in 1538, he presented to Henry of Valois, Dauphin of France, later to become King Henry II (1547–59). It is on this version that the present translation or paraphrase is based. It is not a literal translation, for the Italian text is frequently repetitive and unnecessarily verbose; and some of the passages of it have been only summarised or condensed. It was first published in printed form at Lucca in 1550 and then, with numerous inaccuracies, at Florence in 1551; and it was this printed form, with all its defects, which was reproduced by Sansovino in 1654.[20] The full text, however, was first published by the Greek scholar and statesman Constantine Sathas in 1890, in the ninth volume of his great collection of documents concerning the history of Greece in the middle ages; and this is the text which I have had before me.[21]

Sathas furnished his edition with a long Preface in French but with no commentary or notes on the bare text. It is partly to fill this gap that I undertook the present study. For although Spandounes was no systematic historian and many of his factual errors can be demon-

---

[20] See Nicol, *Byzantine Family*, pp. xvi–xvii.

[21] C. N. Sathas, Μνημεῖα Ἑλληνικῆς Ἱστορίας. *Documents inédits relatifs à l'histoire de la Grèce au moyen âge*, IX (Paris, 1980), pp. iii–l (Preface), pp. 133–261 (text). The text edited by Sathas is from a manuscript in Paris (Bibliothèque Nationale, fonds italien, 881). A full list of the various manuscripts containing the surviving redactions of Spandounes's treatise is given by Christianne Villain-Gandossi, 'La cronaca italiana di Teodoro Spandugino', *Il Veltro. Rivista della civiltà italiana*, 2–4, *anno* XXIII (Rome, 1979), 151–71 (reprinted in C. Villain-Gandossi, *La Méditerranée aux XIᵉ–XVIᵉ siècles* (Collected Studies: London, 1983), no. III).

strated, much of his material is original, unique and sometimes entertaining. One extract from the final redaction of his treatise he presented to a friend called Constantine Musachi whom he seemed to have met in Rome in 1535 and who compiled a number of notes and annals about his own family and ancestors in Epiros and Albania. The text of Spandounes's contribution to this curious compilation was published in 1873 by Carl Hopf in his *Chroniques gréco-romanes inédites ou peu connues* (Berlin, 1873), pp. 315–35, under the title: *Breve memoria de li discendenti de nostra casa Musachi.*

The sources from which Spandounes derived his information are hard to determine. It is evident that he had access to many oral and perhaps documentary accounts of family history and even to eye-witness records of certain events. The written narrative sources which he may have used, however, are elusive. He makes much of his reliance on what he calls the 'annali di Turchi'. But there is no clear evidence that he had read any of the works of the Turkish annalists and chroniclers that have survived, such as Mehmed Neshri, Tursun Beg or Ibn Kemal. There is no doubt that there were other Turkish writers whose works have not survived; and one may therefore allow Spandounes the benefit of the doubt on this matter.[22] The same does not, however, hold good for the Greek historians of the fifteenth century whose writings should have been available to him. Notable among these is Laonikos Chalkokondyles, often called the last of the Byzantine historians, whose record of events spans the years from 1298 to 1463, with numerous digressions and accounts of affairs between the years 1484 and 1487. Chalkokondyles, like Spandounes, laid his emphasis more on the progress of the Ottoman Turks than on

---

[22] Spandounes, ed. Sathas, pp. 138, 260–1 ('annali di Turchi'). See F. Babinger, *Die Geschichts-schreiber der Osmanen und ihre Werke* (Leipzig, 1927); A. Bombaci, *Storia della letteratura turca* (Milan, 1956).

the demise of the Byzantines and he clearly had access to Turkish sources. Spandounes could have read some of this account; but the only direct reference that he makes to Chalkokondyles is inaccurate or at least misleading.[23]

Of the Greek historians of the fall of Constantinople in 1453 and of the reign of the Sultan Mehmed II, Spandounes makes no mention. This is perhaps not surprising. Of the *History* of Doukas, which covers the years from 1341 to 1462, there are now only two known manuscripts; and the first printed edition appeared in 1649, although there was an Italian translation made about a hundred years earlier. Of the *Histories* of Kritoboulos of Imbros (1451–67) the only known manuscript is in the Seraglio Library in Istanbul and belonged to Mehmed II to whom its author dedicated it. Sathas claimed to detect echoes of the text of Kritoboulos in Spandounes and suggested that he might have read it in Constantinople or in the library of his great-aunt Maria-Mara in Ježevo. But the echoes are hard to find.[24] Of the *Memoirs* of George Sphrantzes (1401–77) there are no known manuscripts earlier than the sixteenth century and no printed edition before 1796. The *Greek Chronicle of the Turkish Sultans* (1373–1512) was probably written by a Greek living in Venice or on Venetian-held territory and could have been useful to Spandounes. But in its present form the Chronicle is no older than 1573.[25] Finally, there is the so-called *Voyages* of Nikandros Noukios, a native of Corfu who settled in Venice where he seems to have worked as a copyist and editor of Greek manuscripts. He was present at the Turkish assault on Corfu in 1537–8 and his account of that event is therefore especially

---

[23] Spandounes, ed. Sathas, p. 261. N. Nicoloudis, Επιδράσεις τῶν "Αποδείξιαν Ιστορίων" του Λαόνικου Χαλκοκονδύλη στο έργον του Θ. Σπαντούνη, *Hellenic Historical Society: 14th Panhellenic Historical Conference* (Thessaloniki, 1994), pp. 135–42.

[24] Spandounes, ed. Sathas, pp. xvii–xviii.

[25] Elizabeth Zachariadou (see *Chron. Turc.*) has shown that the Chronicle was largely based on the 2nd edition of the *Annali* of Sansovino (1573).

valuable. But his work was not complete until 1451 at the earliest and cannot therefore have been available to Spandounes.[26]

Spandounes was not the first to attempt a history of the Ottomans in Italian. Nor was he by any means the last.[27] Sansovino's collection of such treatises, including the earlier version of Spandounes, testifies to their range and popularity; and one need not accept the patronising opinion of Franz Babinger that: 'It is hard to think of anything sillier or more degrading than the anti-Turkish literary exercises that the venal humanists of Italy turned out in those years.'[28] Only the earliest of these productions, however, could have been available to Spandounes; and of these two names stand out: Nicola Sagundino and Giovanni Maria Angiolello. Sagundino, who knew Greek, had been in the service of the Venetian Republic in Negroponte (Euboia) and in Thessalonica; and when that city was captured by the Turks in 1430 he had been taken prisoner and held for thirteen months before getting back to Negroponte. He acted as an interpreter at the Council of Florence in 1438–9. In 1456 he wrote for Aeneas Sylvius Piccolomini a work entitled: *Liber de familia Autumanorum id est Turchorum*, or *De origine et gestis Turcarum liber*, which Babinger hailed as 'the first European attempt at a history of the Ottomans'. It may or may not have been consulted by Spandounes. The first printed edition of it appeared in Vienna in 1551.[29] Angiolello of Vicenza wrote a *Historia turchesca* covering the years 1300 to 1514. It is not included in Sansovino and was not published until 1909. He served the Sultan Mehmed II as a slave from 1470 and then in the Ottoman army under the command of Mehmed's son Mustafa in the campaigns against Uzun Hasan in 1472–3. After Mustafa's defeat and death in 1474 he

---

[26] Fuller details of these and other Greek sources are listed in the Bibliography, section I.A.
[27] See especially A. Pertusi, 'I primi studi in Occidente sull'origine e la potenza dei Turchi', *Studi Veneziani*, 12 (1970), 456–552.
[28] Babinger, *Mehmed*, p. 198.
[29] Babinger, *Mehmed*, p. 111. On Sagundino: A. Pertusi, *La Caduta di Costantinopoli*, 2 vols. (Verona, 1976), II, pp. 126–7; Pertusi, 'I primi studi', 471.

reverted to the Sultan's service and took part in campaigns against Stephen the Great of Moldavia (1476), against Matthew Corvinus in Bosnia (1476–7) and against the Venetians in Albania (1478). After Mehmed's death in 1481 he escaped home to Vicenza. Later, however, he returned to the east, to Persia; and he also wrote an account of the life and deeds of Uzun Hasan. Angiolello's works, perhaps rather more than those of Sagundino, might have been helpful to Spandounes in his researches; but there is no clear indication that he knew of either.[30]

Nor, it seems, was he acquainted with the writings of Paolo Giovio, which are so similar in form to his own. Giovio's commentaries on the origins of the Ottoman Empire, the lives of its Sultans and the nature and strength of their armed forces probably appeared too late for Spandounes to consult them, although one of them was published in Rome before 1531. The only Italian chronicler of his day to whose work Spandounes makes specific reference by name is Marino 'Scodrense', or Marinus Barletius. Marinus wrote an account of the siege by Mehmed II of Skodra (Shkodër) in Albania in 1474, which was printed at Venice in 1504. He also wrote a Life of the celebrated Albanian leader George Kastriotes Skanderbeg, which was first printed at Rome in 1509 or 1510. It is evident that Spandounes knew the first of these publications if not both.[31]

Three other chroniclers of his time whose writings could have been known to Spandounes were Constantine of Ostrovica, Felix Ragusinus and George of Hungary. Constantine Mihailović, born at Ostrovica about 1430, served in an expeditionary force commandeered from George Branković, Despot of Serbia, by the Sultan Mehmed II to assist in the siege of Constantinople in 1453. After that

---

[30] See Bibliography, section I.B, under Angiolello. Pertusi, 'I primi studi', 480–2. An English translation of Angiolello's account of Uzun Hassan is given in *A Narrative of Italian Travels in Persia in the Fifteenth and Sixteenth Centuries*, trans. Charles Grey (London, 1873), pp. 73–138.
[31] See Bibliography, section I.B, under Giovio and Barletius.

he went back to Serbia and was taken prisoner by the Turks when they captured Novo Brdo. He was then forcibly enrolled in the Janissaries, became a Muslim, and fought on various campaigns. In 1463 he was at Zvečaj in Bosnia, where he welcomed the liberation of part of the country by Matthew Corvinus. He reverted to Christianity and finally settled in Poland; and there he composed his *Memoirs* between 1490 and 1498, perhaps originally in Serbian, then translated into Polish and Czech. The historical section of his work (chapters 9 to 37) narrates Ottoman and Serbian history from Osman to the capture of Kilia and Akkerman by Bayezid II in 1484. One note-worthy feature of his account is that nowhere does he make mention of Venice or the Venetians. Spandounes, when emphasising his own reliance on Turkish sources, makes a passing remark about 'German, Polish and other chroniclers'. This might be construed as a reference to Constantine of Ostrovica.[32]

Felix Ragusinus or Felix Petancić was a scholar who worked at the Biblioteca Corvina at Buda from 1487–90. He was then a notary and judge at Dubrovnik (Ragusa) in 1496. Later he was again at Buda at the court of Matthew Corvinus's successor, Vladislas II, who sent him on diplomatic missions to Rhodes (1502), to Venice (1504), to Spain, to France and to the court of Selim I at Constantinople in 1513. In 1512 he wrote for Vladislas II a *Historia turcica* (unedited) and in 1516 a work entitled: *De origine et militari disciplina magni Turce domi forisque habitata libellus*, which was published in 1530.[33]

Finally, there was George of Hungary, or 'Brother George' of Mühlenbach. George was among the thousands captured during the Turkish raids on Transylvania in 1438. He was then still a boy and he remained a prisoner, or a slave, for twenty years. After his escape he

---

[32] See Bibliography, section I.D, under Constantine of Ostrovica. Pertusi, 'I primi studi', 482–4. Spandounes, ed. Sathas, p. 261.
[33] See Bibliography, section I.D, under Felix. Pertusi, 'I primi studi', 489–92.

became a Dominican friar; and in 1479 he wrote his *Tractatus* on the Turks. It was first printed in Rome in 1480 and was remarkably popular. A German translation of it was published at Wittenberg in 1539, with a Preface by Martin Luther; and in its Latin or German editions it was reprinted many times in the sixteenth century. Its popularity stemmed from the fact that it was not so much a call to arms against the Muslims as a handbook for survival for those Christians who had the misfortune to be taken captive by the Turks. He knew them well, however, and, like Spandounes, he was not above commending some of their characteristics and customs.[34]

These were the sort of works which were of interest and concern to westerners in the sixteenth century. Ordinary readers were fascinated by the origins of these orientals who were so defiantly anti-Christian and who had risen to such heights of power and influence over the world. Statesmen were interested to discover all that could be known about the military structure and governmental system of the Ottomans. Theodore Spandounes, like others before and after him, set out to provide information about the historical development of the Ottoman Empire, but also about the form of its government and society and its military and naval strength. The second and shorter part of his treatise aims to record this statistical information. His efforts to transliterate Turkish words and titles produce some strange and occasionally baffling results. His near contemporary Angiolello drew up a similar though smaller list; and I have thought it worthwhile, where applicable, to note his renderings of equivalent Turkish words.

One has to bear in mind that Spandounes was not a trained or even a very well-organised historian. His chronological sequence is often very perverse, as if he had jotted down various events as they

---

[34] See Bibliography, section I.D, under George of Hungary. R. Schwoebel, *The Shadow of the Crescent* (Nieuwkoop, 1967), pp. 208–11; Babinger, *Mehmed the Conqueror*, pp. 16–17, 418–19.

occurred to him without much system. This is especially true of the last sections of his history. At the very end of his work he apologises to his readers for his illiterate style, claiming that he had never intended to be a writer and had never been instructed in the art of historiography. This is evident; but the fact remains that he provides a wealth of information. It is also evident that the several redactions of his work were widely circulated and widely read in the sixteenth century. Apart from the editions printed in Lucca and Florence in 1550 and 1551, a French version was printed at Lyons in 1569, 1590 and 1591; and manuscripts exist of a Spanish version dedicated to Charles V as early as 1520 and of a German version in 1523. Spandounes did his best to prick the conscience of western Christendom; and he deserves to be given a better hearing than he has hitherto received from more sophisticated modern historians who have judged his work only from incomplete or imperfect versions.[35]

---

[35] Franz Babinger, e.g., describes Spandounes as being 'none too trustworthy', 'not always reliable' and 'often given to exaggeration'. These are fair comments; but it seems that Babinger had consulted only the French version of the first draft of the text produced in 1519. Babinger, *Mehmed*, pp. 384, 411, 431, 458. Another modern scholar, however, who likewise knew only the French translation of 1519 and the imperfect Florence edition of 1551, believed that Spandounes produced 'one of the best of the earliest accounts of Ottoman history'. R. B. M. Merriman, *Suleiman the Magnificent, 1520–1566* (Cambridge, Mass., 1944), p. 305; and Robert Schwoebel, in his remarkable book on the Renaissance image of the Turk, rated the treatise of Spandounes still more highly for 'its reliability, objectivity and comprehensiveness', although he too judged it only from the French translation. Schwoebel, *The Shadow of the Crescent*, p. 209. Christianne Villain-Gandossi, a more recent authority on the text of Spandounes and its worth among the first western accounts of the Ottomans, concludes that its author 'rates a special position of honour for the objectivity of his account and his profound knowledge of Turkey'. Villain-Gandossi, 'La cronaca italiana di Teodoro Spandugino', 152.

Genealogical table

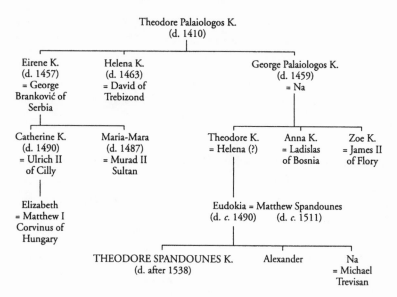

Theodore Palaiologos K.
(d. 1410)

Eirene K.
(d. 1457)
= George
Branković of
Serbia

Helena K.
(d. 1463)
= David of
Trebizond

George Palaiologos K.
(d. 1459)
= Na

Catherine K.
(d. 1490)
= Ulrich II
of Cilly

Maria-Mara
(d. 1487)
= Murad II
Sultan

Theodore K.
= Helena (?)

Anna K.
= Ladislas
of Bosnia

Zoe K.
= James II
of Flory

Elizabeth
= Matthew I
Corvinus of
Hungary

Eudokia = Matthew Spandounes
(d. c. 1490)   (d. c. 1511)

THEODORE SPANDOUNES K.
(d. after 1538)

Alexander

Na
= Michael
Trevisan

K. = Kantakouzenos, Cantacuzene

Abbreviations

CFHB	*Corpus Fontium Historiae Byzantinae*
Chron. brev.	*Chronica Byzantina breviora*
Chron. Turc.	*Chronicle of the Turkish Sultans*
CSHB	*Corpus Scriptorum Historiae Byzantinae*
DR	F. Dölger, *Regesten der Kaiserurkunden des oströmischen Reiches*
EI	*Encyclopaedia of Islam*
Nicol, *LCB*	D. M. Nicol, *The Last Centuries of Byzantium, 1261–1453*
PLP	*Prosopographisches Lexikon der Palaiologenzeit*

Map of Greece and the Aegean by Jacopo Gastaldi, *c.* 1575

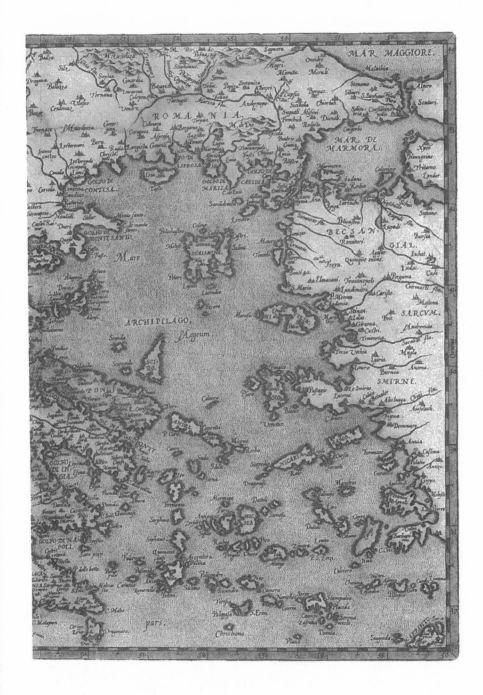

On the origin
of the
Ottoman
Emperors

Dedication

———

To the most serene and invincible prince and lord Henry, by the grace of God Dauphin of France, I beg your humble servant Theodore Spandugnino Cantacusino, patrician of Constantinople.

Most serene prince and my lord: All authors, ancient and modern, Greek as well as Latin, strive to treat of matters which are delightful, novel, beneficial and readable by everyone. This my present work, however, may cause the reader to sigh, weep and lament; for its subject is the ruin and total desolation that has for so long been inflicted on my own illustrious and excellent fatherland. Yet, bearing in mind how greatly the Christian religion would benefit if your Majesty would peruse and digest this treatise, I have gladly taken the trouble to record it. The last time that I went to Constantinople, my purpose was to meet again my dearest brother, Alexander. I spent quite a while in those parts, endeavouring to retrieve some of our property which had been sequestered by the Turkish Emperor Bayezid at the time of his war with the Venetian Senate. It was my misfortune to discover that my brother was dead and that our goods were iniquitously confiscated and lost. After some days of grief and mourning, I thought to alleviate my misery and transcend my obsession with the sad fate which had deprived me of all my worldly goods. I made myself investigate with all studiousness and care everything that I could learn about the origins and the deeds of the house of the Ottomans, to see how such people had ascended to such heights and grandeur. I felt qualified by the fact that I had long experience of the country and that I was able to consult two of the nobility who were on most intimate terms with the Emperor of the Turks; they were

———

3

———

among my closest friends and my relations, men of rare talent and great knowledge of these matters.[1] I was not content merely with a short history of the deeds of the Ottomans, such as one finds in the several annals written by the Turks. I wanted to explore further, giving the matter time and diligence, to present an understanding of the ritual of the court, the dignitaries, ministers and officials of the Turks in times of war and peace, with a general account of their manners, fashions and customs and a commentary on my findings. /

136 It seemed to me that such a study might be of no little value and advantage for those wishing to know more about a principality and empire which is far from humble; for it has indeed become a great power in peace and war, to be numbered among the greatest states and nations, including those of Christendom. I have presented a copy of this study in an abbreviated form to the Pontifex Maximus Leo X in Bologna, and also to the father of your Majesty, the most Christian King Francis ('Francesco').[2]

In the years since I made this dedication, the last two Emperors of the Turks, Selim and his son Suleiman, who now reigns, have substantially enlarged their dominions. They have subdued Cairo, Egypt and Syria ('Sora'), which belonged to the [Mamluk Sultan] 'Soldano'; part of Mesopotamia, which Selim took by force from 'Sophi', and the land of Anadolu ('Annadoula'); and the present Emperor Suleiman has acquired Belgrade and Rhodes and, like Selim, has added not only to his dominions but also to the numbers of his Janissaries and other troops.[3] Wherefore I have now extended my study to include these events; and I have dedicated it to the Most Revd Joan Mattheo di Giberti, secretary of the Pontifex Maximus Clement VII, whom I have been advising in monitoring the progress of the Turks.[4] Since that dedication, however, the reigning Emperor Suleiman has extended his empire still further. The unfortunate Louis ('Lodovico'), King of Hungary, has died; Suleiman has conquered Persia, taken Baghdad ('Bagdet') and other places and has multiplied the ranks of his officials; and, after his recent war with the Signoria of Venice, he is preparing an innumerable force to make war upon the Christians by land and sea. Like a dragon with his gullet wide open, he has no other thought but to devour the Christians.[5]

Yet I note that at the present time the most merciful God has worked through the mediation of His Holiness Pope Paul III who, for all his advanced years, has spared no effort and no energy to do all in his power as a dutiful and zealous pastor of his Christian flock; and he has travelled in person to Nice ('Nizza') and, to his eternal praise and glory, has effected a full accord between the two principal and most exalted princes of Christendom.[6] Thus has he demonstrated that the Apostolic See is the most holy, pious and divine institution that ever was; and we can now envisage and confidently predict a certain victory, the which Our Lord will promote and accomplish when their sacred proposals are put into effect.

In France and wherever else my aforementioned works are to be found, it is my intention to expand them and bring them to their conclusion once these proposals have been successfully achieved. I shall then send the completed treatise, dedicated and entitled to your Majesty – and a small gift to so great a prince; and in that work you will find faithfully recorded all that has occurred up to the present year 1538, fittingly presented to so deserving a prince in the hope that he will excel all other Christian princes in taking up arms, as did your blessed predecessors – and that you will deign to read it, written though it is in my rude and uncultured style, inasmuch as it is a true and faithful exposition of affairs. / And may God grant your Highness many happy years. 137

I have also composed a new 'operetta' which treats of the origins of the two Kings of Persia, 'Sach Ismael and his son Sach Thamas, commonly known as Sophi'.[7] The Persians should be considered as powerful counterweights to and enemies of the Turks. I am taking this work with me to Rome to show it to the Pope [Paul III], the main benefactor of myself and of the Greek nation, which was once so outstanding and successful but is now more miserable and down-trodden than any other. It is my hope that the Pope together with the Christian princes will invite the same 'Sophi' to co-operate in the holy, pious and glorious campaign against the Turks. I shall append a manuscript copy of this to the end of my treatise on Turkish affairs and send it to your Highness; and you will be the first among Christian princes to read it, as you will also be the first to take up the sword against these people; and you will find that the ruler of the Persians at present called 'Sophi' commands an army that conforms in every respect to Christian standards, being quite different from the style and usages of warfare among the Turks. I hope that your Highness will accept the sincere best wishes of one who has your welfare constantly in his mind.

Notes and commentary

1 The friends and relations at the Ottoman court to whom Spandounes was indebted for information included Sinan (Ahmed) Pasha Herzegoglou, the brother of Ladislas, Duke (Herzog) of Bosnia. See below, text pp. 160, 170. The other might be Mesih Pasha (Palaiologos) to whom Spandounes claimed to be related through his grandmother. See below, text pp. 164, 176; and above, Introduction, p. xviii.

2 Leo X, of the family of Medici, Pope from 1513 to 1521; Francis I, King of France from 1515 to 1547.

3 'Sophi' is Ismail I Safavi, Shah of Persia (see below, n. 7). 'Annadoula' here means not Anatolia, which Spandounes regularly calls 'Natalia', but Cilicia or Lesser Armenia, which Selim I captured from Ismail in 1514–15. See below, text p. 181. Angiolello, *Historia turchesca*, ed. I. Ursu (Bucharest, 1909), p. 153, names the country between Kayseri and Syria as 'Anadular'.

4 Giovanni (Matteo) Giberti was Bishop of Verona from 1524 to 1543. He was sent to Venice as legate of Pope Clement VII (1523–34). K. M. Setton, *The Papacy and the Levant*, 4 vols. (Philadelphia, 1976–84), III, pp. 223, 225, 356.

5 Louis II Jagiellon, son of Ladislas, King of Hungary, was killed at the battle of Mohacs in 1526. See below, text pp. 189–90.

6 Pope Paul III (1534–49) engineered a peace settlement between the Emperor Charles V and Francis I of France at Nice in July 1538. See below, text p. 201.

7 Ismail I Safavi was Shah of Persia from 1502 to 1524. His son Tahmasp ('Thamas' or 'Tomas') succeeded him in 1524. See below, text pp. 160 and n. 78, 177 and n. 129. Spandounes's 'operetta' on the Persian Kings is printed in Spandounes, ed. Sathas, pp. 252–61. See below, text part III.

I

Having with the utmost diligence and care searched the historians of the Turks who treat of the origin of the mighty house of the Ottomans, I have found so far as I can see that they are descended from shepherds of Tartary of the race of one called Ogus. It is said that in the reign of the Sultan Aladin [Alaeddin Kayqobad], who was lord of various places and of Konya ('Cogno'), a district lying between Caramania and the land of the Persians, a number of families of Tartars came to live on his territory, among them that of Ottoman. This lord Aladin fought a great war with the Emperor of Constantinople Alexios Komnenos ('Alessio Comgnino'); and one of his warriors was a most valiant Greek knight who vanquished all that fought with him in single combat. Among those whom he defeated and killed was one most courageous man, a great favourite of the said Aladin. He, being much distressed, turned to his knights and said: 'Which of you will take on this Christian man who has already killed so many of my men and among them my favourite?' None could be found willing to do battle with this valiant Greek because of his proven prowess. But one of the descendants of the shepherd race of Ogus came forward, a man of peasant stock and of such lowly estate that none of the Turkish writers give him any other name but Pazzo, the fool. He in great excitement exclaimed: 'My lord, I will take revenge on this Christian for his murder of so many brave men.' The lord [Aladin] turned to his colleagues in arms and said: 'How strange it is that from so many warriors I can find no one but a rustic idiot prepared to go to his death to wreak my vengeance.' The peasant said: 'Let me do it, my lord, for I care little how many men he

---

has already sent to their death.' With some difficulty he obtained permission, presented himself for battle and in single combat worsted and killed the Greek knight; and as a reward for his victory the lord Aladino gave him the place called Ottomanzich, from which his descendants took their family name of Ottomans.

His exploit brought this Turk much fame, so that most of those who were in Tartaria together with many others came to the said Ottomanzich to live. It was his wish that they should share everything in common, which made it easier for him to assemble crowds of people around him and greatly to enlarge his territory. In prophetic anticipation of the future ruin of the Christians / he and his small band of men used the opportunity of a period of truce to burn and plunder a number of the surrounding villages, among them one which was called in Greek 'Dimbos', which in Turkish means 'breaking of faith'; and in truth his later successors gave substance to this presage.

When the lord Aladino heard of this, he sent one of his ministers to bring the man to his presence as a wrongdoer, because he had violated the prevailing truce. The minister could not find him because he had gone pirating again and captured a village called Sar. When he got back with his booty he learnt that the lord Aladino was much displeased about his pillage of Dimbos and had sent for him. So he decided to go with the booty which he had amassed in his house to present it to Aladino and make his voluntary submission. This he did, and the lord absolved him of the crime that he had committed and commanded him not to molest his neighbours any more. Agreement was reached between them and the lord let him keep the male children of the said village of Sar. It was from them that the name of Janissaries originated, which in Turkish means 'the young men of Sar'. There is no further record of the achievements of this man. The common opinion of the Turkish historians is that he was poisoned by the lord Aladino. Of his house no other memorable deed is recorded in the long period before the appearance of Ottomano as the first Emperor of the Turks.

The unconquered conqueror of Constantinople, Mehmed II ('Mahometh Ottomano'), would surely never have had people believe that his family were descended from shepherds who came from Tartary, as the Turkish historians say. He believed that they derived their origins from the Emperor of Constantinople, Komnenos ('Comnigno'). It was said that, during the wars between the Emperor and the lord Aladino, the Emperor was joined by a courageous knight from the west ('Ponente'). He fought so brilliantly in one feat of arms that the Emperor ordered one of his own nephews called Isaac to dismount from his horse and give it to the western lord ('Ponentino'). Isaac took great umbrage at this, went over to the Sultan Aladino, abjured his faith and became a Mahometan. Aladino gave him his daughter in marriage together with some estates and villages, among them that of Ottomanzich. The Sultan Mehmed believed that this Ottomano, of whom and of whose successors we shall speak later, was descended from Isaac. Yet others, Christian writers, have not clarified the matter by their various and diverse accounts of the origin of the Ottoman house. For my part, I incline to give credence to the Turkish historians who, as we have related, say that it was descended from that humble peasant among the shepherds of Tartary of the race of Ogus who slew the Greek knight. But that is enough about the beginnings of the house of the Ottomani.

The strength and power of the Ottomans increased largely as a consequence of the discord and disunity between the Greek and Latin Christians. For more than 700 years there was no disagreement between them in the church universal. But the influence of the Emperors in Constantinople began to decline; and they had always wanted to intervene in the election of the Popes. / The Supreme Pontiffs decreed that their election should be a matter for the clergy alone and quite properly drew up a constitution to that effect. Then

140

11

they altered their rites and as a result neither side could comprehend the other and they took to speaking ill of each other. The Patriarchs of Constantinople refused any more to obey the Popes and encouraged their ignorant people to imitate their disobedience; and this plague became cancerous a few years before the Ottoman house came into being. The Council of Florence in the time of Pope Eugenius IV took place a mere fourteen years before the fall of Constantinople. The Christians had left it too late to defend their own cause against the vast and growing might of the Turks; and Almighty God allowed them to be humiliated because of our sins.

It is well known that the French, the Venetians, the Genoese and the Marquis of Montferrat embarked at Venice for the just and pious purpose of recovering the Holy Land. At Zara they found a son of the Emperor of Constantinople who had recently been deprived of his throne. This Alexios ('Alessio') had gone to the Emperor of Germany, who was his mother's brother, to seek his help. Since no help was forthcoming, he found himself in deep despair in the said city of Zara. When the above-mentioned armada reached there, he made an agreement with their leaders to pay them a certain sum of money if they would reinstate him in his palace. So it came about that the armada sailed on to lay siege to Constantinople, where they stayed for more than a year due to the great dissension that there was in the city.[1] Some were in favour of the Emperor within, others with those outside, while some were neutral; so that in the space of the year while the city was under siege, three Emperors were created inside it. The last of them was called 'Murzufolo' [Alexios V Mourtzouphlos], who held held the throne for only forty days. Under him Constantinople was taken, for those outside gave battle and, acting on intelligence from within, assaulted the city. In the fighting the new Emperor Murzufolo was killed and also the young man for whom they had brought their armada to besiege and capture Constantinople. The city was sacked with great savagery and the victorious army appointed a

12

French Emperor, while the Venetian Senate created the Patriarch and the clergy. The Greek nobility and gentry, not content with this state of affairs, left Constantinople and crossed over to Anatolia ('Natalia'), where they set up an Empire of their own ruled by the house of Lascaris. In the sixty-five years during which Constantinople was in the possession of French and Venetians, there reigned three French Emperors. Likewise, the Greeks in Natalia were governed by three Emperors of the said house of Lascaris, namely Alessio Laskaris, John his son and Alessio the son of John.[2] The last Emperor of that house had four daughters and one son, and he took for his son-in-law one Michael Palaeologo who was a most energetic soldier and a favourite of the army. He was a liberal and magnanimous man. When the Emperor Laskaris died, he usurped the Empire with the support of the soldiers. For the army preferred to have as their ruler an experienced captain rather than an infant boy of five years old; and, to put the matter briefly, [the usurper], who had taken the title of Caesar, was prepared to do violence to secure the throne and had the boy, who was his relative, blinded. / This was the cause of the greatest discord and altercation in all Greece [and a break with all the sensible and laudable tradition that had prevailed in that country as in our part of the world. For they were accustomed to gouge out the eyes of their enemies rather than putting them to death. The said youth was sent into exile by the Emperor; and when he came of man's estate, though blind, he married and had issue and his line endures to the present day. Through the direct male line are descended three most valiant gentlemen whom I know, two of whom distinguished themselves in arms and one in letters. One was called Signor Demetrio Lascari, a captain who died in the service of the Venetian Republic in Dalmatia during the second war with the Turks, in the time of the Sultan Baiazit; the second was the Signor Juan Lascari, who was most erudite and died in Rome in the pontificate of his Holiness Pope Paul III [1534–49] who is at present the Supreme Pontiff; the third is

141

Alessio Lascari who is still a captain and now in the service of His Beatitude of the Holy Church.]³

During his reign the said Michael Paleologo made a truce with the Frenchman in Constantinople; and during that truce he ordered one of his officers called Alexios Strategopoulos ('Giovanni Straticopolo') to go and fight the Bulgars with an army of 25,000 men. Now this officer, when he was about twenty miles from Constantinople, fell in with an old man of Greek race who lived in the city and said to him: 'My lord, God does not grant me the favour of dying under a Greek Emperor. If your lordship so wills, I can direct you and your army into the city, for I know of an aperture in the walls through which a man on foot can easily get in. I use it myself when going back from my fields and finding the gate locked.' So the officer sent some of his most trusted men and they found that what the old Greek had said was true. He therefore planned to make an attempt on Constantinople without consulting his Emperor. In the early evening he gave the signal to his cavalry and advancing with caution he reached the city walls. Some of his men then crept through the aforesaid hole and came to a gate through which the whole army went in. He commanded that most of them should station themselves by the gates so that the enemy would not escape their clutches. When day came the enemy, seeing that they were already defeated and had no means of getting out, took to fighting. Many were killed. Others set fire to some of the finest buildings and churches in the place and they were more successful in getting away because the Greeks ran to put out the flames. Then the French Emperor fled and reached Napoli in safety. And a courier was sent to take the news to Natalia, where there was great rejoicing and feasting as is to be expected in such cases.⁴ There was, however, a Greek gentleman of mature years and judgment, rich in experience, called Theodore 'Tornichio', who listened to the news of the recovery of Constantinople from some who came to visit him on his sick bed. He burst into tears saying: 'Alas, this is the ruin of Christendom.'

They replied: 'What are you saying, sir? We have won back our homeland and you are weeping!' He said: 'I weep not without cause. / You see how much controversy there is in the Empire of the Greeks now that it has passed into the hands of Michael Paleologo. He, to strengthen his position now that Constantinople is restored, will transfer his capital there; and all the brave men who have for so many years been accustomed to bear arms and have fought and still fight against the Turks and have made the most of the discord among the Christians [will leave]; and our young noblemen will flock to the city with the Emperor and abandon their warfare against the Turks. They will discover the delights of the city and forget their military prowess; and the Turks who command these neighbouring heights and almost control the plains, when they see that the Emperor and his army have gone, will overrun everything and in time will cross over into Europe and pillage Constantinople and all our Empire.' Having uttered these words, he turned over in his bed and expired.[5]

Now in the time of Michael Paleologo, the first of his house to reign as Emperor in Constantinople, there were four lords of the Turks in the vicinity. One was called 'Michauli', the second was Turachan, the third Evrenes, the fourth Ottomano. Each was no more than a petty chieftain. They knew that the Emperor Michael had left their frontier. But as they were, they were too divided and scattered to attack their enemies as was their wont; rather they thought of defending themselves. They saw that the power of the Christians was too great for them to resist it singly, and they soon decided to look not to their own self-interest but to their common good; and they did something generous and memorable – something which the Christian princes of the time could not bring themselves to do for the promotion of their faith. One day they assembled together to elect one lord from among them. Each of those present had his own say but all were agreed that none could match Ottomano in authority, courage and strength of character. They found it hard to decide, for by common consent they would rather have had a brother than a sovereign lord. But they elected Ottomano as such; and he became the first Emperor of the Turks and ruled over them for forty-nine years.[6] Once in power he showed a valour and genius greater even than expected. He wanted to assess all their military strength and he held an inspection of their combined infantry and cavalry and staged a splendid assembly, exhorting them to stir themselves for the propagation of their faith and to defy subjection to the Christians. He directed their minds to great objectives. He was a just and worthy prince who did much good and enacted salutary laws which are still observed in Turchia. He was merciful, liberal, yet warlike, to such an extent that his fame will last as long as the Turks exist. Whence they are wont to say at the election of one of their Emperors: 'God grant that his excellence compares with that of Ottomano.'

This Ottomano [Osman] made war on all the lands in Natalia which were subject to Constantinople, because once Michael had left Natalia to make his capital in Constantinople Osman found the going easy. He made himself lord of the district without any difficulty, for Michael Paleologo had enemies among the Greeks who detested him for having usurped the throne. He was also anxious about the French Emperor 'Balduino' and especially about his enemies in Italy, the Venetians and the King of Naples, to whom the French Emperor had fled to seek help, since they were related. / Michael Paleologo went to France to the Council at Lyons ('Leone') to try to make the rite of the Greek church accord with that of Latins.[7] This was the prime cause of dissension between the Christians; and he believed that by agreeing on this issue they would be able to settle their other differences. During the period while he was away from his Empire, it was easy for Osman ('Ottomano') to pursue his aims and he mastered much of the territory of the Empire of the Greeks in Natalia. Michael came back from France with nothing achieved and then died. He was succeeded as Emperor by his son Andronikos [II] ('Andronico') who

143

was not so dedicated as his father to warfare and military matters.[8] He was a most just and 'catholic' prince, but more committed to rhetoric and the state of the church than to the armed defence of his dominions against the infidel. So not only did the infidel prosper at his expense, but so also did his Christian rivals. The French, the Navarrese, the King of Naples and the Venetians formed a league against him. It included the Peloponnese, whose conquerors made it over to the church, as well as the island of Corfu, which the King of Naples held for himself, and the islands of Cephalonia, Ithaca, Zakynthos ('Jacinto') and Santa Maura, which their conquerors sold to a Neapolitan of the house of Tocco. And being at odds with the prince of Gothia and with the Bulgars, as well as with King 'Stephano' of Serbia, whose son George was subsequently to be made Despot, Andronikos was more involved in fighting the Christians than in the defence of his realm against the Turks.[9] So that Osman was encouraged to lay siege to the fine city of Bursa ('Bursia'), to fight a land battle and capture it. When he died he was succeeded by his son Orhan ('Orchano'), aged twenty-four, who later built a tomb for Osman in the said city of Bursa, which can be seen in all its glory to this day.[10]

Orhan, who succeeded Osman, was truly a most energetic and excellent ruler who achieved great things in his day. Some Christian writers have it that he caused his three brothers to be put to death so that he would have no rivals. The Turkish historians, however, make no mention of this. They say that it was his son Murad ('Amurat') who was the first of this line to stain his hands with the blood of his own brothers to safeguard his authority. Fortune was kind to Orhan, for he reigned for fifty-six years.[11] During that time it seems that the son of 'Andronico Paleologo' conspired against his father and the plot was revealed. A son of Orhan did the same. Both were apprehended by their fathers. 'Andronico' had his son Constantine blinded, for it was the custom of the Emperors of Constantinople not to put culprits to death but instead to deprive them of the light. Nobles were blinded; the lower orders had their eyes gouged out. Orhan caused the eyes of his son Mustafa to be removed.[12] For some time he was at peace with the Emperors of Constantinople who followed one another; and for our sins God allowed it to happen that these Emperors, while they were at peace with Orhan, continually took up arms with their neighbouring Christian princes, which resulted in a pitiful state of affairs and the total ruin of Greece and all of Christendom. /

144 The Empire passed to one 'Emanuel', son of 'Andronico', who had become elderly. 'Andronico' had a grandson called John [V] ('Gioanne Paleologo'), a man of great talent and military prowess.[13] He ('Emanuel' [?]), against the wishes of his father, wanted to take a wife; and when John heard of this he made an agreement with his own father-in-law, whose name was John Cantacuzene ('Joanne Cantacusino'), a great man of action, of noble blood and endowed with every virtue. These two together made war against the above 'Emanuel Paleologo' and called on Orhan for support. This he gladly provided, sending his son Murad ('Amurat') with 12,000 Turks; for in those days the rulers of the Turks used to appoint their own sons to the office now known as the Pasha ('Bassa'). These Turks were the first to cross over into Greece; and they drove the said 'Emanuel' out of his dominion. But about the division of the spoils there was the greatest disagreement between John Cantacuzene and John Palaiologos. It lasted for twenty years. Some took the side of the father-in-law, others of the son-in-law. The grandees favoured John Cantacuzene; and he evicted his son-in-law John Palaiologos. Cantacuzene then reigned as the Emperor John [VI] in Constantinople for twenty years, during which he made war against his son-in-law, which played into the hands of Orhan.[14] To strengthen his position and authority, Cantacuzene married his son Matthew to a daughter of the King of Serbia, who brought him the whole of Albania as her dowry; and [then] to secure his hold over the Albanians, he

rounded up all their leading men. Some of them he settled near Constantinople, divided among the towns and castles; a large number of them he settled in the Morea or Peloponnese which he had conquered, having driven out the Pope's governors.[15] This deportation of the ruling class of Albania by Cantacuzene was to contribute to the ruin of that country and of all Christendom. Cantacuzene designated his son Matthew as Emperor and had him crowned; though he died before long.[16] John Palaiologos, however, who was in exile at 'Eraclea', sought by every way and means to recover the Empire and expel his father-in-law Cantacuzene. We learn from the annals of the Greeks that these two fought each other with armies of 50,000 horsemen on one side and 60,000 on the other; and the casualties on either side were incalculable.

At the same time there was a most savage conflict between the rulers of Venice and Genoa. The Venetians took the side of Cantacuzene, the Genoese of Paleologo. Things went badly for the Venetians; and [Paleologo] made a determined attack by sea, with the help of one Gattilusio ('Cathalusio') to whom, after he had attained power, he gave the island of Mytilene ('Metellino') and some other places.[17] The Emperor Cantacuzene was stronger by land and had a fine army through having on his side all the nobles and grandees of Greece as well as the alliance of the King of Serbia. John Paleologo, to further his cause, gave one of his illegitimate sisters-in-law as wife to Orhan, ruler of the Turks, and then paid him, decrepit though he was, to bring over 60,000 Turkish troops to end the war and restore the house of Paleologo. The Genoese were engaged to ferry them over from Anatolia to Greece for 60,000 ducats in 'AD 1383', according to the Turkish historians; / though some Christian writers 145 give a different date. The first place that the Turks occupied in Europe was Gallipoli, which John Paleologo assigned to them to make the crossing and which was near to 'Eraclea'. Orhan, having crossed over, went on to lay siege to Constantinople; and John

19

Cantacuzene was forced to abdicate and became a monk with the name of Joasaph.[18]

John Paleologo then entered the palace and paid Orhan all that he had promised. Orhan then wanted to go back to Asia, or Natalia. But when he was about four days' distance from Constantinople, not far from Gallipoli, the day before he was due to embark, there was an earthquake so severe that almost all the walls and buildings in the neighbourhood collapsed; and the soothsayers persuaded Orhan that he should not leave Europe. Orhan replied: 'Since God has opened the way we shall stay here.'

As soon as Cantacuzene had left Constantinople, King Stephen of Serbia made war on John Paleologo to recover Albania. Orhan heard of this and promptly made an agreement with the Serbian King and with the Vlachs ('Valacchi') against Paleologo. One George 'Glava', then lord of Didymoteichon ('Dimotico'), went to pledge loyalty to Paleologo at Constantinople; and [while he was away] some rebels, corrupted by bribes, handed the castle over to Orhan, who marched in and pillaged the country. The news prompted John Uglješa ('Unglesi'), lord of Serres, to assemble a huge [army of] Christians to blockade Orhan in Didymoteichon. He had very few troops; but he broke out by night and made his way towards Bulgaria. The Bulgars failed to realise what was afoot since there were so few Turks; and in any case the Bulgars were sodden in drunken sleep. Their army was totally defeated and scattered; and this was the first victory which God, for our sins, granted to the infidel on the soil of Greece.[19]

Orhan, having conquered some other places, died three years after he had crossed to Greece and he was buried in a village near Gallipoli called 'Plagin'. His tomb still stands there and is the centre of ceremonies and festivals [here described].[20]

His place was taken by Murad ('Amurath'), the first of this name and the third Emperor of the Turks. He was called Gazi Hüdavendigar ('Caxi Condichiaro'). As soon as he had assumed power, he turned on his two brothers. One he had strangled; the other fled and escaped to Karaman ('Caramano'), some of whose men, bribed by Murad, poisoned him. The Turkish historians say that the prince Murad, called Gazi Hüdavendigar, was the most powerful of the line of the Ottomans for there was no one to be found who could defeat him in battle. He was always the first to strike and for this he was known as Gazi, which in Turkish means valiant and spirited. He was also the first of the Ottomans to be entitled Hüdavendigar ('Condichiaro'), / a name still preserved in Turkey, meaning Emperor in our language.[21]   146 He was the first of the Ottoman rulers to bring experts to Gallipoli to build galleys and other ships for warfare by sea. He was often at war with the Emperor of Constantinople because, at the beginning of his reign, he fought in alliance with the King of Serbia against him over the matter of Albania. Then he fell out with the Serbian King and joined forces with the Emperor; and he captured more and more places in Serbia and reduced it to a tributary province. Then he allied with the Bulgars, the Wallachians ('Valacchi') and the Goths and with the Emperor of Constantinople against the Kingdom of Hungary; and they attacked Hungary from two sides.

Murad, called Gazi, took with him more than 80,000 Turkish soldiers to invade Hungary; and had it not been for the intervention of divine providence Hungary would have fared badly. Murad came to a place in the forests of Serbia called Kossovo ('Consogno') near Novo Brdo. There twelve knights in the pay of Hungary conspired to murder him; and it happened that a certain Miloš Kobilić ('Miloi Copilovichio') was chosen for the deed. He was a Serbian in the service of Hungary. What he did was brave and memorable and much celebrated. He pretended to defect from Hungary to the camp of the Turks and he asked to speak to Murad, who agreed, having heard that he was a fine man in form and stature and well armed. Entering the pavilion of the Grand Turk, the knight made to kiss his hand but instead struck him with his fist and killed him. He did not get

21

out of the pavilion alive, for he was savagely wounded and struck down.[22]

This Murad was the first to institute the order of Janissaries ('Janizari'). At first they were only 500 in number, though later, in the time of the second Murad ('Amurath'), they were increased to 8,000. They formed the guard of the Emperor of the Turks. The Sultan Selim raised their number to 10,000. It was the above-mentioned 500 who brought down Miloš Kobilić; and from that day to this, if anyone goes to kiss the hand of a lord of Turkey, two of the guards hold his hands. Murad was buried in the place where the deed was done and a monument was raised on the spot where he died. His corpse was interred in Kossovo, though later, in the time of his son Bayezid, it was taken to Adrianople; and there a sepulchre was built and a hospital was endowed for charitable purposes by the Turkish rulers. His son Ildrim Bayezid succeeded him.[23]

Bayezid I was the fourth Emperor of the Turks and no less talented than his predecessors, as witness the fact that he was called Ildrim, which in Turkish means Thunderbolt. First he disposed of his seven brothers by murder. He then observed how greatly divided among themselves were the princes of Christendom, especially the King of Serbia, / the Goths and the Wallachians, who were all at war with the Emperor of Constantinople, Manuel ('Emanuel'), son of the aforesaid John [V]. Bayezid made war on this Manuel, invading and plundering more and more of his territory; and he captured the great city of Adrianople, earlier known as 'Horestiade' because it had been founded by 'Horestias'. This greatly contributed to the fall and ruin of Greece, since all at once the Turks controlled a city so rich in corn and all other good things. He made it his headquarters and pillaged more and more places in Greece, so much so that his bandits seemed to be everywhere.[24] We have already described how the King of Serbia had given Albania to the son of [John] Cantacuzene as dowry, and how the Emperor Cantacuzene had rounded up all the potentates

147

and lords in Albania and appointed governors and landlords who were his servants. When he died, having voluntarily forfeited his sovereignty and become a monk, Albania was wholly denuded of fighting men and was peopled by more petty lords fighting one another than there were towns and castles in it. Ildrim Bayezid, who was always on the watch, invaded Albania and perpetuated unbelievable butchery and destruction. He captured Valona and then turned on Greece and took 'Solana' [Salona], on the left at the entrance to the Gulf of Patras.[25] Then he went on to lay siege to Constantinople.

The city might well have fallen to the Turks had it not been for the foresight of the Emperor Manuel [II]. He sent to the Emperor of the Tartars, the Grand Sachatai, to inform him of the siege and of the bellicose activities of Ildrim Bayezid. He suggested that it would be more honourable if the great city of Constantinople surrendered itself to a most noble Emperor, Sachatai, than fall into the hands of the Ottomans, who were the descendants of mere shepherds. Sachatai responded by putting several thousand warriors in the field to attack and plunder all Natalia, killing men, women and children of the Turks, as though they were not Mahometans of the same faith but most deceitful dogs.[26] Ildrim Bayezid had not anticipated that such a huge army would descend upon him with such wrath. He crossed into Natalia with his own army; and with him was the son of the King of Serbia, Giorgio, who, after his father's death, was named Despot; and they suffered more and more damage from their enemies. Finally, in a pitched battle, Ildrim Bayezid was taken prisoner and the rest of the Turkish army was completely destroyed and dispersed.[27] The great Tamburlan Sachatai then came and established himself in Bursa, where the Emperor Manuel sent ambassadors to offer him obedience. But Sachatai, like the magnanimous lord that he was, exercised a courteous liberality, for he replied to the ambassadors: 'It is not God's wish that a most splendid city, full of nobility and urbanity, should be made a slave and a subject. I am not moved by ambition or by greed to acquire cities, lands and countries. I have enough of these. My motive is the defence of nobility, as is the duty of a good emperor. Live therefore under your ancient laws, and I shall chastise anyone who is so rash as to want to enslave you.' He went back whence he had come; and he kept Ildrim Bayezid continuously bound by golden ropes and took him with him wherever he went in an iron cage, and made him serve as a mounting block with his shoulder.[28] /

148 When Sachatai got back to 'Scytia' he staged a magnificent triumph for his victory over Bayezid and a great assembly attended by almost all the lords and princes of Scytia; and the cage containing Bayezid was brought in. Then [Sachatai] did something very out of keeping with his grandeur and noble character. He had Ildrim's wife, who was also his prisoner, brought in and he caused her clothes to be ripped down to her navel so that she showed all her pudenda; and he made her wait upon and serve food to all his guests. Idrim, seeing his wife thus shamed, bewailed his fortune and wanted to kill himself at once. But he had no knife or other means. So he banged his head against the iron bars of his cage so hard that he dispatched himself miserably. After him his son Mehmed ('Mehemeth') came to power. He was the first of that name and also the first to call himself Sultan.[29]

So Sultan Mehmed [I], the fifth Emperor of the Turks, succeeded his father Ildrim Bayezid; and when Sachatai died he recovered his kingdom and chased out the governors whom Sachatai had installed. After the battle in which Bayezid was captured, one of his sons, Mustapha, died. There were three other sons whom he had left at Adrianople, namely: Sultan Mehmed and two others. As soon as he heard of his father's capture, [Mehmed] summoned his brothers and fled to Karamania ('Caramano'); and there he stayed until Sachatai's death, after which he assumed the Empire of the Turks, ruined and fragmented though it was.[30] The Turkish historians did not praise him very highly because he did not acquire any more territory. Still, in my opinion he was a most valiant prince. He found his affairs in total disarray; yet he constantly defended, conserved and restored all the lands that had been lost and devastated. He was enabled to achieve this because of the weakness and dissension among the Christian princes who, when they should have taken advantage of the ruin and defeat of the Turks and joined forces, abandoned Greece and devoted themselves to their diabolical quarrels with one another. The Emperor Manuel [II] was generally beset by all his neighbours. It was during this period that the Sultan Mehmed stabilised his position in Greece; while Manuel in Constantinople negotiated with his neighbouring Christian rulers; he had no other means of driving the Turks out of Greece since his treasury was empty. But he acted contrary to the policies of all his predecessors. For while each of them had several sons, one alone was destined to become Emperor and to inherit everything, while the others had nothing. Manuel Paleologo had seven sons and he divided his Empire into seven parts, giving each son his portion. This led to dissension among the brothers, which God allowed for our sins and was the cause of our ruin and that of all Christendom. This Mehmed Sultan died and was buried in the city of Adrianople, leaving two sons, Murad ('Amurath') and Mustapha.[31]

The Sultan Murad, the second of that name, became Emperor of the Turks / by strangling his brother Mustapha and consolidating his power. He observed the ceaseless division and discord among the Christian princes, and this was for our sins and arose because the Empire had been divided into seven parts with seven heads. In the division Salonichi had fallen by lot to a son of Manuel called Andronico 'Desposto', who was an invalid. Seeing the quarrelling between his brothers, he sought to strengthen his own position by making an arrangement with the Signoria of Venice. He promised to give them Salonichi if they would let him live in Treviso. The Venetians thus acquired possession of Salonichi. Andronico died on his way to Venice and the Venetians sent governors of their own to

149

Salonichi, who administered the place in a manner quite different from its previous administration. When the Sultan Murad heard of this he was provoked and, with the encouragement of many of the greatest in the land, he marched on the fine and famous city under pretext of demanding the tribute which Andronico Paleologo had paid him, none of which had been received during the four and a half years that the Venetians had held Salonichi. He besieged it for some months and finally conquered it. The Venetian governors and soldiers were captured and killed and the sons of the locals were taken to Adrianople as hostages. Others were left in possession of their belongings on payment of the *haraç* ('carazo') or customary tax.[32]

Another of the Emperor Manuel's sons, the Despot Andreas, had been allotted the lordship of Vizye ('Visu') with its district. He died childless and Murad took over the place.[33] Murad then saw that Albania, or rather Epiros, was in utter disorder. This was because, when the Emperor [John] Cantacuzene controlled it, he had sent to Janina a member of the family of Spata and made him Vice-Despot and governor, along with another called Musachi Theopia. One of these resided in Janina which was the capital of the realm of Epiros; Musachi resided in Durazzo and governed certain places which were known as 'la Musachia'.[34] The Spata who governed Janina found himself monarch of the place by succession after the death of the Emperor Cantacuzene. For many years he was at odds with the lord of Angelocastro, and he enlisted the help of one Carlo Tocco. Tocco's father, as we have recorded, had bought the islands of Ithaka, Zakynthos ('Itacha, Jacinto'), Cephalonia and Santa Maura from those who had acquired them by conquest from Andronico [II] Paleologo, son of Michael [VIII]; and the King of Naples had made him Duke of these islands.

This Carlo Tocco was a gentleman from the Capuano side of Naples. He sold his services to the said Gin Spata as a mercenary, together with his brother Leonardo. Leonardo brought a naval force and Carlo a land army; and they easily dislodged the said lord of Angelocastro and reduced him to subservience to Janina. Carlo then demanded his pay from Gin Spata, who had no money with which to pay him. So Carlo occupied and held / Angelocastro; though later 150 others intervened and arranged the matter. Carlo took to wife the only daughter of Gin Spata, who died soon after and left Carlo Tocco as his heir to all his possessions. He was the first of his house to be named Despot.[35] [The title] was granted to him by Manuel Paleologo who divided the Empire of the Greeks, as we have indicated. This title of Despot was not an office that passed by succession from one to another. It came by imperial appointment and was usually granted to brothers, sons, near relatives and other grandees by favour of the Emperor.[36] The said Carlo Tocco reigned in Janina for eleven years, lording it over the Albanians in the Italian style with a severity to which they were not accustomed. When he died, the men of Janina at once went to Murad and proclaimed him their lord; and he sent a captain called Turahan ('Turacanbei') with other officers and took over Janina, a stronghold and capital of all Epiros.[37] For our sins it was God's will that Carlo had no legitimate children by his aforesaid wife, only five bastards. His brother Count Leonardo was already dead. He left a legitimate son called Carlo who, after his uncle's death, would have liked to go to Constantinople to be invested as Despot; but he called himself lord of Arta, Carlo de Tocca. He fought bitterly with the aforesaid bastards, and some of them sought the help of Murad, claiming that their father's lordship belonged to them; for they knew that the Turks make no distinction between legitimate and bastard sons. Others of them went to the Despots of the Morea, and one to the Signori of Venice. Murad and his army invaded Epiros, occupied Arta and Angelocastro and many other places; and the said Carlo Tocco was forced to live in Santa Maura, where he still held Zakynthos, Ithaca and Cephalonia, and to pay annual tribute to Murad. He also surrendered his son Leonardo as a hostage, and

Murad made him over to his son Mehemeth [Mehmed], though later he left the Seraglio a Christian as he had entered it. This Carlo [II] recognised the Venetians as his lords in respect of the islands which he ruled, so that all appeals in civil and criminal cases went to be decided in Venice. But Murad, having settled affairs in one part of Albania, turned to the other. He saw that Janina and the places within its jurisdiction were rent by discord and tumult. Certain petty lords came to him on a three day journey to ask that 'Musai Carlo', reputedly the leading man in Epiros, should take control. Others, for one reason or another, disputed this; and the said Musai Carlo, in desperation, went to Murad and was made his captain. After Musai Carlo's death, his sons were made *Sanjak beys* ('sanzacchi'), and Murad found ways and means of curbing the disunited Albanians, continually harassing them with raids and incursions and every day he carried off innumerable prisoners into miserable captivity.[38]

Manuel Emperor of Constantinople was succeeded by his son John [VIII] Paleologo, who had no children by his wife. / The power of the Turks was growing and John realised that he could not resist it on his own; also the Despot Theodore who had reigned at Selymbria ('Silivrea') had died with no male issue, only a daughter married to the King of Cyprus, who was the mother of Queen Carlotta, who died at Rome.[39] [John] therefore decided to go to the council [in Italy]; and he summoned from the Peloponnese the Despot Constantine called Dragasi, a most belligerent soldier, who was, in view of the death of the Despot Theodore, destined to succeed as Emperor when John died. [John] left him [Constantine] in Constantinople and himself set out on the journey to Italy; he took with him his other brother, the Despot Demetrios, who ruled Lacedemonia and Misithra. There was such rivalry between Demetrios and his brother Thomas, who ruled at Patras, that the one seemed likely to eat out the heart of the other. This is why the Emperor John [VIII] thought it wise to take Demetrios with him, as well as a large number of lords and gentlemen.[40] The Despot Constantine took with him to Constantinople John Cantacuzene, a famous captain of the time, and several other soldiers also, among them George Cantacuzene called 'Sachatai', who was the grandson or son of the son of the Emperor John [VI] Cantacuzene. [George was a prince endowed with all the virtues and highly esteemed among the Greeks because of his lineage and his talents. He went to visit his sister 'Helena' [Eirene], wife of the Despot George of Serbia, where he found that the Despot was at war with Hungary. So he elected to stay there and was instrumental in building the strong fortress of Smederevo ('Sfenderono').] This prince was accompanied by a large body of men.[41]

Murad saw that the Peloponnese was denuded of fighting men. The Despot Thomas was still there but he had no control over the unruly and quarrelsome Greeks. Murad was eager to go there and demolish the 'Examili', the six-mile wall stretching from sea to sea. And so he did, not once but twice, after a five-year interval. This led to the total ruin of Greece.[42]

The Emperor John [VIII] came to Italy in the time of Pope Eugenius IV and they began to hold the Council at Ferrara, later moving to Florence on account of the plague. There they were in discussion for three and a half years, until the Greek and Latin rites were brought into harmony. John then went to Rome to visit the holy places, and from there to France, to 'Borgogna', and he called on many other Christian princes to incite them to war against the Turks. He was away from Constantinople for seven years.[43] During that time Murad gave all the Christian rulers cause to fear for their religion as John VIII had personally or by letter forewarned them. Only the King of Hungary and Philip, Duke of Burgundy, took action / against the Turks in 1444, though the most reverend Cardinal Juliano Cesarini went as legate from the Apostolic See. The Christian army encountered Murad at a place called Varna and such were their talents and their discipline that the Christians were victorious, breaking and scattering the army of the Turks, so that Murad and his Janissaries were forced to retreat to the top of a small hill nearby, together with a very few others who thus escaped death. There they were surrounded by the victorious Christian army. After three days of siege and starvation, Murad was forced to capitulate, on these terms: he himself would be allowed to go free; all the other Turks would be at the mercy of their conquerors. When the terms were brought to him for signature, Murad began to cry like a baby. One of his Janissaries then accosted him and said: 'Do you think that you can mitigate the wrath of your victorious enemies by tears? Emperors defeat their enemies by the sword not by tears.' Murad replied: 'I weep for the mean capitulation forced upon me . . . '. Then the Janissary suddenly took out his sword and said: 'You stupid, deceitful traitor! You have brought us here to save your own skin and leave the rest of us to perish by the sword, a prey to our enemies. You will die with the rest of us.' So saying, he struck down Murad's horse. Our Christians, trusting in the capitulation, were disarmed and not prepared when the Turks in arms unexpectedly attacked them. They had no time to put their hands to their swords, and they were routed and defeated. Among the dead were King Vladislav of Hungary and Poland and the Cardinal Cesarini, the Pope's legate. To this day at Varna there can be seen a huge mound of the bones of the Christians who died in that rout.[44] After the battle, the Duke Philip of Burgundy ('Bergonia') was brought to the presence of Murad, who arrogantly asked him: 'What led you to come and make war on me when you have no common frontier with me anywhere?' He answered: 'My lord I came to defend my Christian religion.' Murad said: 'If your Christian religion were better than mine, God would not have allowed me to defeat you with such dishonour and loss.' He summoned that Janissary of whom we spoke above and bade him insult the Duke, a prince whose truth and honour need no comment. Having filled him with dread, he took him to the block to cut off his head. However, he was ultimately ransomed for 200,000 scuti and the money was given to the Janissary. The Duke of Burgundy then went home and prepared for [further] war against the Turks. But it pleased God to call him to Himself. He left a curse upon his son if he failed to pursue his vendetta. The son disobeyed. The arms that he should have turned against the Turks he turned instead against his relatives for eleven years, for which God justly punished him.[45]

The Sultan Murad took to wife Maria, daughter of George Branković ('Jurgo'), Despot of Serbia. He had no children by her.[46] Two of her relatives, Stephen and Gregory [Grgur], aged fifteen and sixteen, he caused to be blinded. They had gone to visit their sister [Maria] in Adrianople. When out hunting with Murad they shot a deer that he was chasing. / He was suspicious and remarked: 'ogni lupo fa il suo lupato' [like father like son]; and at supper he had their eyes removed and had the orbs sent direct to their father. Then he went to war with the Despot George, drove him out and conquered all of Rascia and Serbia. The Despot escaped and found refuge with his wife Eirene Cantacuzene and their children in the city of Ragusa. There the said Eirene had banked much money which she had amassed unbeknownst to her husband; and with this he enlisted John Corvinus Hunyadi ('Janco Vaivoda'), father of King Matthew ('Mathias'), and recovered his realm.[47] Next Murad went to lay siege to Athens, whose Duke was then a Florentine of the house of Acciajuoli ('Acciaoli') called Nerio. He surrendered and gave Murad his son Franco as a hostage.[48] Murad then went to Albania and besieged the stronghold of Krujë ('Croia') which was then held by Skanderbeg. But during this operation Murad fell ill and died. His corpse was taken to Adrianople and there buried; and his son had a fine mosque and a hospice built in which prayers were offered for his soul; and it is the general opinion among Turkish historians that, for all his triumphs, Murad was outshone by his son Mehmed ('Mehemeth').[49]

So the Ottoman Sultan Mehmed, the second of that name and the seventh Emperor of the Turks, succeeded his father Murad. He was a strong and warlike, yet liberal and magnanimous prince. As soon as he came to power he had his five-year old brother strangled. He then turned on Constantine, Emperor of Constantinople, who had come to his throne in Murad's time in place of his deceased brother John [VIII] Paleologo.[50] He captured the great city of Selymbria ('Silvrea'), an event that heralded the ruin of Constantinople, for the Turks could then make constant incursions right up to the gates of the city.[51] Mehmed then brought a huge army by land to besiege the city. By sea he had ships dragged over the hill of Pera and launched into the harbour of Constantinople. The Emperor Constantine had sent envoys to Rome to Pope Nicholas V and had written round to all the Christian princes appealing for their aid. But, for our sins, none of them responded, for all the Pope's exhortations and the Emperor's pleas – except for the Venetians and the Genoese. For one of their provveditors, of the house of Armer, happened to be there with three galleys; and when the enemy attacked he was constrained to defend the place.[52] The Venetian Senate deliberated whether they should send help or not; but their deliberations went on for so long that they were not in time, for the captain who led the relief got to Negroponte only to learn that the unhappy city was already taken. There were some soldiers of Genoa who bravely defended the walls. But Mehmed held the city under siege for fifty-four days; and when he mounted his attack the Genoese constable was wounded and God willed it, for our sins, that the Turks broke in at that spot on 29 May 1453.[53] It was God's will that, as Constantinople had been built by a Constantine, son of Helena, / so also it was lost by force of arms in the time of another Constantine, son of Helena. And the seventh Emperor of the Ottomans defeated the seventh Emperor of the house of Paleologo. The Christian Emperor could have saved himself but he refused to do so. When the Turks were almost inside the walls he said: 'My God, I

154

32

do not wish to be an Emperor without an Empire. I wish to die with my land.' And to some nobles who were standing round him he said: 'Whoever wants to save himself may go; whoever wants to accompany his Emperor, follow me and come with me to death.' So a crowd of more than 200 went with him on horseback to the streets of 'Chinigo' where the Turks had broken in; and they engaged the whole Turkish army in fighting for four hours, so that the enemy could get no further. But when the Turks had taken the city the Christians were surrounded from every side and the blessed Emperor was killed with 200 other martyrs, not without a great slaughter of their enemies.[54] No human tongue could tell the savagery with which they [the Turks] treated the churches and the Christians. They turned churches and shrines into brothels and stables for horses. They broke into convents of holy nuns devoted to God; they took from the churches the icons ('anchone') of saints on the altars, putting out their eyes and throwing them on the ground; they violated the holy nuns and blasphemed against the infinite providence, saying: 'If your faith is good, let God work a miracle at this time!' They also broke open and shattered the gorgeous tombs of the Emperors and other princes of Greece to steal the Crowns, the golden spurs and other military decorations with which princes and lords were wont to be buried. The cruelty of the Turks and the debasement of Christianity made the good Pope Nicholas V so sad and melancholy that he fell ill and died.

The Turkish historians write that Mehmed made a search for the corpse of the Holy Emperor and that when he was found he mourned over it and honoured it and accompanied it to its grave. But the Christians say that the body was never discovered, for in truth no grave was ever found in Constantinople.[55]

When the savage slaughter of Christians was over, Mehmed did not want to live in the palace of the Caesars. He took for his residence a convent of the friars of St Francis.[56] On the next day he issued a decree that all who were holding prisoners must present them on pain of death. When they were presented, he ordered that those of rank should be set free, saying that it was not right that noblemen should live as slaves to someone else. Of the common people, some were killed, some taken as slaves along with their wives and children. Later, Mehmed decreed that all proven gentlefolk should be more abundantly provided for than they had been under the Christian Emperors, for it was wrong that a gentleman should suffer and have to go begging. Some foolish ones among them went to register and a day was fixed on which they would receive their promised provision. It was the day of St Peter. / And on that day, by command of Mehmed, they were all executed.[57] As Vergil says [Aeneid, 1. 94–6]: 'O terque quaterque beati, quis ante ora patrum [Troiae sub moenibus altis contigit oppetere!].' God was merciful in not allowing them to survive or their descendants to prove how hard it is for noblemen to have to live on the mercy of others, like dogs. This is what happened to me and my companions in the time of Hadrian VI when he declined to pay us that which previous Pontiffs had paid, and some of us died from starvation while others were cast into prison on the pretext that we had dealings with the Turks.[58]

Mehmed then learnt that the prince of Gothia had murdered his elder brother and usurped his place. So he sent his *Beylerbey* ('biglerbei'), his captain-general on land, to make war on the said prince. An agreement was reached to the effect that his person and property were safe. But in the end Mehmed had him brought to Constantinople and decapitated, telling him that he had broken his agreement. He made one of the King's little sons a Turk; and I saw him still alive when I was last in Constantinople.[59]

[Now the Christian princes, seeing Constantinople occupied by the Sultan Mehmed whose power grew by the day while their own strength grew feebler and feebler, did not, as they should have done, take common military action against their common enemy. Instead they fought and quarrelled among themselves. There was at that time fierce warfare between the Despot George ('Jurgo') of Serbia and the King of Hungary, as though they were at each other's throats. The Despot George observed the Greek rite, the King of Hungary the Latin; and there were many bloody battles between them and great carnage on either side. The Hungarians were more often the losers, though in the end, in a savage feat of arms, they took the Despot captive and with him the lord Theodore Cantacuzene. Both were taken to prison in Hungary. Theodore, however, was allowed to go on oath to Serbia to collect and provide 300,000 ducats as ransom. This he was unable to find; but, so as not to break his oath, he returned to prison in Hungary until the money was paid. The Hungarians were barbarised by war. They wanted to keep the Despot as well as Cantacuzene in their hands. They sent a huge army to lay siege to the famous city of Smederevo, called Semendria by the Turks who now occupy it. They were unable to take it because within its walls was the celebrated warrior prince George Cantacuzene who had built the fortress. He defended it with all his might and all the strength and tenacity that he possessed; and this he demonstrated when the Hungarians led his son, their prisoner [Theodore] up to the walls and threatened to kill him before his father's eyes if he would not surrender. The son bravely declared that he did not care, for [in death] he would have liberated his country from servitude. All these discords God permitted because / of our sins; and as a consequence Mehmed found these places enfeebled and occupied them all.[60]]

He made war on the Bulgars and butchered them, depriving them of their lives and occupying their country. Then he turned on the ruler of Karamania ('Caramano'), who was evicted and fled to the King of Persia, where he died a miserable death. He took Smyrna, Phokaia ('Foghie') and other Christian towns. The lord Gattilusio ('Cathalusio') ruled over Mytilene, Ainos ('Eno'), Samothrace, Lemnos ('Stalimeni') and some other islands which the Emperor John [V] Paleologo had given to his forebear [Francesco] Gattilusio

156

35

after he expelled John Cantacuzene from Constantinople. He had murdered his brother and usurped power. When Mehmed got hold of him he said: 'I shall treat you as you treated your brother to obtain your position.' And he had him executed. His wife and some of his household were taken as prisoners.[61] Mehmed next planned to occupy the Peloponnese. This was made easy for him by the great dissension prevailing between the Despot Demetrios and his brother the Despot Thomas. After their father Manuel [II] died, these two brothers were so quarrelsome that they seemed like to eat each other's heart out. After the fall of Constantinople and the death of their brother Constantine, the Greek nobles and lords were for appointing Demetrios as their Emperor because they saw him as a reasonable man. But his brother Thomas would not budge, for all that Demetrios was the elder.[62] The leading men of Greece none the less concerted their efforts to bring peace between the brothers. They never succeeded. Thomas, who really was a bad lot, schemed to take over the realm of his relative, the prince of Clarentza ('Chiarenza'), and other places in what was still called the Principality of Achaia. He summoned his relative to come under safe conduct to Patras, then broke his pledge and put him in prison, where he was left to die of hunger together with his sons. Then he seized a nobleman called Theodore 'Dissipato' [? Disypatos], who had married his daughter while the Prince of Achaia was in prison, cut off his hands, ears and nose and gouged out his eyes, a truly savage and terrible deed. He also captured one Theodore Bochalis ('Boccali') who was under safe conduct. He was a man of high estate and the leading figure of all the Peloponnese. He had the right to mint coinage and he held the court title of 'Megaduca'. Thomas had him blinded and seized his estate, though he was to be liberated by Dissipato with some of his sons who were in custody, returned and recovered his property.[63] Another noble gentleman was Manuel Cantacuzene, brother of that George called Sachatai, who was my mother's grandfather ('mio avo materno'). He held sway over all the promontory of Mani ('Mayna') and was most highly regarded as the leading lord among the Greek nation. He too was invited by the said Thomas to present himself under safe conduct; but being prudent and sensible he declined the invitation and put up so brave a resistance that Thomas wanted to destroy him. The courage and resistance of Manuel Cantacuzene gave heart to many of the Albanians who were subjected to and badly treated by various Greek lords and masters. They were inspired to liberate themselves from servitude; and they acclaimed Manuel Cantacuzene as their own Despot. / They changed his name to Gin Cantacusino and called his wife Cucchia instead of Maria, these being Albanian names.[64] Such were the hostilities between these Despots that each was a prisoner of his own ambition, Thomas being besieged in Patras, Demetrios in Mistra or Lacedaemonia, and Manuel lording it all over the country. Mehmed, who knew all about it, took swift military action, marched into the Peloponnese and impatiently devastated and occupied it all.[65]

Thomas did not wait for the wrath of Mehmed but left Patras by boat, taking with him the head of St Andrew the Apostle, which he presented to the Pontifex Maximus, Pius II. The Pope came out to the Ponte Molle to receive it and to this day there is a chapel commemorating the reception of the holy relic.[66] Thomas also took with him his two sons, the Despots Andrew and Manuel, and also his daughter who, after Thomas's death, Pope Sixtus IV gave as wife to the Grand Muscovite Ivan III ('Gioanne'). Andrew lived in Rome in abject poverty and misery. His brother Manuel, a generous and virtuous man and superior to Andrew in character, prudence and way of life, despaired of his brother's miserable condition, left Rome and went off to find the Sultan Mehmed. He expected the worst but on the contrary Mehmed received him with kindness, provided for him and honoured him at court more than any other prince; and he was allowed to die as a Christian like all his forebears.[67]

The Despot Demetrios who ruled at Mistra seems to have allowed the Sultan to conquer the Peloponnese because Mehmed had promised to take his daughter to wife. She was his only child and heiress to all that he had. Manuel Cantacuzene also came to agreement with Mehmed and surrendered to him. Mehmed, however, no longer wanted to marry Demetrios's daughter; and she died as a virgin at Adrianople. Manuel Cantacuzene, though well provided for by the Sultan, did not trust him and fled to the King of Hungary, where he died. Demetrios, accused of some fraud over the collection of the salt tax, was deprived of all his sustenance and soon died of grief.[68] Note also that when Mehmed invaded the Peloponnese and the Despot Thomas fled, another who escaped was the son of the lord Carlo Tocco called Leonardo whom the Grand Turk held as a hostage; and Mehmed ordered a search party to find him and bring him back.[69] Another victim was the Duke of Athens, Franco Acciajuoli, who was obliged to serve as a vassal of the Sultan. He sent a Janissary with some colleagues to pretend to dine with the Duke and they brutally murdered him.[70] One place in the Peloponnese that Mehmed failed to capture was Mouchli ('Mucli'), although he tried for fifty-four days. But it was defended by its most valiant lord, 'Andrea Paleologo di Grizza'. Nor did he attempt to capture Monemvasia / ('Malvasia'), an impregnable fortress, which was held by Nicolo Paleologo in the name of the Despot. When Mehmed left, however, Paleologo Grizza abandoned Mouchli and went to Venice, where the Senate welcomed him and made him captain-general of their light cavalry, although he died soon after. The other, Nicolo Paleologo, having little hope that the Christian princes would mount an attack on the Turks, sold his stronghold of Monemvasia to the Venetians for a trifling sum of money. On his way back to Adrianople Mehmed took possession of Athens, since its Duke had died without sons. In Adrianople he celebrated his great victories with a triumph.[71]

Now when the Despot George [Branković] of Serbia died he left two daughters: one called Maria had been married to the Sultan Murad of whom we have spoken; the other, Catherine, had married the Count of Cilly ('Cil'), a brother of the Emperor Frederick of Austria. Both were widows. Maria had no issue; but Catherine had a daughter who was the first wife of Matthew ('Mathias') King of Hungary.[72] The Despot George [Branković] also left three sons: first the Despot Stephen ('Stefano'), second the Despot Gregory ('Curgur'). Both of these were blinded by Murad, as mentioned above. The third was the Despot Lazar and his father arranged for him to marry the daughter of Thomas Paleologo, Despot of the Morea. They were closely related, for Thomas's father, the Emperor Manuel [II], had given him in marriage to a sister of the Despot George, and George was Lazar's father. Experience has shown that these marriages arranged among relatives, although contracted by dispensation of the church, seldom end happily. Now because the said Lazar had his eyesight, while his elder brothers had been blinded by Murad, Lazar was more active than they in affairs of state; and he succeeded to the government when his father George died. His mother, Eirene Cantacuzene, sister of that prince George Cantacusino who was my mother's grandfather ('mio avo materno'), was content to be regent and guardian of her sons' realm. Lazar, however, was not content. He wanted it all and, with no fear of God, he poisoned his said mother Eirene, a princess endowed with every virtue. Thus did Lazar make himself shunned and hated by all his vassals and his neighbours and in the confusion earned the implacable wrath of Mehmed, who resolved to take over Rascia and Serbia. This news caused Lazar to fall ill, and before long he died, leaving no sons but only his three daughters.[73] Stephen, the first-born [of the sons of George] was, as I have said, blind and he fled the wrath of Mehmed. He went first to Albania with his retinue and there he met and married a virtuous lady called Angelina, daughter of Signor Golemo Araniti; and they did not lack offspring. At his death he left two sons, George

and John, called Despots, and a daughter called Maria who married
Boniface, Marquis of Montferrat. George's second son, Gregory
('Gurgur'), went to Hungary where he died without legitimate
offspring.[74] / The aforementioned Lazar had, as reported, three
children: the first, Maria, married King Stephen of Bosnia ('Bossina')
while her father was still alive; the second, Milica, married Leonardo
Tocco; the third, Eirene, married John Kastriotes ('Ioanne Castrioto
Duca di San Pietro'), who was the son of Skanderbeg whom we have
mentioned. Mehmed invaded and occupied the whole of Rascia and
Serbia and all the possessions of the Despots of Serbia; and those of
their lands that did not surrender were taken by force with unheard-
of cruelty to their poor inhabitants.[75]

Not content with this, Mehmed declared war on David Komnenos
('Commino'), Emperor of Trebizond, and, having captured several
places on his way, he encircled the city. David was forced to
capitulate and in return Mehmed spared his life and allowed him
to leave with his belongings and settled him in the city of Serres.[76]
Mehmed then captured Kaffa ('Capha') which belonged to the
Genoese, 'Scandiloro', Sebastia, Tana and many other places in
Natalia. Some of their inhabitants he killed, some he took captive to
Constantinople and some stayed disconsolately in their homes.[77]
Next, ravenously thirsting for Christian blood, he had some letters
forged which appeared as if written in Rome. This was two years after
he had settled the Emperor of Trebizond in Serres. The letters told of
a crusade against the Turks. On this false pretext Mehmed had the
Emperor David Komnenos brought before him in chains with his
wife Helena, who was the sister of my mother's grandfather ('sorella
di mio avo materno'), and their eight sons and one daughter. In
Constantinople he announced to them that they would all die if they
refused to become Turks and renounce their Christian faith. When he
heard this, David comforted his sons and committed them to holy
martyrdom. He and seven of his sons were decapitated. The eighth,

being but three years of age, was made a Turk together with his sister and were given as a gift to Uzun Hasan ('Uzum Cassano'), King of Persia. The son later escaped and went to the King of Georgia called 'Gurguiabei', who was converted to Christianity and gave him his daughter to wife, by whom he had children who are still alive today. His sister who had married Uzun Hasan had two daughters, one of whom became the mother of Ismail [I] ('Signor Sophi Jach Issmail'), who was the father of the present King of Persia, Tahmasp ('Sac Tomas re di Persia').

Mehmed confiscated all the property of the imperial family of Trebizond and condemned the Empress to pay 15,000 ducats within three days or be executed. Her servants, who were Mehmed's prisoners in Constantinople, worked from dawn to dusk to raise the money and paid it. I cannot pass over, however, the virtuous conduct of this pious and saintly Empress Helene Cantacuzene in her pitiful state. Having lost her husband and her sons, she had no desire to remain in this world; and, clad in sackcloth, she who had been accustomed to regal finery, refused to eat meat any more and built herself a hovel covered in straw in which she slept rough. Mehmed had decreed that no one was to bury the bodies under pain of death. They were to be left for the dogs and ravens to devour. But the sainted Empress secretly acquired a spade / and with her own delicate hands   160 as best she could dug a trench in her hut. All day long she defended the corpses against the animals and at night she took them one by one and gave them burial. Thus did God give her the grace to bury her husband and her sons; and a few days later she too died.[78]

Mehmed then made preparations for war against the Venetian Senate and took a large army to conquer the island of Negroponte. He constructed a bridge from the mainland to the island and occupied the land of Negroponte. The Venetians had appointed one Nicolao da Canale, who was a doctor, as captain-general of their armada and their large and well-armed fleet of ships. Now if Canale had resolutely done his duty by attacking and destroying the bridge as he had been advised to do, Mehmed would have been trapped on the island and he and all his men would have been like to die of hunger. But Canale did not have the courage for such glorious deeds and Mehmed and his troops prepared to come back across the bridge. He was prevented by a certain Pasha of Constantinople called Mahmud ('Maumuth') who held him by the reins of his horse and persuaded him to stay and fight. Mehmed therefore staged a great battle on the island. The Turks fought fiercely. They had an agent inside the castle called Pietro Schiavo; and in the end they killed nearly all the male inhabitants and took all the women and children into pitiable captivity.[79] The Venetian Senate responded by sending Sigismondo Malatesta of Rimini ('Arimino'), a well-known captain in Italy, with 1,200 picked men and the fleet to the Peloponnese. Within three days he had occupied most of it, except for the heavily fortified castles of Corinth and Calavrita, for the Greeks were glad to see the back of their hated Turkish oppressors. Sigismondo Malatesta was, however, short of supplies, and he went on to pillage Lacedemonia which is now called 'Misitra'; and there he found and exhumed the bones of the famous philosopher George Gemistos Plethon ('Gemisto Plitona') who, in the opinion of learned Greeks, was the most erudite Greek since Aristotle. He had been at the Council of Florence in the time of Pope Eugenius IV. Sigismondo, who was versed in Greek and devoted to scholarship, erected a splendid and ornate tomb for Gemistos Plethon which can still be seen in his city of Rimini.[80]

In the place of the lord of Rimini the Venetian Senate appointed the excellent Bertoldo. He went to lay siege to Corinth and gained the keys of the lower city. But the rock remained in the hands of the Janissaries / and [Bertoldo] was killed when a woman threw a rock down on him and smashed his head, whereupon his army withdrew.[81]

When Mehmed heard that Nicolao da Canale had refortified Vostizza and the Hexamilion wall ('Xamili') and some other places,

161

he sent an army commanded by his captain Omar Bey ('Amarbei'), who invaded the Peloponnese and destroyed all these places. At that time a Venetian provveditor was at Patras with many ships along with a Greek commander called Michael Ralli. Together they scored a victory over Omar Beg and his Turks; and 'Barbadico', the provveditor, being overexcited and inexperienced in warfare, was for going on to capture Patras, against the advice of the captain 'Ralli Isi' who was more prudently cautious.[82] Barbadico's impetuosity led him to cause the destruction of his army. He and about 10,000 Christians were slaughtered; and the good Michael Ralli was carried into a swamp by his horse. He might have been saved if a priest had not betrayed him and accused him to the Turks, who seized him and cruelly impaled him.[83] The other Christian armies, hearing of this and of the death of Bertoldo, retreated to a place called Calamata near Coron and there they were butchered and dispersed by the Turks, some being captured as prisoners. And when I was a lad in Gallipoli I saw some of these who, up to that time, had not been ransomed. The Venetian Senate, having recalled Nicolao Canale, put him in prison at Portogruer in Friuli, and they made Pietro Mocenigo, later to be Doge of Venice, their captain-general of the sea.[84] The Apostolic See sent Olivier Carapha, who was apostolic cardinal legate; and King Ferdinand of Aragon sent some warships which, together with those of Mocenigo and some others, totalled more than 100 armed ships; and they made war against Omar Bey ('Amarbei') to punish his incredible and lamentable cruelty towards the Christians since he had taken over the Peloponnese, so inhumanly impaling and savagely killing those who had rebelled against the Turks. The good captain Mocenigo, zealous for the catholic faith, advanced against them; and he recruited for his army certain light cavalry from various parts of Greece that were then owned by the Venetians; and having assembled a strong force he overran all the maritime possessions of the Turks, burning, sacking and plundering them. He then captured and sacked the city of Ainos ('Eno') and destroyed its saltpans which were guarded by the Turks. He also captured Lemnos and from there crossed over to Natalia to the land of Karamania occupied by Mehmed / and put it to fire and sword. He sacked other places as well; and almost all his company came back rich with spoils from the enemy. This famous captain and Doge lies buried in his native city of Venice in the church of Saints John and Paul which belongs to the friars of the Dominican Order in an ornate marble tomb with an epitaph that reads:

EX HOSTIUM MANUBIIS.[85]

Mehmed then decided to occupy the Duchy and realm of Bosnia ('Bossina') where there lived a Duke of S. Saba, called in vulgar parlance the Herzog ('el Cersecho'), who shared a frontier with the Ragusans, his rivals. His first-born son Ladislas was married to a sister of my grandfather called Anna. The said Duke, being elderly and having little respect either for his son or for morality took a loose woman for his concubine and installed her in his palace. Ladislas and Anna took offence at this; but his father made matters worse by declaring that he was master in his own house and could do what he liked. Ladislas was indignant and with the support of others chased his father out. The old Duke was furious. He appealed to Mehmed for help and handed over his younger son as a hostage. Mehmed made a Turk of him and later on a Pasha and called him Sina[n] Pasha Herzegoglou. At the time when Mehmed invaded Bosnia [1463], the old Duke was dead, and Ladislas wasted no time in fleeing to Venice with his wife and sons. He stayed at our house for a few days before going on to Hungary, where he died [in 1489]; and Mehmed occupied the country, leaving to the other son of the old Duke, called Vlatko ('Vlatheo'), only Castel Nuovo and a few other places to support himself as a tribute-paying vassal, until Bayezid, Mehmed's son, drove him out. He died in Bar ('Arbe'), a city of Dalmatia.[86]

Mehmed then put pressure on the Ragusans, obliging them to pay him the tribute which up to now they still pay. He then turned on the Kingdom of Bosnia ('Bossina') where reigned King Stephen who had married Maria, daughter of the Despot Lazar of Serbia, as we have said above. Stephen reigned in peace, until one of the local princes took it into his head to make himself King of Bosnia; and he went to seek support from the King of Hungary, alleging that Stephen had reached the throne by murdering his father and that he was in league with the Turks. Furthermore he said that most of the local people wanted him [and not Stephen] for king. The King of Hungary gave him a relative as a wife and an army; and he began to make war on Stephen. When the Turk heard this, he sent his *Beylerbey* to negotiate with Stephen, promising him his possessions and his life if he would surrender. But Mehmed intervened, broke his promise and had Stephen decapitated. His Queen was captured and given to one of the Sultan's courtiers, an officer of the Spahis ('dell' ordine de Spacogliani') who made her his wife; but she remained sterile. Mehmed then marched on the Hungarians. They were slow to withdraw and were all routed and scattered. Among the dead was their captain / who had wanted to seize the throne, as well as an infinite number of others. Mehmed went back in triumph to Constantinople.[87]

The following year he attacked the strong city of Belgrade which, after the ruin of the Despots of Serbia, had fallen into the hands of the King of Hungary. The Hungarians refused to surrender it at Mehmed's command and he went to war against them. Belgrade was saved by John Hunyadi ('Iancho Vaivoda'), father of King Matthias and a renowned soldier of Hungary, and by the Franciscan friar Giovanni ('Ioan') Capistrano, who came from Germany ('Alamania') with a cross on his shoulder and more than 20,000 troops ready to die for the Christian religion. The Turks were beaten off and their Sultan withdrew in disgrace and with heavy losses. The saintly Capistrano, however, who had led the field with his cross and given

163

heart to the others, was killed as a martyr along with other good Christians.[88]

Nothing daunted, Mehmed went on to attack and besiege the strongholds of Stephen the Great ('Carabogdan'), at 'Chieli' and 'Moncastro' [in Moldavia]. Stephen became his tributary. The lord of the other Valachia was obliged to pay twice as much tribute as Stephen ('Carabogdan') and also to go every second year to kiss the foot of the Emperor of the Turks. Stephen, however, they held in high esteem because of his strenuous and successful defence of Chieli and Moncastro. As a result he was granted certain concessions and was not obliged to go and kiss the Sultan's foot nor to give hostages. Mehmed went back to Constantinople; and the 'Sciotti' [lords of Chios ?], in terror, of their own free will offered to pay him the tribute which they still pay him to this day.[89]

Now the Venetian Senate, looking for every means of opposing Mehmed, sent ambassadors to Uzun Hasan ('Ussum Cassan'), King of Persia, to persuade him to take up arms against the Sultan. Uzun prepared for war and demanded the tribute which Mehmed's ancestors had paid to Persia; and this led to savage warfare between the two. Mehmed lost many men and Uzun Hasan lost a son; and Mehmed employed some 'schiopettieri' [Shqipetars] in his army, who were unfamiliar to the Persians. / In the end Uzun was put to flight. Mehmed was victorious and celebrated his triumph throughout his dominions.[90]

Mehmed also sent a force to lay siege to Rhodes. It was led by one Mesih Pasha ('Messit bassa'), who was of the house of Palaiologos.He was a brother of my father's mother. At the capture of Constantinople he had been taken by the Turks along with his two brothers. He was only ten at the time, and they were all made Turks. Mesih rose to the rank of Pasha; and it was he who was sent to lay siege to Rhodes with 200 warships and all the armies of Greece and Anatolia. It was in the time of the Grand Master d'Aubusson ('d'Ubuson'), who was joined

164

by the army of France. The Turks, however, failed to capture the island and retreated.[91]

The Sultan was concerned by the discord in Albania; and he thought it best to be done with it by taking over the place. For some years it had been ruled by Skanderbeg, a most valiant man of Serbian origin. He had taken to wife the daughter of Golemo Arianiti, mentioned above. He also had sisters whom he married off in Albania – one called Mamiza who married Musachio Thopia ('Musai Theopia'), a noble of great power and authority among the Albanians. Thus did Skanderbeg affiliate himself to all the grandees of Albania; and his military prowess was beyond compare and description. Those interested in the life of Skanderbeg should read the work of one Marino Scodrense. It was said that he had a sword with which he could cut an ox in half at one stroke. Mehmed asked to see this sword and Skanderbeg sent it to him. He then summoned one of his strongest men. An ox was led in to him but he proved unable to slice it in one blow. Mehmed complained that he had been deceived and sent the sword back saying that it was not the same weapon. Whereupon Skanderbeg had an ox brought to him and demonstrated to the Sultan's ambassador how to slice the beast in half at one blow with the same sword; and he sent the weapon back to Mehmed, who returned it saying: 'God will not be pleased if I deprive so strong a man of such a sword'; and he sent it back to Skanderbeg with many other presents. Having done wonders in battle against the Turks, Skanderbeg died [in January 1468]. / So also did his father-in-law Golemo Arianiti and many of the other princes of Albania.[92] Mehmed therefore invaded the country with a large army, devastated it, annihilated its rulers and made himself master of it all. Skodra ('Scutari') he besieged. It was defended by Antonio Lauredano who later became captain-general of the Venetians. It was he who fought back when Mehmed pitched camp at the Boiana [river], in defence of the Christian faith not only in Albania but also in other places. For the

Sultan was at war with the Venetian Senate. Mehmed therefore abandoned his siege of Skodra and, having subjugated all the rest of Albania he went back to Constantinople.[93] From there he sent a Pasha called 'Ali Eunucho' and the celebrated Omar Bey ('Amarbei') with 40,000 Turks to lay siege to Lepanto. But Antonio Loredano, who was in command of its defence as captain-general of the Christians, obliged the Turks to abandon their siege and retire.[94]

At this time there lived in Florence Lorenzo the Magnificent and Juliano di Medici, both wealthy noblemen. One day at Mass in the Sancta Reparata, now called S. Maria de Fiore, they were set upon by some conspirators. Juliano was killed and his brother Lorenzo was wounded. Cardinal San Giorgio, nephew of Pope Sixtus, also died. Lorenzo had great trouble in restoring order. But all the criminals were brought to justice and put to death except for one, Bernardo Bandini. He escaped and made his way to the Sultan Mehmed, who gave him asylum in Constantinople. Some days later Lorenzo sent a messenger to Mehmed to warn him that he had a murderer on his hands. Mehmed had him arrested and delivered to Lorenzo's man. Thus was Bandini taken to Florence where he was most cruelly punished; and Lorenzo remained a close and honoured friend of the Sultan.[95]

Mehmed sent an army under the command of his captain Iskender Bey ('Schender bassa') to raid the coast on the Venetian territory in Friuli. The Venetians appointed Girolamo Novella ('Count Hieronymo di Verona') to fight back, but he was defeated and killed; and the Turks took 20,000 prisoners from Friuli.[96] The Venetian Senate then sought out Maria, the daughter of the Despot of Serbia, who, as related above, had been the wife of Mehmed's father Murad. Mehmed honoured and respected her as if she were his own mother. She resided at Ježevo ('Exova') near Serres; and it was there that the Venetians sent ambassadors to find her and ask her to use her influence by arranging a pact with Mehmed. She was not successful.[97]

/ They they sent a young man called [Giovanni] Dario, who was secretary of their Senate and had great experience, to Constantinople. Dario spent a long time there and eventually arranged a peace treaty on the following terms: Venice was to cede to the Turks the fortress of Skodra ('Scutari') in Albania, which the Turks had failed to capture. Also to be surrendered to Mehmed were the islands of Lemnos and of Tridognia near Lepanto. The Venetians were in addition to pay 80,000 ducats in eight years – this in compensation for the seizure of certain taxes due to the Turks which had been appropriated by a gentleman of the 'cà Zorzi' who had escaped to Venice.[98] Peace was concluded, but the terms did not include Leonardo di Tocco who ruled S. Mavra, Leucada, Ithaca, Jacinto, Cephalonia. His wife was Milica, a daughter of the Despot Lazar of Serbia by whom he had one son and three daughters. She died as a prudent and blameless princess. Leonardo married again to a daughter of the prince of 'Rosano' [Francesca Marzano of Aragon], a relative of King Ferdinand of Naples, an enemy of Venice.[99] Wherefore, as I have said above, at the time when Pietro Mocenigo was deputy captain-general against the Turks, King Ferdinand sent an armada led by his son Frederick, later to become King, which with many ships entered the Gulf and blockaded 'Curzola'. But, being unable to capture it, they left; and the Venetians sent a fleet of their own and captured and sacked 'Galipoli'. A few days later peace was concluded between Venice and Ferdinand [of Naples].[100]

The Signoria of Venice was annoyed that Leonardo [Tocco], who was its vassal, had married a relative of the King [Ferdinand] at a time when the King was at war with them; and for this reason he was not party to the peace [with the Turks]. He [Leonardo Tocco] was obliged, every time a *Sanjak bey* arrived at Janina and Arta, to pay him 500 ducats, over and above the customary tribute payable to the Emperor of the Turks. It happened that a new official arrived as Pasha. He was a young man of seventeen called 'Fait bassa'. He was related to Leonardo who, relying on this fact, sent him a basket of fruit instead of the usual cash. Fait was cross and complained, vowing that Leonardo would soon see the error of his ways. He wrote at once to the lord of the Turks, since Leonardo was his tributary, pointing out that during the Veneto-Turkish war Leonardo had maintained a number of light cavalry from Venice on Zakynthos and that these had repeatedly attacked places belonging to the Turks and remained there with the support and goodwill of Leonardo, who had not been party to the peace treaty. Whereupon Mehmed sent twenty-eight warships under / command of his celebrated captain Gedik Ahmed Pasha ('Gidi Cadmath bassa') to fight Leonardo, who, anticipating their approach and being hated by the people for his tyranny, promptly embarked with his new wife and sons and all his relics and treasures and fled to King Ferdinand of Naples. The King granted him some castles in Calabria. Shortly after the death of Mehmed [in 1481], Leonardo's brother Antonio [Tocco] got some ships from the King of Naples and drove the Turks out of Cephalonia. But the Venetians, unwilling to break their truce with the Turks, sent four warships to Cephalonia to fight Antonio and restore the island to the Sultan Bayezid. As to Leonardo, he left Calabria after a while and went to Montferrat, then to Rome, where, in the time of Pope Alexander VI, he died. His son Carlo also died in Rome, in the pontificate of Leo X. Gedik Ahmed took over the islands, killing all Leonardo's officials and rounding up most of the inhabitants. They were taken with their wives to Constantinople, where Mehmed ordered that they were to cohabit with black Ethiopians, male and female, to engender a race of half-coloured slaves. He confined them to the islands of the Marmara and other islets close by between Gallipoli and Constantinople.[101]

At this time the King of Naples was at odds with Leonardo di Medici and other potentates. Mehmed was persuaded that the time was ripe to send Gedik Ahmed with a fleet to attack Otranto in Italy; and he captured it and slaughtered all its men who were capable of bearing arms and enslaved all its women and children. He plundered most thoroughly the surrounding countryside, towns and castles. King Ferdinand in despair wrote to all the Christian princes to tell them how Mehmed had set foot in Italy and taken Otranto, what you might call the 'key to Italy'. Hearing this lamentable news everyone volunteered to go to the rescue of the said King of Naples Ferdinand and his son Alfonso, then Duke of Calabria and later King. But on the death of Mehmed (May 1481) Gedik went back to Constantinople, leaving Otranto garrisoned by numerous Turkish troops. He had occupied it for a year.[102]

[The Sultan Mehmed (died 3 May 1481)]

The Emperor Mehmed was a most fortunate and excellent prince / and in his time his captains achieved many victories and brought him many prizes in diverse Christian countries, in Hungary, Poland, Istria, Dalmatia, 'Corniola' [Carniola], Carinthia, Austria and Friuli, places not then subject to him but raided and plundered by his horsemen.[103] Mehmed was lucky in matters of war and very liberal and magnanimous, especially to his fighting men. If one of them distinguished himself he was handsomely remunerated and went from one extreme [of wealth] to the other. If Mehmed saw one valiantly mounting the wall of a city he would reward that man with 3 ducats a month; and this might be increased to 8,000 a year, as an example and incentive to others, so that his servants would more readily and voluntarily expose themselves to serious dangers on his behalf. He did not waste his money on maintaining buffoons, actors and other useless persons. One day at a banquet when he was a young man and flushed with wine a jester came into the hall and began his buffoonery, which gave Mehmed great pleasure. He said to the jester, 'Go to the treasury and they will give you 500 ducats.' The jester replied, 'No they will not, without your authority.' Mehmed said, 'Just go and

168

demand it and insist. If they refuse, come to my court in the morning with the treasurer and I will make him do it.' Off he went to the treasurer and asked him for the money. The treasurer said, 'I cannot give it to you without other authority. Wait till the morning when I go to the court, and if my lord orders me to do so I shall willingly give the money to you.' The jester passed the night in happy anticipation of getting it. In the morning the treasurer mentioned the matter to the Emperor. Mehmed laughed and said, 'You did well not to give it to him.' When the jester heard this he was furious. Mehmed summoned him and asked what he was complaining about. 'You', he said, 'gave me an hour's pleasure. I gave you a whole night's pleasure. It's a fair deal. You are indebted to me, not I to you. Go your way.'

He preferred to spend his money on warfare and the support of troops, his nobles and other useful and honourable purposes. He was also most charitable and every week as a rule he would distribute to the poor and needy infinite amounts of money and clothes, as much to the Christians and Jews as to the Turks impartially. In Constantinople he demolished the beautiful church of the Holy Apostles and built in its place a superb mosque, which is a church of the Turks, endowed with hospitals, doctors and medicines for the sick which he maintained as a charity, giving it more than 150,000 ducats a year. This Mehmed was gifted with a singular and wide-ranging intellectual ability. He understood Arabic and Greek and had as his master a Greek monk called 'Scholario' [George Gennadios Scholarios] who was a most erudite theologian and had attended the Council of Florence. Scholarios composed a work in Greek entitled 'To Mahomet the Emperor' – a most beautiful work defining the nature of the Father, the Son and the Holy Spirit. It is easy to convince a Christian of the truth of such matters but to make them intelligible to a Turk is another matter. / This book comprises all the articles of the Christian faith and is a fine work to be read and studied by all. He often read out of it to Mehmed, so much so that some say that the

169

Emperor adhered more to the Christian faith than to any other, especially in the years before his death.[104] He always kept by him some relics of saints with lamps burning before them either, as some say, to enhance their reputation so that he could sell them to Christians at a great price or, as others say, out of a genuine devotion to them. Many, however, and among them trustworthy men, say that Mehmed was the cruellest Emperor since the time of Nero. Here is one example of his cruelties: one day when he was wandering at random in one of his gardens he saw a young melon ('cuchumero') and forbade anyone to touch it because he wanted it to mature. But one of the boys who followed him as personal servants, provoked by childish gluttony, picked it and ate it. The Emperor turned round and, not finding the melon or the culprit, was determined to find him by any means; so he had the stomachs of fourteen of the boys opened. It was the fourteenth who proved to have eaten the melon. An instance of his liberality was the case of his servant Gedik Ahmed, so called because he had a front tooth missing. Gedik once remarked to Mehmed that a prince is not great if he cannot make a small person great or a great person small. Whereupon Mehmed was provoked and raised Gedik from the status of a servant to the rank of Pasha or captain. This was the man whom he sent to capture Leonardo Tocco and who took the city of Otranto, as we have said above. He had a beautiful wife. Mehmed's son Mustafa Čelebi, coming one morning to kiss his father's hand, saw her and fell in love with her; and one afternoon he forced his way into the ladies' bathroom, no guard daring to bar the way to the Sultan's son; and he found the lady naked and violated her. When Gedik heard of this he went straight to the Emperor Mehmed to seek justice for the crime. Mehmed asked him why he made such a fuss. Was he not the Sultan's slave and therefore the slave of his son? If Mustafa had done this deed he had done it to his slave. / None the less he confined Mustafa to his own quarters and 170
three months later had him suffocated, although it was generally

believed that he died of a fever. Another instance of Mehmed's cruelty: a *Kadi* or judge in Bursa was found to have more than once accepted bribes. He was brought to Constantinople and there skinned alive. Mehmed had the man's son brought before him and told him that he was to take his father's place as a judge at Bursa. In case of offence he would suffer the same fate as his father. The carpet on which he sat in the court at Bursa was the pelt of his late father.[105]

Mehmed was more cruel than Nero. The Turkish annals record that in the thirty-three years of his reign and at his command 873,000 people were put to death. Finally, he had prepared a great armada, some said to attack Rhodes by land and sea, others to fight his own son, others to make war on the Sultan of Egypt ('Soldano'). But he was taken gravely ill on his journey at a place in Natalia called Chalcedon ('Calcedonia') and he died. He was aged fifty-six. His corpse was taken to Constantinople and buried in a chapel of the great Imaret ('Marat') which he had built, as we have said above. There lamps continually burned, tended by many 'Talasumani', their priests, who from vigil to vigil sang psalms for his soul. He was dressed in his robes and his turban and festooned with seasonal flowers, as was the custom with all Emperors of the Turks; and on his tomb was inscribed a Turkish epitaph recording the names of all the Emperors, lords, Kings and princes and all the lands that he had conquered. It concluded with the words: 'He had in mind to make war on Rhodes and on arrogant Italy.' But divine goodness willed that such wickedness should not occur.[106]

Mehmed's son Bayezid succeeded him. He was the second of that name and the eighth Emperor of the Turks, and he found his Empire much expanded in countries, nations, subjects and wealth. Some say that Mehmed did not really want Bayezid to be his successor, for all that he was his first-born. He would have preferred another son called Jem ('Cem') to be Sultan, who had not so many sons as Bayezid and was more severe and bellicose; wherefore the Pasha, knowing

Mehmed's intentions, notified Jem first about his father's death. However, the messenger with the news fell into the hands of the pasha Herzegoglou ('Cherzegogli'), who was the son of the Duke of Santa Saba and *Beylerbey* of Natalia and related to the said Bayezid.[107] That messenger was hanged. A second courier went to Jem by another route; his name was Gedik ('Gidich') Mustafa. In the event the news reached Bayezid before his brother Jem and he got to Üsküdar ('Scutari'), a fortress in Natalia on the way to Constantinople, first. / He was fortunate in having a son in Constantinople called Korkud ('Curchut'), who was eight years old; and he acted as regent and quelled the Janissaries who were up in arms, holding the pass until his father Bayezid entered the city and restored peace and order.[108]

171

His brother Jem was thus forestalled, but he was not discouraged. He assembled a huge army and occupied Bursa; and it was near there that Bayezid joined battle with him at a place called 'Sultan Humi'. Jem was defeated, shattered, and fled to Rhodes. From there he was sent on to the Duke of Savoy and thence to King Charles VIII of France who sent him to Rome to Pope Innocent [VIII]. In the time of Pope Alexander VI, Charles of France had a mind to conquer the Kingdom of Naples and then to take Constantinople, and Bayezid was afraid that the Turks might lose the coastline of Greece. But by bad luck Jem died on his way to Terracina and was buried in the city of Capua – to the great relief of Bayezid, who had been paying the Apostolic See 40,000 Venetian gold ducats a year for his upkeep and had also, to ingratiate himself with Pope Innocent VIII, presented to him the iron of the Holy Lance, the sponge, the reed of Our Saviour and many other relics which Mehmed had held in great reverence.[109]

As soon as his brother [Jem] had been disposed of, Bayezid went to war against 'Carabogdan', prince of 'Valachia' and captured Kilia ('Cheli') and Akkerman ('Moncastro'), strongholds which his father Mehmed had tried and failed to conquer. By these achievements Bayezid struck universal panic into all Christians.[110] He also made war on the Sultan of Egypt ('Soldano'); but near Adana ('Addena') and Tarsus in the space of three years he suffered three great defeats in which it is estimated that more than 120,000 Turks perished. There then arose a quarrel between the King of Poland and 'Carabogdan' and the latter freely sold the pass to the Turks.[111] /

172 The sins of the Christians blinded the eyes of their own leaders. Whenever they had a difference among themselves they called on one of the Ottomans for help against their rivals; and the poor wretches never saw that this was their own clear ruin. Thus have the Ottoman princes reached their dominating position at the present day, aided by the constant discord among the Christian princes.

Bayezid then sent a captain called 'Marco Zogli' with a large army, mainly *Akinji* ('Achinzi'), for war against Poland. His enemies were unprepared and 40,000 Christian prisoners were taken; and the following year, when the King of Poland and 'Carabogdan' had made peace together, Bayezid sent 'Marco Zogli' again to Poland with 20,000 *Akinji*; but there was famine and extremely cold weather, which caused the death of all of these Turks. Bayezid next occupied the land of Vlad ('Vlatheo'), son of the Duke of San Saba. Vlad subsequently died in the city of Bar ('Arbe') in Dalmatia, as we have said above.[112]

Bayezid determined to put a stop to the ceaseless banditry and piracy of the men of Chimara ('Cimariotti'). So he advanced upon them by land. Some believe, however, that his real objective was Corfu. But there he found the place well defended, victualled and prepared. This was why he turned on Chimara instead and totally destroyed it. But its people were indomitable and before six months had passed most of them escaped from captivity and returned to their houses, where they still are.[113]

Bayezid then overran the district of Kotor ('Catharo'), expelling its lord Črnojević ('Cernovichio'), who had married a Venetian lady of the family of Erizo. He had been imprisoned for conspiring against the Venetian Senate; but he escaped and went first to France and then to Rome, and finally, in desperation, he went over to Bayezid and became a Turk by faith. Venice then made a pact with the King of France for the ruin and destruction of the Duke of Milan, Lodovico Moro, who sent one Giorgio Buzardo of Genoa with gifts as ambassador to Bayezid to persuade him that the time had come to make war on Venice. Wherefore Bayezid, notwithstanding that the Venetians had sent him an ambassador of their own called Andrea Zanchani to arrange a peace treaty of twenty-five years, reopened hostilities. For the law of Mahomet decreed that it was not necessary to keep faith with Christians. Bayezid therefore sent an army under Iskender Pasha ('Schender bassa'), of whom we have already spoken. It was he, who in the time of Mehmed, had ravaged Friuli. Now he was to attack Friuli again; and there he took 16,000 prisoners, male and female, apart from those that were killed.[114] /

Bayezid had built a great fleet of more than 400 ships. The   173
Venetians too had a large armada which, though smaller in number, was more powerful. Their captain was Antonio Grimani, later to be Doge of Venice. The Turkish captain was Davud ('Tauth') Bey, *Sanjak bey* of Gallipoli, who was based at Coron. There the war began [1499].[115] The Turkish fleet retreated to Porto Longo [near Navarino]; and if the Christians had done the right thing they would have blockaded the Turks there. But they got out, not without danger, and sailed up to Patras. If the Christians had started a fight there in the Gulf of Patras they would have won, especially as the Venetians were joined by eighteen French ships arriving by way of Clarentza ('Chiarenza'). If all the men of Venice had acted like Andrea Loredano and Alban d'Armer the Venetians would surely have scored a great victory, for their two ships attacked the huge vessel of the Turks commanded by Barak Reïs ('Barach Raisi'). Though they looked big, their two ships were small in comparison. Yet they might have boarded the Turkish ship and raised the

Christian flag on it. But Barak set fire to all three of them and they were burnt together with all their crews. The French ships, blown on by a high wind, attacked the Turks vigorously, until of a sudden God blew out the candle of their wind and they were becalmed. They withdrew to a safer position, except for their ship called 'Chiaranta' which was enormous and fought on for hours, until the Turks gave up and left it to sail on with the rest. The French captain was so cross with the Venetians for not coming to the help of the 'Chiaranta' that he left for Marseilles. The Turks sailed off 'Verso il Papa', where many were killed by the guns of the Venetian ships. They then made for Patras, while the Christian captain went to Cephalonia, though he was unable to take it. Those in Lepanto, seeing the Turkish fleet upon them, surrendered; and the Turkish armada wintered in the Gulf of Patras.[116]

The Venetians appointed another captain, Melchior ('Marchio') Trevisano, who led some ships and men to Cephalonia; but they failed to capture it.[117] In the next year [1500] the Sultan Bayezid, who never slept, led a great force by land and sea to join his fleet which had been wintering in the / Gulf of Patras to lay siege to the city of Modon. Six Venetian captains of galleys (whose names are here recorded) volunteered to go to the rescue of 'poor Modone'. Its defenders were so excited to see their rescuers arriving that they left their posts in the fortress and ran down to the sea to welcome them. The Turks, seeing the walls abandoned, climbed up and captured the place. The first over the walls was a Janissary who had but five aspers a day for his pay. Bayezid was to reward this man by making him a *Sanjak bey* with an annual stipend of 8,000 ducats. The conquerors treated the faithful people of Modon with the utmost cruelty. It is said that on the day after his conquest Bayezid went to give thanks in the Christian church and, on crossing the bridge to enter the city, he observed the great depth of the moat; and he exclaimed that neither the talent of his *Beylerbey* Sinan Pasha nor the prowess of his Janissaries had won this place for him. It was the work of God alone.

Zonchio [Navarino] was Bayezid's next stop. It surrendered; and from there he went on to Coron, whose people were so frightened that they gave him the keys of their city. He sailed on to Nauplion ('Napoli di Romania'), but it was too well defended. So he went back to Constantinople to celebrate his triumph; and he had the gates at the entrances to Modon and Coron turned to face Mecca, where their prophet Mehemet is buried.[118]

In the next year [1501], after the death of Melchior Trevisano, the new Venetian captain was named as Benedetto di cà Pesaro; and he sailed to Corfu to raid Vjosa ('Voiosa') near Valona, where some of Bayezid's warships were stationed. His operations were, however, disturbed by a great storm at sea. He was there joined by Gonsalvo Fernando ('Consalvo Ferrante di Corduvo'), Duke of 'Terra Nova', the grand captain of his Catholic Majesty of Spain, with sixty-five well-armed ships. The two captains sailed to Cephalonia and succeeded in capturing it; less than 100 of its Turkish defenders survived, so strongly had they resisted.[119]

It was in the time of Bayezid that the Despot Manuel Palaiologos, of whom we have spoken above, died as a Christian in Constantinople. At Bayezid's command, / he was buried with great honour and solemnity, his funeral being attended not only by Christians but also by Turkish lords and nobles of the court. Manuel left two bastard sons born of two slaves. The elder died as a Christian after his father's death. The younger was made a Turk by Selim, son of Bayezid, and lived in the seraglio.[120] About the family [of Palaiologos], the annals of the Greeks say it came from Rome, being a Roman patrician family that went to Constantinople with the Emperor Constantine the Great. Then, in the days of the exarchs, they moved to Italy and one of them married in Viterbo; and in the days of the Lascaris Emperors there was a celebrated soldier of the family who came to the aid of the

175

Emperor Lascaris. He married in Greece and was the father of the Emperor Michael Palaiologos, of whom we spoke above. There were seven Emperors of the imperial line of Palaiologos. There is now no remaining legitimate descendant in the male line, except for the illustrious Gian Giorgio, Marquis of Montferrat, who is descended from the younger son of the Emperor Andronico Palaeologo called Theodore, who married the female heir to the Marquisate and produced two sons, of whom Gian Giorgio is the last – and even he is now dead.[121]

On leaving Cephalonia, Gonsalvo Fernando, the grand captain, made for Naples. Benedetto of Pesaro took aboard some 'strathioti' and other light cavalry and sailed with his fleet to Natalia to a place called Perama.[122] The Turks there were unprepared and he plundered the district and went back to Candia with much booty and many prisoners. While he was there one Kemal ('Camali') with a few ships raided Zonchio, which some brave Greeks had wrested from the Turks a few months before. It was impregnable by land. The Venetians had four galleys there and a small garrison commanded by a castellan. Kemal arrived unexpectedly by sea, captured the Venetian ships and killed all the soldiers who fell into his hands. Ali Pasha ('Hali Bassa Eunucho'), then *Sanjak bey* of the Morea, came to the scene by land with an army; and Kemal, who was already there, opened the gates to him. The Venetian castellan surrendered his fortress. Ali Pasha spared the lives of its defenders. The captain [Pesaro] rushed to the rescue only to find that Zonchio was already in the hands of Ali Pasha. Ali handed over his prisoners and Pesaro took them with him to Corfu. There he had the castellan and his constable beheaded along with some others. The rest he let go free.[123] /

176   Then one evening the Turks surprised and captured the city of Durazzo. An armada of the French came to the rescue under the command of the lord of Ravenstein ('monsignor di Rovesten').[124] They could put ashore 10,000 men at arms all clad in white. With

Ravenstein were the Duke of Albania, the Infanta of Navarre and many other French lords. From Durazzo, accompanied by the afore-said Venetian captain [Benedetto of Pesaro], they sailed to Mytilene and blockaded it. But they were unable to take it, although they attacked the outskirts of the place, battered its walls and fought some battles. The Grand Master of Rhodes, Pierre d'Aubusson ('Pietro Dubusone') arrived with twenty-eight warships and brave knights to help the Christians but withdrew to Rhodes when he learnt that they had abandoned their assault. Bayezid, not knowing this, and fearful of losing Mytilene, at once sent reinforcements with Mesih ('Mesit') Pasha, whom we have already mentioned [p. 164] in connection with the siege of Rhodes. This Mesih, for all that he was the brother of the mother of my father, was a fierce enemy of the Christians; and in the course of his operations at Mytilene he broke his neck. But Bayezid's fleet found that the Christians had already left Mytilene. For the lord of Ravenstein and the French armada encountered a great storm at sea and were scattered in various directions, his own vessel being wrecked off Cerigo with much loss of life. The general Pesaro thereupon decided to make for the Gulf of Arta, for a place called Preveza there, where some Turkish galleys had stopped to collect ammunition. The Venetian captain-general went in through the narrow mouth of the Gulf and set fire to their munitions and blew them up. But when the *Sanjak bey* arrived with many Turkish cavalry the Christians went back to their ships and managed to get out of the Gulf with the loss of only one man. Another French fleet then arrived commanded by the captain 'Pier Ian' who, together with the general Pesaro and the Bishop of Paphos ('Baffo'), the apostolic legate who had twenty ships sent by Alexander VI, went on to attack the island of Santa Maura. There they constructed a rampart to defend the crossing from the mainland; and this was held by the French and Venetian ships which could prevent any force from The Levant getting across to the island. And they built another rampart which was manned by the papal legate with the Pope's warships. The *Sanjak bey* ('frambularo') arrived with an army but found the causeway blocked and the island cut off. He was unable to do anything and he retired under fire from the Christian guns. / So Santa Maura was taken and the Venetians restored its fortifications.[125]

None the less, Bayezid did not relent in his aggressive hostility towards and damage to the Republic of Venice, as much in time of peace as in time of war, in a manner more deceitful than his forebears. This was especially so in the district of Dalmatia which was subject to Venice, for he visited the Venetians there with a wave of persecution, capture and hangings on the grounds that they were thieves and pirates from the sea. The Venetians brought it on themselves by not taking precautions in the days of peace; and it is my opinion that they suffered more in peace than in war; for the Turks arrested almost all of their merchants and put them in prisons from which they could escape only by paying great sums of money which they did not have. I can testify to this, for it was such exactions and payments that caused the ruin of my family in those parts, especially of my brother Alexander.[126] The Venetian Senate made many fruitless attempts to reach a settlement with Bayezid. In the end they appointed a most prudent man called Andrea Gritti, who is now Doge of Venice. He had been released from prison; and it was he who persuaded Bayezid to make peace on the following terms: Cephalonia was to remain in Venetian hands; but Santa Maura was to revert to its former [Turkish] status; the money and goods which the Sultan had filched from Venetian merchants were to remain in his hands, to help pay for the repair of the defences of Santa Maura.[127]

In the year 1509 ('1510') there was a mighty earthquake which caused a large part of the walls of Constantinople to collapse. Bayezid decreed that throughout his Empire every twenty households must produce one man to work on the repair and restoration of the ruined walls; and the task was fully completed in the short space of one summer. I myself saw 73,000 men at work in Constantinople. Another 10,000 were commissioned to repair the walls of Didymoteichon ('Demotico') in Europe, which was the Sultan's birthplace.[128]

Next Ismail I Safavi ('il Sophi') of Persia declared war on Bayezid, entered Anatolia and advanced as far as the vicinity of Bursa. Bayezid sent an army against him under the command of Ali ('Halil') Pasha the Eunuch. But he was killed and his army was destroyed. / Ismail ('Sophi') recalled his troops to Persia and made peace with Bayezid.[129]   178

The three surviving sons of Bayezid [II], all called 'sultam', were Ahmed ('Acmat'), Selim and Korkud ('Curcuth'). It was his intention that Ahmed should succeed him, for he was more like himself in character, being of a peaceable and charitable nature. All three sons were born of the same mother. This was unusual among the Turkish rulers, although the present Sultan Suleiman has several sons born of the same mother. / Selim, however, was restless and ambitious for the   179 throne, and he had the support of the Janissaries in Constantinople. They were glad to accept him as their Emperor. Selim went to kiss his father's hand and Bayezid handed over his sword and abdicated his authority. The court went over to Selim; and after about twenty days in Constantinople, Bayezid, abandoned by all, moved to Didymoteichon ('Dimotico') near Adrianople, where he had been born. He died at a place called 'Saslidere' and his corpse was taken to Constantinople and buried in the Imaret which he had built there. /

Selim [1512–20] was the ninth Sultan of the Turks. He was   180 magnanimous, bellicose and liberal; and he had it in mind to outdo Alexander of Macedon in the magnitude of his achievements. After his father's funeral he went to Bursa; and there he ordered the execution of a number of Pashas, among them that Mustafa who had gone as ambassador to Rome and presented Pope Innocent [VIII] with the holy relics, as recounted above. Other victims of Selim's executioner were the 'basa Ducaginogli', 'Taut bei', his major domo and 'Zaiusbassi', because they had taken sides with his brother Ahmed

Pasha. There was then warfare between Selim and his two brothers Ahmed and Korkud. He defeated both of them and had them strangled with a bowstring. Back in Constantinople, Selim had all his grandsons with their wives and children brought to him and strangled in like fashion – a total of twenty members of the Ottoman family.[130]

The same Selim was, however, very partial to the Christians. In the case of a dispute between a Christian and a Turk, he would take the side of the former, which was not in keeping with the religion of Mahomet. Once, when some Muslims had tortured a Christian into changing his faith, Selim had the offenders punished; and all Christians who had denied Christ and become Muslims against their will were encouraged to revert to their Christian faith.[131]

Selim made war on Ismail, King of Persia ('Sophi Sac Ismail'). /
181   Ismail fought back but he could not resist the great multitudes of Turkish troops; and he retired to the great city of Tabriz ('Thauris'), his Persian capital. Selim followed him and entered the city. He emptied its treasury, stole two of the king's concubines, and took with him to Constantinople as prisoners 3,000 masters of various arts and wealthy citizens of Tabriz.[132] In the following year Selim made war against the [Mamluk] Sultan of Cairo, 'Camsoingani', and defeated him and the troops which Ismail ('Sophi') had sent to help him in a
182   battle near Aleppo, on 24 August 1516. / [Here follows an Italian translation of the text of a letter, written in Greek, which Selim sent to all his governors and officials as well as to the podestà of the island of Chios ('Schio'), dated 27 August.][133] Of the Mamluks only 8,000 were left. They found a new Sultan called Tuman Bey ('Tomobei'). But Selim, with 130,000 camels, succeeded in crossing the desert in eight days, and made camp at a place called 'Bulacho'. The Mamluks, unable to fight so huge an army, withdrew to Cairo; and Selim captured their new Sultan and displayed him from the walls before going on to Alexandria, where he slaughtered all the Mamluks. While he was there he got word from his son Suleiman that Pope Leo X of

blessed memory had preached the crusade in Rome inciting all Christian princes. So Selim appointed a viceroy in Cairo and left for Constantinople, / taking with him all the contents of the Mamluk treasury and many rich and prominent men as prisoners. 'I shall not go on to tell of 'Aliduli' and the other Arab princes, nor of the many places that Selim acquired and the many who died at his hands, since other writers have fully described the life of this emperor who day and night thought of nothing but war.'[134] [There follows a list of his victims.] In Constantinople, however, he had a splendid arsenal built at Pera for his fleet, roofed over like that of the Signoria at Venice. He also had it in mind to reconstruct the arsenal of the Christian Emperors. But death prevented the fulfilment of these projects. He also planned a great expedition to Sicily. But he fell ill and died [1520].

The Janissaries in Constantinople kept his death a secret until his son Suleiman arrived there to take over the sovereignty. He met the corpse of his father at the Adrianople gate of the city and, out of his love and respect, dismounted and helped shoulder the coffin to the Imaret of the Sultan Bayezid. There it was laid with great pomp and ceremony, until such time as the Sultan Suleiman will have completed the construction of his own sumptuous Imaret which is now in progress and which will stand above what was in the days of the Christian Emperors a fine cistern supplying an aqueduct.[135]

Thus did Suleiman become the tenth Sultan of the Turks. The news of Selim's death sparked a rebellion in Egypt and Syria led by an Arab called Ghazali ('Gazeli') supported by some Mamluks. To crush the revolt, Suleiman sent his brother-in-law Ferhad Pasha, and Ghazali was killed in battle. / His head, together with others, was sent to Suleiman.[136] Suleiman then elected to make war on the Hungarians to punish them for the great injuries which they had inflicted on him. He was aware that the princes of Christendom were divided among themselves by great altercations and internecine warfare. So he took personal command of a vast army to attack the city of Belgrade. He

183

184

laid siege to it with such savagery that its defenders, seeing their fortress destroyed and with no prospect of help coming from any quarter, surrendered and offered to make peace in exchange for their survival. None the less many of them were put to death and there was much looting and pillage. Suleiman then ordered that all the captains between the rivers Danube and Sava, for all that so many of them had surrendered, be put to the sword or taken as prisoners; and when he went back to Constantinople, he took with him the body of 'Santa Teta', the body of Santa Veneranda, an effigy of Our Lady and an arm of Santa Barbara, all of which were objects of veneration in Belgrade. These he offered to the Greek Patriarch in Constantinople at a price for the charity of Christians; otherwise he would throw them in the sea. The poor Patriarch did all he could to save the relics; he handed over some money and kept them in the Patriarchate with the greatest veneration. And I may say that the Patriarch was not alone in finding the means to ransom many Christians. Throughout the Empire the bishops adjured all Christian people, merchants and foreigners to do God's will by subscribing to the liberation of Christian slaves; and they did so willingly. I know of someone in Adrianople who three times sold one of her houses to raise ransom money to set free the slaves who were taken at Modon.[137]

When Pope Leo X of blessed memory died, the cardinals in conclave elected as Supreme Pontiff Hadrian VI. He had been the teacher of Charles V ('Carlo'), Emperor of the Christians in Austria; and he was much revered as a man of saintly life.[138] His arrival in Rome from Spain was for so long delayed that Suleiman, / seeing the Christian church without a leader and in discord, decided to abandon his campaign against Hungary and to concentrate on taking the island of Rhodes, 'the key of Italy', whose Knights of Jerusalem had caused him so much damage and trouble. The French were not able to come to the aid of the poor city of Rhodes as they had been wont to do; for they were being harassed by other Christian princes. But there had come to Rome with Pope Hadrian VI a contingent of Spaniards, together with the Archbishop of 'Matera and Chiarenza'.[139] Pope Clement VII had made this Archbishop a Cardinal and he died under Pope Paul [III]. He saw that Pope Hadrian was doing very little to help 'poor Rhodes'. So he offered to go and fight the Turks at his own expense and he was ready to pay the Spanish troops that he had brought with him. His name was Matteo Palmieri ('Palmero'). He came from Naples and he was the honour and glory of Christendom. He realised that Pope Hadrian was too involved with other matters to give much thought to the plight of Rhodes and would not support him. Indeed he told the Archbishop that Rhodes was a small place surrounded by walls with quite enough knights behind them to defend it. In the face of the Pope's constant plea that he had no money and that St Peter was impoverished, the troops who were assembled in Italy for the purpose of going to Rhodes made their own arrangements to raise the funds; / and, with the assistance of the Emperor 186 Charles V, they gathered together at Naples and Sicily. They were joined for the relief of Rhodes by some ships and men from Castille, England, Portugal and other places. But it was too late, for Rhodes fell to Suleiman and his Turks in December 1522. The Grand Master, Philippe de Villiers de l'Isle Adam ('Philippo Devilers Lisle Adam Francesce'), was forced to surrender his fortified city of Rhodes, which had been granted of old by the Christian Emperors of Constantinople to the Order of the Knights of Jerusalem.[140]

Now Suleiman intimated to the Grand Master that no treaty could be arranged and no ship could leave the island until the son of Jem Sultan ('Cem'), who was known to be in their hands, was found and delivered. A dear friend of mine was offered ten ducats a day for his pains by one of Suleiman's Pashas if he would reveal the whereabouts of the said son of Jem, whose name was also Jem. But my friend, mindful of his Christian faith, refused to reveal it. Finally, however, the Turks scoured all the highways and byways of Rhodes and found

Jem together with his children, two sons and two daughters. They asked him whether he would prefer to die as a Turk or as a Christian; and he bravely replied that he and his children would all wish to die as Christians. So Suleiman had Jem and his sons secretly put to death. The daughters were sent to Constantinople. And my readers should note that the death of this Jem together with his two sons was neither helpful nor expedient for the Christian cause; for Jem was favoured not only by the Janissaries but also by many of the Turks. This was shown by the way in which the Janissaries mourned his passing; and certainly when he was alive Jem had the power to perform a great service to Christendom by creating dissension among the Turks.[141] /

187 His death was thus a great loss to the Christian cause. Yet a still greater loss had been the death of Pope Leo X who, in contrast to Pope Hadrian VI, had laboured day and night for the defence of the church and resistance against the common enemy of all Christians, the Turks. Often, when I was with him, Leo would consult me about the way that the Christians could impede the Turks and prevent them from following up their victory at Belgrade. It would have been a great advantage to have in our hands Jem the Ottoman, the son of Jem, and to have brought him to Rome and sent him to Hungary. I had advised the Pope to do this and so to promote disaffection from the Sultan Selim. The glorious Pope Leo had wanted to do this. But he wanted still more to collect a great army, a solemn crusade, to fight the Turks, as he publicly declared; and he would have gone on it himself had death not cruelly prevented him.[142]

When he had captured Rhodes and dismissed the Grand Master, Suleiman prepared to go to Natalia from Constantinople. He disbanded his fleet, though some sailed for Chios ('Scyo'); but before they got to the Straits nearly all their ships were destroyed in a storm. Back in Constantinople, Suleiman celebrated a great triumph and ordered the construction of a new fleet of many galleys, planning to wreak havoc among the Christians, as he had promised his Janissaries.

Suleiman was very hard on the Christians. He decreed that no Christian in his dominions should ride a horse of more than four ducats in value; and he imposed other restrictions with penalties and punishments which made his reign more tyrannical than any of his predecessors.[143] At this time he was intent on restoring and refortifying the stronghold of Skradin ('Scardona') in Dalmatia, which his men had captured before Pope Hadrian left Spain, and which was on the frontier of Hungary. But that Pope, who had so disgraced Christendom by neglecting 'poor Rhodes', sent the cardinal Gaetano / of San Sisto to Hungary with some money. He did not stay there for long. Hadrian's successor Clement VII, however, at the start of his reign, heard that the Turks were laying siege to Kliš ('Clissa') and ordered the Bishop of Skradin with 'Thomasi Nigro' and 'Zuan Francesco Brancha di Fuligno' to go to the relief of Kliš, which they did.[144]

188

Now when the viceroy of Cairo died, the man whom the Sultan had appointed as his deputy there, Suleiman sent out to replace him one Mustafa Pasha. He was a Dalmatian, having been born near Kotor ('Cattaro'). When he arrived in Cairo, Mustafa was blockaded by the Arabs and other rebels against Turkish rule. He appealed to the Sultan for help. The news greatly distressed his wife. She was a sister of Suleiman and she went to him in tears, lamenting that life had been so cruel to her; for their father had given her in marriage to the *Bostançibaşi* [the head gardener of the palace], and she had little joy out of that marriage, for her husband had soon been executed. Now she was married to a Pasha who was holed up in distant Cairo and she knew not whether she was a widow or a wife. She begged that she might be sent to die in Cairo with her man or that he might be recalled and rescued from his predicament. Suleiman at once ordered Ahmed Pasha ('Acmat bassa'), who had been born in Trebizond and promoted by the Sultan Selim, to take an army to the scene; and he liberated Mustafa and took over the government of Cairo as Sultan.

But as soon as Mustafa had left and was back in Constantinople, Ahmed Pasha staged a rebellion in Cairo and was hailed as Sultan by his Arab conspirators. This news prompted Suleiman to postpone his campaign against the Christians. He sent an army to Egypt under the command of Ibrahim Pasha to deal with Ahmed. When the rebels knew that the army was almost upon them in Cairo they changed their minds and reverted to their allegiance to Suleiman. They found Ahmed in his bath, cut off his head and sent it to Constantinople, to the great delight of Suleiman. This Ibrahim Pasha was born at a place called Riniasa ('Regnassa') below Parga and opposite Corfu. / He

189 was a notable soldier and a great favourite of the Sultan Suleiman, who found a wife for him and even attended his wedding and joined in the festivities, for which no expense was spared; and this was an unheard-of event for a Sultan.[145]

Suleiman, not content with so many victories, led a huge army to Hungary in 1526. Its King, Louis II ('Ludovico'), was only twenty years old, but he raised a force of 25,000 men to fight the Turks; and he was joined by contingents from Transylvania and elsewhere. But they came too late, for Suleiman advanced from Belgrade and reached a place called Mohacs ('Noaz') which was in the plain; and there on 26 ('28') August Ibrahim, with the army of the *Beylerbey* of Natalia, defeated the Christians. The King fled and met his death trying to ford a swollen river or swamp on horseback. His body was later found. [A list of the Hungarian casualties follows – a total of 15,000.]

190 / The Queen of Hungary fled from Buda and took refuge in 'Cossonia' near Austria, as also did the Count Palatine 'Stephano Batori'. The Turks then marched on Buda, found it abandoned and pillaged it; and Suleiman took with him to Constantinople many of the city's treasures and antiquities which are still to be seen on public display.[146]

When he had left Hungary, its barons and people elected as their King the Voivode of Transylvania. He was John Zápolya ('Zuane').

His election was disputed by the Count Palatine Stephen Batori on the grounds that the Voivode of Transylvania had caused the ruin of Hungary by failing to come to the aid of the late King against Ibrahim Pasha and his Turks. He maintained that the Voivode had an arrangement with the Turks. So the Diet was summoned again; and 'Ferdinando of Austria' [Ferdinand, Archduke and brother of Charles V] was elected King of Hungary and crowned as such. John [Zápolya] fled back to Transylvania, hoping that the Turks would come to his support. They did so in 1529 when Suleiman returned to Hungary with a huge army, expelled King Ferdinand and restored John / [Zápolya] to the throne. He then sent Ibrahim to lay siege to   191 Vienna, which he did; but after a while he had to give it up; and Suleiman, having reduced Hungary to ruins and taken many prisoners, went back to Constantinople. He filled a whole room in his palace with all the jewels and precious stones that he had collected; and he took to using a dining table and stools 'in the Italian fashion', a thing that the Turks had never done before.[147]

In 1530 Suleiman celebrated the feast of the circumcision of some of his sons and he sent invitations to all the lords of his Empire and to other potentates and princes who were in alliance with him. He was the first of the Sultans of the Turks to write to Christians in the Turkish language. I have to hand a copy of the letter which he addressed to the Signoria of Venice [to the Doge Andrea Gritti], which I here transcribe as translated from the Arabic into the common tongue; and it will be observed that he makes the most of his honorific titles: ' . . . Suleiman Sach, son of Selim Sach, invincible Emperor, I who am the ruler of rulers and a wonder among men, the legitimate sovereign of all the realms on the face of the earth, the shadow of God over the two lands, of the White Sea and the Black Sea, of Romania and Natalia, of Karamania and Greece, of the countries of Dulkadir ('Bulchadria') and Dyarbakir, of Kurdistan ('Caldi') and Azerbaijan ('Dirbazan'), of Persia ('Rizen') and Damascus, Aleppo and Cairo,

Mecca and Medina and Jerusalem, of all the lands of the Arabs and the Yemeni ('Hemeri'), of the Tartars and many other places . . . '. The invitation is addressed to the Doge Andrea Gritti of Venice, most honoured among the lords of the Christians, most revered among the potentates of the followers of Jesus, to attend the feast of the circumcisions of his sons the Sultans Mustafa, Mehmet, Selim and

192   Bayezid. / This feast was the greatest ever held in Turkey.[148]

In 1531 ('1532') Ferdinand attacked John Zápolya ('Juane') in Hungary and laid siege to Buda. Suleiman sent an army to intervene and a treaty was arranged through the arbitration of the King of Poland in 1532. Before this, however, there was continuing discord over the possession of Kliš ('Clissa') in Dalmatia; and the Christians demolished the fortress which the Turks had built on the coast.[149] /

193   In 1531 the Knights of Rhodes, now in Malta, sailed to Modon and made a spirited attack on it. The enterprise was inspired by a Greek called 'Isidoro Scandali', who had been on Rhodes, had been captured by Moorish pirates and ransomed from Barbary by the Grand Master of the Knights in Malta. He had friends in Modon; but his clever scheme to drive out the Turks misfired. Also involved in this venture was a Knight called 'Zuan Maria Straticopulo'.[150] /

194   Suleiman, seeing that the King of Poland had failed to bring an end to the trouble in Hungary, set out again for Vienna. The Emperor Charles V, Ferdinand King of the Romans, France and the whole of Germany joined forces to meet him there. But the Turkish armies were brought to a halt and half destroyed by rain and floods and the Christians were saved.[151]

In the same year as the episode of Scandali at Modon [1531], the [Genoese] lord Andrea Doria brought a fleet to the Levant and, passing Modon, succeeded in getting ashore at Coron. The Turks strenuously defended the rock but after ten days they were driven out by the Christians. Andrea Doria left a garrison of seasoned Spanish soldiers at Coron and sailed up to Patras. This too he captured and

sacked; and all of the Morea broke out into rebellion. / Lepanto
resisted Doria's attack, although it very nearly fell to the Christians.
In the following year [1532] the Turks sent a purposeful fleet of ninety
ships to Coron. The garrison there reported to 'Cesare' [?] and
Andrea Doria sailed down with twenty-four galleys and twenty-four
flat-bottomed boats ('barze'). The Turkish ships were at Sapienza.
The Christians sailed through the narrows and blockaded them; and
as luck would have it their first shot killed the leader of the Janissaries.
Doria went back to look for two of his ships which had got becalmed
and taken by the Turks. He found them and went on to attack the
Turkish fleet. The Christians then held Coron for eighteen months,
until an envoy from Ferdinand went to Constantinople to arrange
a treaty. Doria then left Coron after taking aboard all those who
wanted to come to Christendom. All who stayed behind were brutally
murdered by the *Sanjak bey* of the Morea.[152]

When he had made peace with the Kings of France and of the
Romans [Francis I and Ferdinand I], Suleiman sent Ibrahim Pasha
with the army of Anatolia to winter in Aleppo to keep an eye on the
King of Persia.[153] He also sent Haireddin ('Caradin Bey'), commonly
known as Barbarossa, as captain-general with an armada to Barbary;
and he sent Lodovico ('Alvise') Gritti [the Venetian envoy in
Constantinople] to Hungary. Barbarossa on his voyage passed near
Salerno, then Gaeta, and sacked Fondi and other places before
reaching Barbary and chasing out the King of Tunis. Suleiman ([the]
'Gran Turco') meanwhile set out for Persia with his army, while
Gritti made for Hungary with an escort of 600 Janissaries, 8,000
knights and taking 400,000 ducats. [Gritti was eventually cornered in
Medgyes ('Mevis') and executed as the Sultan's agent by John
Zápolya ('Zuane').][154] /

Having reached Aleppo, Suleiman went on to Tabriz ('Tauris'),   196
taking with him the *Beylerbey* of Mesopotamia. On their advance into
Persia they were helped by the defection of one 'Ullama', a son of that

'Ferisbei' who had been killed in battle against Bayezid. 'Ullama' did the opposite to his father. He guided Suleiman to a place called Bitlis, which was his own patrimony, and thence on to 'Aclat', both of which places still belong to Suleiman. From there he led him on to Tabriz, which Suleiman and his army entered. The Persian King Sac Ismail ('Sophi'), learning of Suleiman's advance, retreated into the mountains, to a place called Khorasan ('Corazzan'). This was a subtle Persian ploy; for the Turks ran short of provisions and were forced to retreat, partly from hunger and partly from the cold. Suleiman therefore made instead for Baghdad ('Bagdet'), which is the ancient Babylonia, with its high tower called 'Nembrot'. And there he spent the winter and passed some time. Before leaving Baghdad, however, he had a fortress built there. The work was done by some Georgian Christians who were rewarded by being granted exemption; and he stocked it with provisions and installed a garrison in it. When he had gone, the present King of Persia, Tahmasp ('Sach Thomas'), the son of Ismail, with a large part of his army, marched to Tabriz. There was a great battle there in which about 30,000 men died, among them 'Ullama'. With him was a renegade Turk called 'Acmet Aga', who had rebelled against Selim. He escaped and found his way to Suleiman at Baghdad. He is now a *Sanjak bey* in Turkey. But Tabriz was lost, retaken by the Persians at great cost to the Turks.[155]

Tabriz was, however, recovered, and is still in Turkish hands. Having spent two years in Persia, and hearing that Barbarossa had captured Tunis, Suleiman left a garrison in Baghdad and went back to Constantinople. Barbarossa came back from his victory in Barbary by way of Sardinia, which he terrorised, taking many Christian prisoners, although he was opposed by two Christian captains, Doria and Don Albarea.[156] / Once back in Constantinople, he went to Anatolia to pay his respects to Suleiman and to kiss the hand of Ibrahim Pasha who was then the Sultan's favourite. Ibrahim rebuffed him, accusing him of having lost all the army and squandered all the money; and when Suleiman was back in Constantinople, Barbarossa plotted with Mustafa Sultan, son of Suleiman and Ibrahim's greatest rival, to let it be known that Ibrahim was in league with the Emperor Charles [V]. A day later, when Ibrahim had dined and gone to bed, Suleiman ordered one of his ministers of justice to go and slit his throat while he was asleep and gave him his own dagger to do the job. He was Ayas Pasha ('Aiasbassa'), who is still alive; and Suleiman said to him: 'See what a pig lies sleeping there.' Ayas Pasha, who was a great rival of Ibrahim, was rewarded for his crime by being elevated to his rank of leading Pasha, with his ring and his fortune.[157]

After Ibrahim's death, Suleiman sent 8,000 men under the command of 'Amurat Vaivoda', a renegade who had been born in Šibenik ('Sebenicho'), to go and lay siege to Kliš ('Clissa'), whose lord Kružić ('Crusich') had built a great fortress on the coast. Pope Paul III set great store by Kliš and had armed and provisioned it under a commissioner called 'Jacomo Dalmoro d'Arbe', who set out from Ancona with an army together with one Niccolo dalla Torre, captain for the King of the Romans, and some German troops. Their intention was to destroy the fortress at Kliš. But their expedition was a disaster. Amurat Vaivoda drove them off. Dalla Torre and the Pope's commissioner managed to escape. But Kružić was killed and his fortress was simply abandoned.[158]

In 1537 Suleiman determined to invade the Kingdom of Naples. / He prepared a great expedition by sea, led by his captain Lutfi Bey, captain-general of Gallipoli. Suleiman went by land with his son and his army and encamped near Valona. Lutfi Pasha sent Barbarossa on with ships from Negroponte to carry supplies to the camp at Valona. Lutfi sailed for the Kingdom of Naples and reached Otranto without much opposition. From there he went on to Castro which surrendered after some resistance, though Lutfi treated its people badly. He then advanced to Tricase ('Tre Case'), to 'Virento near the Conte de Castri', and Galatone [?] ('Galatole').[159]

Now the Venetian Senate had appointed two captains-general of the sea, Girolamo Pesaro ('Hieronymo da Pesaro'), who was at Corfu with forty-four galleys, and Giovanni Vetturi ('Zuan Vetturi'), who was at the Gulf of Kotor ('Cattaro') with about fifty ships. Barbarossa, on his way to Valona with his cargo ships of provisions, came upon Doria in the Archipelago, who followed him and seized seventeen of his vessels. Barbarossa pressed on to Zakynthos where he found no opposition, for the Venetians were not then at war; and from there he made for Corfu followed by his cargo ships. Off Corfu, however, one of his small craft was sunk when the Venetian galley called Zaratina opened fire. This was the cause of great indignation among the Turks. Barbarossa got to Valona, however, with his supplies. Suleiman then sent an ambassador over to Corfu with three ships to lodge a complaint with Pesaro. He was Yunus Bey ('Ionusbei Dragomano') and he demanded compensation from Pesaro for the loss of the goods in the sunken ship. There were three Venetian ships on guard near 'la Glossa' and these challenged the Turkish ships. Doria, who had just arrived back from Messina, joined in and / helped them capture the Turks. Yunus Bey managed to escape ashore but was seized by some pirates ('Cimarioti'), from whom Pesaro ransomed him for 500 ducats and sent him over to the Grand Turk [at Valona], where he reported on the unfriendly activities of the [supposedly neutral] Venetians.[160]

[There followed a number of skirmishes between Christian and Turkish ships in the waters between Corfu and the mainland, resulting in many casualties on both sides. Doria returned to Sicily. But Barbarossa returned to the attack on Corfu; and those that were there say that he was so beset that the sea was blackened by smoke.]

As a consequence Suleiman again declared war on Venice. He ordered his army which had been fighting in the Kingdom of Naples to report forthwith at Valona, which they did, though not before they had done considerably more damage in the region of Otranto. For this Suleiman had their four leaders arrested and executed at Valona.

In anticipation of the Turkish attack on Corfu, Pesaro made for Cephalonia. Suleiman brought his troops by land down to Butrinto; and on 27 August 1537 his fleet sailed over to Corfu. There they created havoc; but after eighteen days they gave up the struggle and sailed off to Constantinople taking with them some 20,000 prisoners.[161] Their captain-general Lutfi Bey returned to Gallipoli. Barbarossa led eighty galleys to the Archipelago and pillaged Aigina ('Lezena') and other places, taking 16,000 captives. The Duke of Naxos ('Nexia') had to agree to buy him off by paying a tribute of 6,000 ducats a year.[162] /

At the time of the attack on Corfu by the Turks and their departure for Constantinople, the Venetian captains Pesaro and Vetturi joined forces at the Gulf of Kotor, from where Pesaro attacked, captured and sacked Skradin ('Scardona'). Vetturi went on to a place called 'Brovazo' [? Brač], where the Christians suffered a disastrous defeat. Winter being upon them, the Venetian Senate then ordered both generals to give it up and retire, leaving only a few galleys to guard Corfu; and the Turks, under command of 'Amurat Vaivoda' with 8,000 cavalry and many infantry, took their chance to come back and recover Skradin which Pesaro had taken and order its repair and reconstruction. Then they went on to 'Nadin' near Zadar ('Zara'), a stronghold in Dalmatia on which the Venetians had spent much money to make it the guardian of Christianity for the whole area. The Turks were unable to take it for all their efforts; but its castellan, corrupted by bribery, handed it over. He was later condemned to death by the Venetian Senate and executed at Zara. The Turks then encamped at the fortress of 'Vrana', whose castellan also handed it over. The Venetians, unable to find him, offered a reward for anyone who captured him alive. The Turks then went on to 'Nova', and that too they captured.[163]

News reached Venice that the Turk was preparing another great armada. Lutfi Bey had been relieved of his command because of his activities around Otranto and had been nominated *Beylerbey* of Anatolia. His place had been taken by Barbarossa in command of more than 200 galleys. The Venetians appointed as their general for the war against the Turks one Vincenzo Capello with more than eighty galleys at his command; and the Pope, Paul III, appointed a commander of his own in the person of Marco Grimani, the Patriarch of Aquileia, with thirty galleys. Barbarossa, when he set out from Constantinople, made first for the Archipelago, to the islands of Skiathos and Skopelos ('Schiati' and 'Scropolli'). Their Venetian governor put up a stout defence; but he was wounded and then murdered in his bed by some traitors who hoped to gain a reward and their liberty by their deed. / But after he had captured the islands, Barbarossa had them all decapitated for their crime. Thence he sailed on to Candia and Suda, where the Venetian troops and some of the locals fought off the Turks who tried to come ashore and frightened them away. Having ravaged some of the towns on Candia, Barbarossa and his men turned on Chios ('Schyo'), where the Genoese pay tribute to the Sultan.[164] There he left some of his ships before proceeding to encounter the Christian forces with 140 of his galleys. The Venetian general was already at Corfu, and there the Pope's commander joined him with some ships from Venice and some from Ancona, having arrived at Corfu by way of Zara and Ragusa. He then sailed across to Preveza without telling the Venetians and bombarded it before being forced back to Corfu.[165]

At Zara the Venetians had appointed a provveditore called Alvise Badoer ('Baduario') and had sent 'Camillo Orsino' ahead to Zara; for many of the Turks had left there to join their Sultan, who had gone from Adrianople to make war on Carabogdan, lord of Moldavia. The Venetians [took their chance] advancing from Zara on Brač ('Broazo') which they captured, sacked and destroyed before going back to Zara. But a few days later 'Amurat Vaivoda' came back with a company of Turks. Some Venetian horsemen descended on his camp, robbed his stable and captured his wife's sister, carrying her off as a prisoner to Šibenik ('Sebenicho'). Amurat went on to Brač ('Broaʒo') and found it razed to the ground. He ordered it to be reconstructed and left a Turkish garrison there.

Suleiman meanwhile with about 120,000 elite cavalry reached Nicopolis, where he hoped to build a bridge across the Danube. But Carabogdan with his 35,000 men prevented this. So Suleiman and his Turks made their crossing of the river at another spot not far away; and the Christians fled over the mountains to take refuge with King John Zápolya ('Zuane').[166]

And at this point, since I have to go for a while to Rome, I shall leave my narrative for some successor to continue. /

The Pope having arranged a peace settlement between the Emperor [Charles V] and the most Christian King [Francis I] and resolved the differences between them, the Emperor left for Spain.[167] The noble Andrea Doria, on the Emperor's orders, came to Genoa and raised some troops in Lombardy. Then, going on to Sicily, he enlisted 'don Ferrante' with some more troops and, leaving Sicily with fifty-two galleys and sixty ships, he sailed on to Corfu. The Patriarch [of Aquileia] had already left Preveza. Barbarossa, coming from Chios, made for Preveza and, having sacked Cephalonia and taken about 1,000 prisoners and packed them off to Lepanto, he entered the Gulf of Arta.[168]

The Christian leaders being now united together, thanks be to God, I have narrated all that happened before my departure from Venice.

202

Notes and commentary

1 The first two pages of the text relate some of the fables and legends about the origins of the Osmanli or Ottoman people and their leaders. What may be called the more strictly historical records begins with this rather garbled

account of the events of the Fourth Crusade in 1204 and its consequences for the Byzantine Empire. Alexios (IV) Angelos was a brother-in-law of the German King Philip of Swabia.

2 Spandounes uses the word 'Natalia' (Greek *Anatoli*) throughout to mean Anatolia or Asia Minor. The three Emperors of the family of Laskaris who ruled the Empire in exile at Nicaea from 1204 to 1261 were in fact Theodore I, John III Vatatzes, his son-in-law, and Theodore II. The rightful claimant to their throne when Theodore II died was his son, John IV Laskaris; and it was he who was dispossessed and blinded by Michael Palaiologos (Michael VIII), who took the title of Despot (not 'Caesar') in 1258 and Emperor in 1259. He was not, as Spandounes asserts, a son-in-law of Theodore II.

3 The passage here in parentheses is not contained in the first printed edition of Spandounes (Lucca, 1550). The account of the subsequent marriage and offspring of the blinded John IV Laskaris is a fabrication, no doubt to support the claims to imperial lineage of later members of the Laskaris family. The story that John IV escaped from his captivity and was lured to the court of Charles I of Anjou in Italy was circulated in the west by Angevin agents. D. J. Geanakoplos, *Emperor Michael Palaeologus and the West, 1258–1282* (Cambridge, Mass., 1959), pp. 217–18. Of the three Laskarids whom Spandounes knew: Demetrios was killed in 1502 during Bayezid II's campaign in Dalmatia, where Theodore's brother Alexander also suffered (see below n. 126). The second of them, 'Juan Lascari', was the celebrated scholar and humanist Janus Lascaris who died in Rome in December 1534 in the time of Pope Paul III (1534–49), when Spandounes was completing the final version of his work. The third, Alexios Laskaris, still in the papal service in 1538, seems to be otherwise unknown. *PLP*, VI, no. 14534 (John IV Laskaris), no. 14536 (Janus Laskaris).

4 The entry of Alexios Strategopoulos and his men into Constantinople in July 1261 is well attested by the Byzantine historians. The 'French Emperor' who fled to Naples was Baldwin II. The news of the recapture of Constantinople reached Michael VIII Palaiologos at Meteorion in Asia Minor. Geanakoplos, *Emperor Michael*, p. 119.

5 The dire prophecy here attributed to one Theodore Tornikes or Tornikios is said by the historian George Pachymeres to have been uttered in somewhat similar terms by a civil servant at the court of Nicaea called Kakos Senachereim. George Pachymeres, *Histories*, ed. I. Bekker, 2 vols. (*CSHB*, 1835), I, p. 149.

6 This account of the emergence of Osman I Gazi ('Ottomano') is largely fictitious. He reigned for rather less than 'forty-nine years' before his death in 1326. The names of his alleged companions in arms are variously recorded. The once Christian families of Michaelogli and Markozogli claimed descent from two of them. H. A. Gibbons, *The Foundation of the*

Ottoman Empire (Oxford, 1916), pp. 52–3. Spandounes, like other western historians of his day, gives Osman the title of 'Emperor' of the Turks, meaning 'Sultan', a title which he never claimed. The first to do so was Murad I (1362–89).

7 At the Second Council of Lyons in 1274 a union of the churches of Rome and Constantinople was proclaimed. The Emperor Michael VIII did not attend the Council in person. See Nicol, *LCB*, pp. 53–7.

8 Andronikos II Palaiologos succeeded when his father Michael died in December 1282.

9 This account of the alleged coalition of the western powers against Andronikos II is too compressed and garbled to be of much value. See Angeliki E. Laiou, *Constantinople and the Latins* (Cambridge, Mass., 1972).

10 Osman captured Bursa (Byzantine Prousa) on 6 April 1326. Nicol, *LCB*, p. 159. He died in the same year and was succeeded by his son Orhan, who may or may not have been twenty-four at the time. Orhan died in 1362.

11 The story of Orhan's violent disposal of his (two) brothers is told with some disbelief by Laonikos Chalkokondyles, *Histories*, ed. E. Darkó, *Laonici Chalcocondylae Historiarum Demonstrationes*, 2 vols. (Budapest, 1922–7), I, p. 13; ed. I. Bekker (*CSHB*, 1843), p. 21. The practice of fratricide, probably initiated by the Sultan Bayezid I in 1389, was not enshrined in law until the time of Mehmed II. Gibbons, *Foundation of the Ottoman Empire*, pp. 180–1. Orhan reigned for thirty-six (not 'fifty-six') years.

12 This is a muddled and misdated account of a much later event – the joint rebellion of Andronikos (IV), son of John V, and Saudži Čelebi, son of Murad I (not of Orhan), against their fathers in 1373. See Nicol, *LCB*, pp. 277–8.

13 What follows is a hopelessly confused account of the successors of Andronikos II and the origins of the civil wars in Byzantium first between Andronikos II and his grandson Andronikos III (1328–41) and then between John V Palaiologos and John Cantacuzene (1341–7). No 'Manuel Paleologo' was involved in either. It is true, however, that John Cantacuzene gave his daughter (Helena) in marriage to John V and so became his father-in-law. It is also true that he called on Orhan for help, though Orhan's son was not 'Amurat' but Suleiman.

14 John (VI) Cantacuzene reigned in Constantinople not for 'twenty years' but only for seven years (1347–54).

15 The tale of the marriage of Matthew, son of John (VI) Cantacuzene, to a daughter (or a sister) of the 'King of Serbia' is told by others, though not by any of the Greek sources. Nicol, *Byzantine Family*, no. 24, p. 121. Matthew's father John subdued the Albanians in a military campaign in 1337 but Matthew himself was not there. The deportation or immigration of Albanians into the Peloponnese was not Matthew's doing. It occurred during the governorship there as Despot of Theodore I Palaiologos later in

the fourteenth century. It was also Theodore who severed the connection of the papacy with the Peloponnese.

16 Matthew Cantacuzene was proclaimed as Emperor by his father in 1353 and crowned as such in February 1354. Nicol, *LCB*, pp. 239–40.

17 John (V) Palaiologos fought his way into Constantinople from his exile on the island of Tenedos (not 'Eraclea') in November 1354. The co-operation of his friend 'Cathalusio' is reported only by the Byzantine historian Doukas, *Istoria Turco-Bizantină*, ed. V. Grecu (Bucharest, 1958), pp. 67, 69. Other sources, however, record that he was rewarded with the lordship of the island of Mytilene ('Metellino') or Lesbos. He was the Genoese Francesco I Gattilusio of that island.

18 It was not John Palaiologos who provided a wife for Orhan but John Cantacuzene. She was his own daughter Theodora and she was not 'illegitimate'. She married Orhan in 1345. The Turks occupied Gallipoli in March 1354 after its destruction by earthquake, as Spandounes goes on to say. The abdication of John Cantacuzene and his entry into a monastery followed in December 1354. No other source indicates that the Genoese were employed to ferry Turkish troops over the straits in '1383'.

19 Didymoteichon ('Dimotico') was first taken by Turks in 1359 and fell permanently in 1361. Nicol, *LCB*, p. 262 and references. Spandounes seems to be alone in suggesting that Orhan was its conqueror. 'King Stephen of Serbia' is presumably Stephen Dušan, who died in December 1355. George Glava, 'lord of Dimotico', may be identified with the George Glabas *skouterios* of Didymoteichon mentioned by John Cantacuzene in his *Histories*, II (*CSHB*, 1831), pp. 195, 401–2, 426; R. Guilland, *Titres et fonctions de l'Empire byzantin* (Collected Studies: London 1976), no. xxv, pp. 85–6. John Uglješa ('Unglesi') made himself Serbian Despot of the city of Serres in 1365 and remained so until 1371. See G. Ostrogorsky, *Serska oblast posle Dušanove smrti* (Belgrade, 1965); B. Ferjančić, *Vizantijski i Srpski Ser u XIV stoletu* (Belgrade, 1994).

20 Orhan died in March 1362. The village of 'Plagin' where he is said to have been buried is called 'Plagiari' in the Lucca edition (1550) of Spandounes. His mausoleum, however, still stands in Bursa.

21 Murad I (1362–89). The title of Gazi Hüdavendigar, or sovereign warrior, which he was the first to assume, may be translated as Emperor, as Spandounes says. H. Inalcik, *The Ottoman Empire* (London, 1973), p. 56. It was commonly believed in the west that Murad was the first of the Sultans to dispose of his brothers by murder. (See above, n. 11.)

22 The battle of Kossovo (15 June 1389) and the heroism of Miloš Kobilić ('Copilovichio') are well attested in Greek as well as Slav sources.

23 The corps of Janissaries seems first to have been founded by Murad I from Christian prisoners-of-war after his conquest of Adrianople (Edirne). Inalcik, *Ottoman Empire*, p. 11. Constantine of Ostrovica, who had been a

Janissary, attributes their origin and that of the *devshirme*, or forcible recruitment of Christian children, to Murad's son, whom he calls 'Sultan'. *Memoirs of a Janissary, Memoiren eines Janitscharen oder Türkische Chroniken*, ed. C.-P. Haase, Renate Lachmann, G. Prinzing (Graz, Vienna and Cologne, 1975), p. 74.

24 Bayezid I (1389–1402), known as Yildirim, made Adrianople (Edirne) his European capital. Its ancient Greek name had been Orestias. It had first been captured by the Turks in 1368–9. *Chron. brev.*, II, pp. 297–9.

25 Bayezid's punitive expedition into Albania after the battle of Kossovo achieved only a temporary success. Valona (Avlona) and its harbour did not fall permanently into Turkish hands until June 1517, when it was taken by Hamza Bey. H. and H. Buschhausen, *Die Marienkirche von Apollonia in Albanien* (Vienna, 1976), pp. 36–7. 'Solana' is rendered as 'Salona' in the Lucca edition (1550) of Spandounes. As such it was the medieval name of Amphissa.

26 Bayezid's blockade of Constantinople began in September 1394. The 'Grand Sachatai, Emperor of the Tartars', is Timur-lenk or Tamburlaine. Nicol, *LCB*, pp. 312ff. There is no certain evidence for the alleged mission of the Emperor (Manuel II Palaiologos) to Timur; and the suggestion that he might take over Constantinople rather than let it be subjected to the Ottomans is surely fanciful. See J. W. Barker, *Manuel II Palaeologus (1391–1425)* (New Brunswick, N.J., 1968), pp. 504ff.

27 If by this 'Giorgio' Spandounes means George Branković he is mistaken. For George was not a son of the 'King of Serbia' but of Vuk Branković, who escaped from the field of Kossovo in 1389; and he did not succeed his father until 1427, being entitled Despot of Serbia in 1429. 'Giorgio' is probably an error for Stephen Lazarević, son of Knez Lazar of Serbia who was killed at Kossovo. Stephen is known to have seen fighting on the side of Bayezid at the 'pitched battle' fought at Ankara in July 1402, as the Sultan's vassal, friend and indeed brother-in-law, for Bayezid had married his sister Despina. He escaped from the battlefield. Doukas, ed. Grecu, pp. 93, 97, 103; *Chron. brev.*, II, p. 370. Gibbons, *Foundation of the Ottoman Empire*, pp. 182–3, 252–3; Nicol, *LCB*, pp. 314–15 and references.

28 It was not Manuel II but his son John (VIII), acting as regent during his father's absence, who, in September 1402, sent ambassadors to Timur to discuss the payment of tribute to him. *DR*, v, no. 3199; Barker, *Manuel II*, p. 507.

29 The stories of Timur's treatment of the captive Bayezid and his wife are commonly reported in similar fashion in eastern and western sources. Bayezid died in March 1403. *Chron. brev.*, II, pp. 376–7. Gibbons, *Foundation of the Ottoman Empire*, pp. 254–7, 260.

30 The four surviving sons of Bayezid were: Suleiman (1402–11), Musa (1411–13), Mehmed (1413–21) and Mustafa (1421–2). Suleiman, the eldest,

is not mentioned by Spandounes, although it was he who took over the Ottoman provinces in Europe after 1402. Perhaps Spandounes confuses him with Mehmed, who did not become Sultan until 1413.

31 Manuel II had six (not 'seven') sons: John VIII who succeeded him as Emperor (1425–48); Theodore II, Despot in the Morea; Andronikos, Despot in Thessalonica; Constantine XI, Despot in the Morea and Emperor (1448–53); Demetrios and Thomas, Despots in the Morea. Mehmed I died in May 1421 at Adrianople and was succeeded by his brother Murad II, who murdered his brother Mustafa in 1422. *Chron. brev.*, II, p. 412.

32 This is a mainly accurate account of the regime of Andronikos Palaiologos as Despot in Thessalonica from 1408 to 1423, when he made the city over to the Venetians, who held it for seven (not 'four and a half' years) until its conquest by the Turks in 1430. It is not true, however, that Andronikos died on his way to Venice. He died either in the Morea or in Constantinople in 1429. *PLP*, IX, no. 21427; Nicol, *LCB*, pp. 325–6, 334–5. The *haraç* ('carazo') was the poll-tax payable by all non-Muslims in the Ottoman Empire.

33 Manuel II had no son called Andrew. 'Visu' (Bizye or Viza in Thrace) was, however, restored to the Byzantine Empire in 1403, though retaken by Musa in 1410. The only source for Vizye at this time seems to be *Chron. brev.*, I, no. 9/40; II, p. 398.

34 This is a very confused and erratic account of some of the ruling families of Epiros and Albania in the fourteenth and fifteenth centuries. No member of the Spata family ever ruled at Ioannina. Their possessions were centred on Angelokastron and Arta in the south of Epiros. The Musachi (Thopia) family were based on the district around Durazzo much further north and were connected with the Angevin rulers of Naples who laid claim to what they called the 'Duchy' of Durazzo. The area which they controlled came to be known as 'Myzeqeja'. Spandounes had among his friends in Italy one Constantine Musachi, who claimed descent from Andreas II Musachi, 'Despot' in the fourteenth century; and he proudly presented Constantine with a copy of the passage of his work relating to the Musachi family. This was to be reproduced in the very fanciful history of that family written in the sixteenth century by one Giovanni Musachi. This was edited by C. Hopf, *Chroniques gréco-romanes inédites ou peu connues* (Berlin, 1873), pp. 270–340; Nicol, *Byzantine Family*, pp. xvi–xvii. See also A. Gegaj, *L'Albanie et l'invasion turque au XVᵉ siècle* (Louvain, 1937); A. Ducellier, *La façade maritime de l'Albanie au moyen âge: Durazzo et Valona du XIᵉ au XVᵉ siècle* (Thessaloniki, 1981), pp. 338–40; D. M. Nicol, *The Despotate of Epiros*, II: *1267–1479* (Cambridge, 1984), p. 197.

35 Carlo (I) Tocco and his younger brother Leonardo (II) were the sons of Leonardo I Tocco, who had been created Count Palatine of the islands of Cephalonia, Ithaka, Zante (Zakynthos), and Duke of Santa Maura (Leukas)

by the Angevin rulers of Naples in 1357. He died in 1375–6 while his sons were still infants; and their mother Maddalena Buondelmonti had their titles confirmed in Naples. The County of Cephalonia was declared to be an autonomous vassal state of the Kingdom of Naples in 1396; and Carlo Tocco made war against the Albanians on the mainland. The details of his campaigns against the brothers Gjin and Sgouros Spata for control of Angelokastron and Arta are narrated in the *Chronicle of Tocco*. Spandounes has confused Gjin Spata, who ruled from 1374 to 1399, with Esau Buondelmonti, who was Despot in Ioannina from 1385 to 1411. It was Esau who married the only daughter of Gjin Spata; and it was when Esau died that Carlo (I) Tocco took over as Despot of Ioannina and Arta. Nicol, *Despotate of Epiros*, II, pp. 147–80.

36 Spandounes is here remarkably correct in stating that the title of Despot was conferred upon Carlo Tocco by the Emperor Manuel II (in 1415) and also in his observation that the title was personal and not hereditary. Nicol, *Despotate of Epiros*, II, pp. 183–4.

37 Carlo Tocco reigned in Ioannina for more like sixteen years (not 'eleven'). He died in 1429; and Ioannina capitulated to the Turks in 1430. The 'captain' who accepted its surrender was not Turahan Bey (who came there later) but Sinan Bey, the *Beylerbey* of Rumelia, who had a few months before forced the bloody surrender of Thessalonica. Nicol, *Despotate of Epiros*, II, pp. 200–4.

38 Spandounes's account of the five fractious bastard sons of Carlo I Tocco and of their disputes with his legitimate son Carlo (II) is, in general, accurate; and his version of the Turkish conquest of Epiros and the refuge of Carlo's descendants in Leukas is at least somewhere near the truth. 'Musai Carlo', however, is hard to identify. Nicol, *Despotate of Epiros*, II, pp. 204–15; and see below, text, pp. 166–7.

39 John VIII Palaiologos succeeded his father Manuel II in 1425. His younger brother Theodore (II), then Despot at Mistra, had married Cleope Malatesta. Their only daughter was Helena who, in 1441, married the King of Cyprus, John II of Lusignan. In 1443 Theodore exchanged his place at Mistra for an appanage in Selymbria in Thrace. He died in 1448. *PLP*, IX, no. 21459; D. M. Nicol, *The Immortal Emperor* (Cambridge, 1992), pp. 18–19.

40 Constantine Dragases Palaiologos, then Despot at Mistra, was later to succeed his brother (John VIII) as the last Emperor at Constantinople. John's 'journey to Italy' was to lead his large delegation to the Council of Florence which began in Ferrara in 1438. On his other brother, Demetrios: *PLP*, IX, no. 21454.

41 On John Cantacuzene and George Cantacuzene: Nicol, *Byzantine Family*, nos. 67 and 80. Elsewhere Spandounes (below, text pp. 156, 158) refers to George as his own mother's grandfather. He was a great-grandson, not a

grandson, of the Emperor John VI Cantacuzene. His title of 'Sachatai' means simply warrior. Spandounes (above, text p. 147) applies it also to Timur-Lenk. Hugues Busac, in his family history, ed. Laurent, 72, 74, describes George as a brother of Andronikos Cantacuzene, the last Byzantine Grand Domestic of Constantinople, the father of nine children. Nicol, *Byzantine Family*, no. 68. Massarellus, in his unpublished genea-logical work 'Dell'Imperadori Constantinopolitani' (Codex Vaticanus Latinus 12127, fol. 351), gives the same information; but he is alone in describing George's father as one Theodore Cantacuzene and crediting him with thirteen surviving children, five boys and eight girls. Spandounes here confuses the sisters of George, Helena and Eirene. He knew quite well that Helena was the wife of David, the last Emperor of Trebizond; and that Eirene was the wife of George Branković, Despot in Serbia. The passage of the text in parentheses above is not to be found in the Lucca edition of 1550.

42 Murad's army destroyed the Hexamilion wall across the Isthmus of Corinth in 1446 and again in 1452. *Chron. brev.*, II, p. 467. Nicol, *LCB*, pp. 364, 381.

43 The Council began in Ferrara in April 1438; the Union of the churches was proclaimed by Pope Eugenius IV in Florence in July 1439. John VIII returned to Constantinople by way of Venice. He was not absent for seven years; nor did he visit Rome, Burgundy ('Borgogna') and other places in the west.

44 This is a simplistic and inaccurate account of the Crusade of Varna which came to grief there in November 1444. Its spiritual leader is rightly identi-fied as Cardinal Giuliano Cesarini. The King of Hungary and Poland was Ladislas III (Vladislav). Philip V, Duke of Burgundy, supplied some ships. But Spandounes makes no mention of the Hungarian general John Hunyadi, who was the only Christian leader to escape the slaughter; nor does he hint at the duplicity of the Christian commanders. He prefers to recount the tale that the Sultan Murad was humiliated into making a temporary surrender and truce. Nicol, *LCB*, pp. 361–3. There was indeed a moment in the heat of battle when Murad's courage failed and his Janissaries had to restrain him by force. A similar tale of Murad's attempted flight is told by the author of the *Chron. Turc.*, pp. 72–3. Chalkokondyles, ed. Darkó, II, pp. 107–8; ed. Bekker, pp. 335–6 (*CSHB*). Constantine of Ostrovica, ed. Lachmann *et al.*, pp. 96–101, gives a different if spirited account of the battle at Varna. See Babinger, *Mehmed*, pp. 36–40; Setton, *Papacy and Levant*, II, pp. 82–91.

45 This story may refer to another of Murad's prisoners, since Philip Duke of Burgundy was not present at Varna.

46 Maria-Mara, daughter of the Serbian Despot George ('Jurgo') Branković, married Murad in 1435. Nicol, *Byzantine Lady*, pp. 110–19. Constantine of Ostrovica, ed. Lachmann *et al.*, p. 104, notes that Mehmed II, her stepson,

let her go home after Murad's death and gave her two properties in southern Serbia, Toplica and Dubočica (or Glabovica). See C. J. Jireček, *Istorija Srba*, ed. J. Radonić, 1 (Belgrade, 1952), pp. 375, 425. Later, he settled her at Ježevo in eastern Macedonia and it was there that she looked after the young Theodore Spandounes, for she was his great-aunt. See above, Introduction, p. xii.

47 Stephen and Gregory ('Jurgo' = Grgur) were brothers of Maria-Mara. Nicol, *Byzantine Family*, nos. 93, 95. They were captured when Murad conquered Smederevo in 1439 and with it all of Rascia and Serbia. He had them blinded, for whatever reason, in 1441. Their father George Branković with his wife Eirene Cantacuzene and their other children are said by Spandounes to have taken refuge in Ragusa where Eirene had a bank account amassed unknown to her husband. (The words 'in Scio' in the text should surely be read as 'sconosciuto'. Such is the version in the printed edition of 1550.) The offspring of George Branković and Eirene are correctly named and listed by Massarellus, fol. 349ᵛ. See Nicol, *Byzantine Family*, no. 71. The alliance of George Branković with John Corvinus Hunyadi, then Voivode of Transylvania, must refer to events in 1442–3, before the battle at Varna. Matthias or Matthew Corvinus, the sixteen-year-old son of John Hunyadi, became King of Hungary in January 1458. *Chron. brev.*, II, pp. 462–3. Babinger, *Mehmed*, pp. 146–7.

48 The Florentine Duke of Athens, Nerio II Acciajuoli (1435–51), was already a vassal of the Sultan; and his son Franco was a hostage at the Ottoman court. Chalkokondyles, ed. Darkó, II, pp. 92, 112; ed. Bekker, pp. 320–2 (*CSHB*). W. Miller, *The Latins in the Levant* (London, 1908), p. 406.

49 Murad II died in February 1451, the year after his failed attempt to dislodge Skanderbeg from his fortress at Kroia. He died at Adrianople but his corpse was taken to Bursa for burial. Babinger, *Mehmed*, pp. 64–5. On Skanderbeg: F. S. Noli, *George Castrioti Scanderbeg 1403–1468* (New York, 1947); *PLP*, XI, no. 26055.

50 Mehmed II was enthroned as Sultan on 18 February 1451 (*Chron. brev.*, II, pp. 478–9). Constantine (XI) Palaiologos, brother of John VIII, had come to Constantinople from the Morea, where he had been proclaimed as Emperor, on 12 March 1449 (*Chron. brev.*, II, p. 475; Nicol, *Immortal Emperor*, pp. 36–9). Mehmed's murder of his youngest brother, Kücük Ahmed Celebi, is recorded by Doukas, ed. Grecu, p. 287, who says that the boy was only eight months old (not 'five years'). This was the first real case of what Mehmed himself was to enact as the law of fratricide. Babinger, *Mehmed*, pp. 65–6.

51 Spandounes's account of the final siege and capture of Constantinople in 1453 is not a major contribution to a well-documented event. For the sources see: Pertusi, *Caduta*; A. Pertusi and A. Carile, *Testi inediti e poco noti sulla caduta di Costantinopoli* (Bologna, 1983). The Turkish attack on

Selymbria (Silivri) and other places surrounding the city on its north and west, led by Haradja Bey, is recorded by Kritoboulos of Imbros, *Critobuli Imbriotae Historiae*, ed. V. Grecu (Bucharest, 1963), p. 75; ed. D. R. Reinsch (*CFSHB*, xxii: Berlin and New York, 1983), and by Doukas, ed. Grecu, p. 321, though he claims that Selymbria resisted capture.

52 The 'house of Armer' (rendered as 'casa degl' armeri' in the Lucca edition of 1550) could refer to some member of the Venetian family of d'Armer (see below n. 116). It might, however, signify 'armiraio' or admiral, referring to the Venetian captain Alvise Diedo, captain of the galleys of Tana, who was made commander of the ships in the Golden Horn. S. Runciman, *The Fall of Constantinople 1453* (Cambridge, 1965), pp. 83, 93, 141–2.

53 The 'Genoese constable' must be Giovanni Giustiniani Longo. Runciman, *Fall of Constantinople*, pp. 83–4, 91–2, 138–9, 150.

54 This version of the heroic death of the Emperor Constantine is similar to several others, although Spandounes makes no mention of his decapitation. Nicol, *Immortal Emperor*, pp. 76–88. The 'street of Chinigo' must mean the Gate of Kynegon in the sea walls along the Golden Horn, which was defended by Gabriele Trevisan and 400 Venetians (Pertusi, *Caduta*, I, pp. lxxi, 332). Two other sources for the siege of Constantinople mention the 'moenia Cynegi' and the Gate called by the Greeks 'Cynagon' (Isidore of Kiev and Ubertino Pusculo: Pertusi, *Caduta*, I, pp. 72, 208). The coincidence of names between the two Constantines and the two Helenas had been noticed by Gennadios Scholarios and others in the fifteenth century (Nicol, *Immortal Emperor*, pp. 74–6). The last defiant words attributed to Constantine XI are similar to those recorded by Kritoboulos, ed. Grecu, p. 157; ed. Reinsch, pp. 80–2.

55 On the uncertainty about Constantine's burial and grave: Nicol, *Immortal Emperor*, pp. 92–4.

56 Mehmed's alleged residence in a Franciscan monastery is not supported by any other source. The first palace that he built for himself was in the Forum Tauri, of the Ox, in the centre of the city. It was completed in 1455. Meanwhile he resided in Adrianople. See J. Inalcik, 'The Policy of Mehmed II toward the Greek Population of Istanbul and the Byzantine Buildings in the City', *Dumbarton Oaks Papers*, 23–4 (1969–70), 231–49.

57 Kritoboulos, ed. Grecu, p. 163, perhaps in order to flatter the Sultan, offers a more favourable account of his treatment of the nobility. See Babinger, *Mehmed*, pp. 102–9.

58 Pope Hadrian VI (1522–3) seems to have docked the pensions which his predecessors (notably Leo X) had granted to some of the Byzantine refugees in Italy, thereby contributing to the impoverishment and ruin of the Spandounes family. See also below, text, pp. 185, 187.

59 The 'prince of Gothia' is hard to identify. 'Gothia' usually means the Crimea, in which case the reference would be to Mehmed's later expedition

there, led by Gedik Ahmed Pasha, which resulted in the Ottoman capture of Caffa in June 1475 (see below text, p. 159 and n. 77). The thousands of Genoese and other prisoners taken were eventually settled in a quarter of Constantinople, where Spandounes claims to have met the 'king's son' among them. *Chron. brev.*, II, p. 517. Babinger, *Mehmed*, pp. 343–5.

60 The passage in parentheses here is not in the Lucca edition of 1550. The Despot 'Jurgo' of Serbia (George Branković) was at war with the King of Hungary from 1453 to 1456, the year of his death. The Theodore Cantacuzene who was taken prisoner is otherwise identified as the son of George only by Hugues Busac, ed. Laurent, 72, and Massarellus, fol. 351. Smederevo was finally taken by the Turks in 1459. Nicol, *Byzantine Family*, no. 67, 82.

61 Mehmed's alleged campaign against the 'Bulgars' is doubtful; but his conquest of Karamania in 1465 is a known fact (Babinger, *Mehmed*, pp. 269–73). The conquest of Lesbos too is well documented. Domenico Gattilusio, Lord of Mytilene (Lesbos), Ainos, Samothrace, Lemnos and other islands (1455–8), was the descendant of that Francesco Gattilusio to whom the Emperor John V had given them. He was murdered by his brother Niccolo II Gattilusio in 1458. He had already lost Thasos and Old Phokaia to the Turks in 1455. He was dispossessed and strangled by the Turks in 1462. *Leonardus Chiensis De Lesbo a Turcis capta Epistola Pio Papae II missa*, ed. Hopf, *Chroniques*, pp. 359–66, and Table IX, 1, p. 502. *Chron. brev.*, II, pp. 487, 502; Doukas, ed. Grecu, pp. 417–19, 433–7; Kritoboulos, ed. Grecu, pp. 179, 295–301; Chalkokondyles, ed. Darkó, II, pp. 267–9; ed. Bekker, pp. 519–21 (*CSHB*); *Chron. Turc.*, p. 112.

62 Mistra surrendered to Mehmed II in May 1460. The subsequent squabbles between the brothers Demetrios and Thomas Palaiologos over what was left of the Despotate of the Morea are well documented (see D. A. Zakythinos, *Le Despotat grec de Morée*, 2 vols. (London, 1975), I, pp. 265–74). Spandounes clearly thought that the greater of the two sinners was Thomas. Constantine of Ostrovica, ed. Lachmann *et al.*, pp. 120–3, mentions only Demetrios in his garbled account of the Turkish conquest of the Morea and Mistra.

63 The principal cities of the New Morea were Clarentza ('Chiarenza') and Patras in the north-west of the peninsula. Thomas's relative, who was prince of Clarentza, is otherwise unknown, as also is his alleged brother-in-law Theodore Disypatos ('Dissipato'). Theodore 'Boccali' was a leading member of the Albanian Peloponnesian family of Boc(c)halis, whether or not he bore the title of Megas Doux; though it is very doubtful that he had the right to mint his own coinage (Zakythinos, *Despotat grec*, I, p. 141 n. 1). For other members of the Bocchalis family: George Sphrantzes, *Chronicon minus*, ed. V. Grecu (Bucharest, 1966), pp. 112, 114, 120; Chalkokondyles, ed. Darkó, II, p. 171; Musachi, ed. Hopf, pp. 285, 331.

64 George Palaiologos 'Sachatai', Spandounes's maternal grandfather: see above, n. 41. He was evidently governor of Mani. Manuel Cantacuzene was more probably his son than his 'brother'. The Albanians called him Gin Cantacusino and his wife Cucchia. Nicol, *Byzantine Family*, no. 83.

65 The Albanian revolt in the Morea was finally put down by Turahan Bey in October 1454. *Chron. brev.*, II, pp. 482–3. The Italian text has it that the Turkish Commander 'prese il sorzo [?sorcio] et la rana' (p. 157), which in the Florence edition of 1551 appears as 'la Topo et la Rana' (p. 44), which I take to imply total devastation, even down to the rats and frogs.

66 The Despot Thomas escaped from the Morea in July 1460 and, by way of Modon and Corfu, reached Rome in 1462. There he formally presented to Pope Pius II the head of St Andrew which he had brought with him from Patras. The presentation was commemorated in the church of Sant' Andrea della Valle. Thomas died in May 1465. *PLP*, IX, no. 21470. Zakythinos, *Despotat grec*, I, pp. 287–90; Nicol, *Immortal Emperor*, p. 114.

67 This account of Thomas's family is reasonably correct. His daughter was Zoe, who married Ivan III ('Gioanne'), Grand Prince of Moscow. His elder son, Andrew, after a chequered career, died in Rome in 1502. The younger son Manuel, as Spandounes reports, defected to the Sultan Mehmed II who made him welcome and treated him with great honour and respect. See below, Spandounes, ed. Sathas, pp. 157, 174–5, 223, 229. Spandounes strangely neglects to mention Thomas's daughter Helena, who married and outlived Lazar, third son of George Branković. She died as a nun on Santa Maura in 1473. A revised view of the career of Andrew is given by J. P. Harris, 'A Worthless Prince? Andreas Palaeologus in Rome – 1464–1502', *Orientalia Christiana Periodica*, 61 (1995), 537–54.

68 Thomas's brother Demetrios also went over to Mehmed II after the conquest of Mistra in 1460 and was settled in Adrianople, where he died as a monk ten years later. His daughter (Helena) was evidently his only child. She was taken, with his consent, into Mehmed's harem at Adrianople, where she too died. *PLP*, IX, no. 21363. Zakythinos, *Despotat grec*, I, pp. 285–7. Demetrios is otherwise known to have fallen out of the Sultan's favour in his latter years. Manuel (Gin) Cantacuzene probably fled first to Ragusa and then to Hungary. Nicol, *Byzantine Family*, no. 83.

69 Leonardo III, son of Carlo II Tocco, is not otherwise known to have been given as a hostage to the Turks. Other sources record that he was deprived of his last remaining mainland possessions in the 'Despotate' when the Turks conquered Angelokastron in 1460 and he retreated to his islands of Cephalonia and Santa Maura. One account records that he was captured by the Turks somewhere near Corinth but escaped. Nicol, *Despotate of Epiros*, II, pp. 210–11.

70 Franco Acciajuoli (1455–6) was the last of the Florentine Dukes of Athens, albeit as a vassal of the Sultan (see above, n. 48). The city fell to the Pasha

Omar Bey, son of Turahan, in June 1456. The tale of Franco's treacherous
murder by a Janissary is told in a different form by others. Chalkokondyles,
ed. Darkó, II, pp. 212–13; ed. Bekker, pp. 454–5, 483–4 (*CSHB*); *Chron.
brev.*, II, p. 489. Miller, *Latins in the Levant*, pp. 436–8, 456–8; Babinger,
Mehmed, pp. 159–60; K. M. Setton, *Catalan Domination of Athens*, 2nd edn
(London, 1975), pp. 209–11.

71 Spandounes appears to confuse the fortress of Mouchli with that of
Salmenikon. Mouchli lay in Arcadia and was first taken by Mehmed's army
in 1458. Zakythinos, *Despotat grec*, I, pp. 258, 266; A. Bon, *La Morée franque*,
2 vols. (Paris, 1969), I, p. 524. Salmenikon was between Patras and Vostitza
(Aigion) (see W. McLeod, 'Castles of the Morea in 1467', *Byzantinische
Zeitschrift*, 65 (1972), 353–63 (357)). It was here that its commander,
Constantine (not 'Andrea') Palaiologos Graitzas, held out so courageously
against the Turks in 1460–1. Chalkokondyles says that the Turkish siege
went on for a whole year, until the surrender of Salmenikon in July 1461.
That Constantine Palaiologos Graitzas retired to Venice where he was
made a captain of the light cavalry seems unrecorded elsewhere. Nicholas
Palaiologos, governor of Monemvasia, first put it under papal protection
and then, in 1463, made it over to the Venetians. Chalkokondyles, ed.
Darkó, II, pp. 235–8; ed. Bekker, pp. 480–1 (*CSHB*); Sphrantzes, ed. Grecu,
p. 124; *Chron. Turc.*, p. 106. *PLP*, IX, no. 21497; Zakythinos, *Despotat grec*,
I, pp. 272–4; D. M. Nicol, 'The Last Byzantine Rulers of Monemvasia',
in *Travellers and Officials in the Peloponnese*, ed. Haris A. Kalligas
(Monemvasia, 1994), pp. 62–7.

72 The information about the Branković family is quite accurate. George
Branković died in 1456. Of his two daughters, Maria-Mara married the
Sultan Murad II (see above, text p. 152), and Catherine married Ulrich,
Count of Cilly (Celje), who was a nephew (not a 'brother') of the
Holy Roman Emperor Frederick III of Habsburg (1452–93). Ulrich was
assassinated in Belgrade in 1456; Murad died in 1451. Mara had no children;
Catherine had a daughter (Elizabeth) who married Matthew I Corvinus,
son of John Hunyadi of Hungary (1458–90). Nicol, *Byzantine Family*,
nos. 92, 94.

73 The three sons of George Branković were: Gregory ('Curgur'), Stephen
and Lazar. The first two were blinded by Murad II (see above, text
pp. 152–3). Lazar therefore succeeded his father as Despot in Serbia; and he
married Helena Palaiologina, eldest daughter of Thomas Palaiologos,
Despot of the Morea, to whom he was, as Spandounes observes, closely
related. Lazar's mother, Eirene Cantacuzene, was a sister of George
Palaiologos Cantacuzene, the 'maternal grandfather' of Spandounes.
Lazar's appalling treatment of his mother is substantiated by other sources,
though Spandounes alone says that he poisoned her. Lazar died in 1458.
Nicol, *Byzantine Family*, nos. 93, 95, 96.

74 Stephen Branković was the second and not the first son of George. He married Angelina Arianitissa, daughter of Golem (George) Komnenos Arianites and a sister-in-law of Skanderbeg of Albania. He had two sons, George and Jovan, and a daughter, Maria, who married Boniface V, Marquis of Montferrat. The eldest son of George Branković, Gregory or Gurgur, died as a monk in the monastery of Chilandari on Mount Athos in October 1459. Despite the testimony of Spandounes, Gregory had at least one son, Vuk Branković, who died as a Despot in Hungary in 1485. Nicol, *Byzantine Family*, nos. 93, 95.

75 Lazar's three daughters are correctly listed as: Maria, who married Stefan Tomašević, of Bosnia; Milica, who married Leonardo III Tocco; and Eirene, who married John Kastriotes, son of Skanderbeg. Mehmed II's conquest of Serbia was completed by his capture of Smederevo in June 1459. Nicol, *Byzantine Family*, no. 96; Babinger, *Mehmed*, pp. 163–4. Most of these genealogical details are confirmed by Massarellus, fol. 350.

76 Trebizond surrendered to Mehmed II in August 1461. Its last Emperor, David Komnenos, was settled at or near Adrianople rather than Serres. Babinger, *Mehmed*, pp. 191–7; Nicol, *LCB*, pp. 407–9.

77 This passage is out of its chronological context. Kaffa and other places in the Crimea were taken from the Genoese in June 1475 by Mehmed's general Gedik Ahmed Pasha. Sphrantzes, ed. Grecu, p. 144; *Chron. brev.*, II, p. 517; Angiolello, ed. Ursu, pp. 72–83. Babinger, *Mehmed*, pp. 343–5. Of the other places mentioned, 'Scandiloro' is Alaia or the port of Alanya, which was known in Italian as Candeloro. Mehmed II captured it in 1471. Babinger, *Mehmed*, pp. 273, 300.

78 The story of the alleged forged letters from Rome about an impending crusade, used as a pretext for murdering David of Trebizond and his family, has no known basis in fact (Babinger, *Mehmed*, p. 215). On the tragic end of David, his family and his wife Helena: Nicol, *Byzantine Lady*, pp. 120–5. The fact that Helena had been a direct ancestor of Spandounes's mother perhaps lends credence to the tale of her martyrdom and death. The daughter of David and Helena who was given in marriage to Uzun Hasan in due course produced two daughters, one of whom (Theodora) became the mother of Ismail I ('Signor Sophi Jach Ismail'), the first Safavid Shah of Persia, whose son Tahmasp ('Sac Tomas re di Persia') succeeded in 1524 and was still Shah when Spandounes was writing. He gives brief accounts of Ismail and Tahmasp below, text pp. 252–60. Much of this information is not to be found in the Lucca and Florence editions of 1550 and 1551.

79 This passage is again out of chronological context. Mehmed's invasion and capture of Negroponte (Euboia) took place in July 1470. It was defended by Nicolo da Canale, captain-general of the Venetian fleet. After several false starts, the Turkish victory was finally achieved by Mahmud Pasha ('Maumuth'). Sphrantzes, ed. Grecu, p. 140; *Chron. brev.*, II, pp. 512–13;

Ecthesis Chronica, ed. S. P. Lambros (London, 1902), p. 33. Giovanni Maria Angiolello of Vicenza was one of the few survivors of the fighting and was carried off to Constantinople as a slave. His own account of the affair is in his *Historia turchesca*, ed. Ursu, pp. 35–7. The traitor in the fortress was Tomasso (not 'Pietro') Schiavo from Dalmatia with his friend Luca of Curzola (Korčula). Both were apprehended by the Venetian authorities and hanged. Babinger, *Mehmed*, pp. 283–4. Mahmud Pasha Angelović who was in command of the Turkish fleet was twice Grand Vizier of Mehmed II (Babinger, *Mehmed*, 272–3, 310; Inalcik, *Ottoman Empire*, p. 95). His brother Michael Angelović was Grand Voivode of Serbia in 1457. They were the grandsons of Manuel Angelos Philanthropenos, the last 'Caesar' of Thessaly in 1392–3. D. M. Nicol, *Meteora. The Rock Monasteries of Thessaly* (London, 1975), p. 68; *EI*, VI, pp. 69–72 (Mahmud Pasha Angelović).

80 Sigismondo Pandolfo Malatesta, lord of Rimini, arrived in the Morea at the port of Modon in July 1464, long before the Turkish capture of Negroponte. His expedition was not as successful as Spandounes makes out, though he certainly rescued the bones of the philosopher George Gemistos Plethon from Mistra and took them back to Rimini, where they still lie buried in the Tempio Malatestiano. Babinger, *Mehmed*, pp. 236–7; Setton, *Papacy and Levant*, II, pp. 252–3; C. M. Woodhouse, *George Gemistos Plethon* (Oxford, 1986), pp. 374–5.

81 The chronology here is again perverse. Venice declared war on the Ottomans on 28 July 1463. Bertoldo, Marquis of Este, was appointed as Venetian commander in the Morea in that year. Malatesta followed him in 1464. Bertoldo (and Alvise Loredano), based on Nauplion, supervised the restoration of the Hexamilion wall and went on to attack Corinth, where Bertoldo was killed in November 1464. Chalkokondyles, ed. Darkó, II, pp. 300–1; ed. Bekker, pp. 557–9 (*CSHB*); Angiolello, ed. Ursu, pp. 32–7; *Chron brev.*, II, p. 507. Babinger, *Mehmed*, p. 227; Setton, *Papacy and Levant*, II, p. 248. This passage of the text is printed from the Sansovino edition of Spandounes in Sathas, *Documents inédits*, VI (Paris, 1885), pp. 100–1.

82 Jacomo Barbarigo (not 'Barbadico') was Venetian provveditore in the Morea in 1465–6, after Malatesta had gone. His dispatches to the Senate in those years are published in Sathas, *Documents inédits*, VI, pp. 1–92. 'Amarbei' is Omar Bey, son of Turahan, who had captured Athens in 1458–60. He was reappointed governor of the Morea in 1451 and was in charge of operations against the Venetians there from 1463. Babinger, *Mehmed*, pp. 159–60, 227–8; Setton, *Papacy and Levant*, II, pp. 248–9, 253.

83 Barbarigo's rash attack on Patras was in the summer of 1466. *Chron. brev.*, II, p. 509; Kritoboulos, ed. Grecu, pp. 345–7; Sphrantzes, ed. Grecu, p. 132. Babinger, *Mehmed*, p. 258; Setton, *Papacy and Levant*, II, p. 284. On Michael Ralli (Raoul) and his son Nicholas Ralli Is(s)is, both of whom were killed

in this venture: S. Fassoulakis, *The Byzantine Family of Raoul–Ral(l)es* (Athens, 1973), nos. 64, 65, pp. 77–9.

84 Spandounes may have visited Gallipoli when, as a boy, he was a ward of his great-aunts at Ježevo in Macedonia (see above, Introduction, p. xii. Nicolo da Canale was tried in Venice and exiled to Portogruaro in Friuli, where, despite the intervention of his friend Pope Paul II, he died. His appointed successor as captain-general of the Venetian fleet was Pietro Mocenigo. Setton, *Papacy and Levant*, II, pp. 306–7.

85 The Pope's commissioner was Oliviero Carafa, Cardinal Archbishop of Naples (1467–1511) leading a crusade for Pope Sixtus IV. Ferdinand of Aragon is Ferdinand (Ferrante) I of Aragon and Naples (1458–94). Setton, *Papacy and Levant*, II, pp. 316–17. Spandounes does not reveal that much of the fervour of Mocenigo and Carafa and their crusaders was prompted by intense diplomatic activity on the part of Venice and the papacy to elicit the support and alliance against Mehmed of Uzun Hasan of Persia. Perhaps their greatest exploits were their destruction by fire of Adalia and of Smyrna in September 1472, though they had set fire to the Sultan's arsenal in Gallipoli in February. Their destruction of Ainos and its saltpans seems to be otherwise unrecorded, as does their attack on Lemnos ('Stalimini'). Carafa and his papal fleet were back in Rome in January 1473. Setton, *Papacy and Levant*, II, pp. 316–18; Babinger, *Mehmed*, pp. 304–5, 307–9. Pietro Mocenigo was Doge of Venice from 1474 to 1476. His tomb built from the spoils of war stands in the church of SS. Giovanni e Paolo. For its relationship to the tomb of Loukas Spandounes in Thessaloniki, see above, Introduction, p. xv.

86 This passage too is introduced out of chronological context and mainly to illustrate another piece of the Spandounes family history. The Turkish conquest of Bosnia began in 1463. Babinger, *Mehmed*, pp. 216–24, 231–3. The Duke ('Herzog') of St Saba at the time was Stjepan Vukčić (1435–66). His eldest son was Ladislas; and it was he who married Anna Cantacuzene who, according to Spandounes, was a sister of his grandfather (Theodore Cantacuzene) and so a daughter of George Palaiologos Cantacuzene. Nicol, *Byzantine Family*, no. 89. The younger brother of Ladislas, whom Mehmed took as a hostage, became a Muslim in the Sultan's service and was later known as Ahmed ('Sinan') Pasha Herzegoglou. See below, text p. 170. His mother Anna and her husband Ladislas took refuge in Ragusa and then in Venice, where they stayed with the Spandounes family before going on to Hungary, where Ladislas died in 1489. 'Vlatheo' was Vlatko, second son of the old Duke. His 'Castel Nuovo' was at Herzegnovi, where his father had been born. He died in Bar ('Arbe'). Nicol, *Byzantine Family*, p. 208 n. 27; Babinger, *Mehmed*, p. 230.

87 Stefan Tomašević ruler of Bosnia, married Maria Jelača, daughter of Lazar of Serbia, in 1459. The events here described took place in 1463. See Nicol,

Byzantine Family, pp. 223–4. The 'Spacogliani' are the Sipahis or Ottoman cavalry. Gy. Moravcsik, *Byzantinoturcica*, 3rd edn, 2 vols. (Berlin and Leiden, 1983), II, p. 291; and see below, text pp. 209, 228.

88 Mehmed laid siege to Belgrade in July 1456 and not 'in the following year', as Spandounes states. The heroes of the resistance were John Hunyadi of Hungary and the Franciscan Giovanni da Capistrano, the crusading friar. Greek accounts are: Kritoboulos, ed. Grecu, pp. 199–205; Chalkokondyles, ed. Darkó, II, pp. 178–85; ed. Bekker, pp. 416–24 (*CSHB*), both of whom tend to play down the significance of Mehmed's defeat; Sphrantzes, ed. Grecu, p. 108; Doukas, ed. Grecu, p. 421; *Chron. brev.*, II, p. 490. Only Sphrantzes mentions Hunyadi and Capistrano, whom Spandounes clearly much admired; though he is mistaken in saying that the belligerent friar was killed in the battle. He and Hunyadi both died a few weeks later, the former from his exertions at Belgrade, the latter of the plague. Modern accounts are: Babinger, *Mehmed*, pp. 138–46; Schwoebel, *Shadow of the Crescent*, pp. 41–50; Setton, *Papacy and Levant*, II, pp. 173–83 (who observes (p. 179) that 'the siege of Belgrade is almost as interesting, almost as important, as that of Constantinople'). It is at this point that the annals of Angiolello, *Historia turchesca*, ed. Ursu, pp. 21–2, begin to become more factual and more reliable, certainly as a check on the statements of Spandounes.

89 'Carabogdan' is Stephen the Great, Voivode of Moldavia (1457–1504), who seemed determined to annex Wallachia. Angiolello, ed. Ursu, pp. 82–93, described him as 'il Conte Stefano, detto da Turchi Carabogdan'. 'Chieli' is Kilia, a port on the island in the Danube in southern Moldavia also known as 'Licostomo', 'Moncastro' is Cetatea Alba (Asprokastro) or Akkerman. Mehmed's not very conclusive attack on Moldavia was in 1475 (Babinger, *Mehmed*, pp. 339–40). His business there was completed by his son Bayezid II (see below, pp. 55–6, text p. 171). The Genoese in Chios ('Sciotti') paid tribute to the Sultan, though not as regularly as he would have wished.

90 Mehmed's campaign against Uzun Hasan is described at much greater length by Angiolello, ed. Ursu, pp. 39–71, and also in his *Breve narratione della vita et fatti d'Uzuncassan Re di Persia*, trans. Grey, *A Narrative of Italian Travels in Persia*. Babinger, *Mehmed*, pp. 310–16. The "schiopettieri" in Mehmed's army must be Shqipetars or Albanian troops. The campaign was fought in 1472–3.

91 The Ottoman siege of Rhodes in May to July 1480 is mentioned here mainly because it was led by another of Spandounes's distant ancestors, Mesih Pasha. Mesih was a brother of the mother of Matthew Spandounes, Theodore's father. She was evidently a Palaiologina. Mesih's own father was one Thomas Palaiologos Gidos (Sphrantzes, ed. Grecu, p. 142; *Ecthesis Chronica*, p. 31. *PLP*, IX, no. 21472). One of the Short Chronicles calls him 'Misel' Pasha (*Chron. brev.*, I, no. 66/9; II, p. 521). Angiolello, ed.

Ursu, p. 106, describes him as ' . . . Bassa della Natolia, il qual' era di natione greco et haveva nome Misit, fu figliolo d'un fratello dell' imperatore di Constantinopoli'. His failed attack on Rhodes is recorded in the *Ecthesis Chronica*, pp. 34–5, where he is called 'Mesik Pasha'. The Sultan disgraced him for his incompetence, but he came to favour again under Bayezid II, who made him *Beylerbey* of Rumelia and then Grand Vizier. He took part in the campaign against Moldavia in 1484. One of his 'two brothers' was Hass Murad Pasha (Palaiologos), a favourite of Mehmed II, who was drowned in the Euphrates during the war against Uzun Hasan in 1473. See also Angiolello, ed. Ursu, pp. 112, 179. N. Beldiceanu and I. Beldiceanu-Steinherr, 'Un Paléologue inconnu de la région de Serrès', *Byzantion*, 41 (1971), 7–17. There can be no truth in the suggestion that Mesih Pasha was Manuel Palaiologos, second son of the Despot Thomas Palaiologos (see A. Th. Papadopulos, *Versuch einer Genealogie der Palaiologen* (Munich, 1938), n. 101; D. I. Polemis, *The Doukai* (London, 1968), p. 163 n. 11). Pierre d'Aubusson was Grand Master of the Hospitallers on Rhodes from 1476 to 1503. Babinger, *Mehmed*, pp. 396–400; Schwoebel, *Shadow of the Crescent*, pp. 119–30; Setton, *Papacy and Levant*, II, pp. 348–62.

92 Skanderbeg married Andronike, daughter of George (Golem) Komnenos Arianites. *PLP*, XI, no. 26055. His sisters were Mamiza, who married Musachio Thopia; Vlaia, who married Ghin Musachi; Maria, who married Stefan I of Montenegro (1427–46); Angelina, who married Vladam Arianiti; and Iella, who married Paul Balša. *PLP*, V, no. 11400, *s.v.* Kastriotes, Ivan, father of George Kastriotes. Skanderbeg died in January 1468. Marino Scodrense, to whose work Spandounes refers his readers, is Marinus Barletius, a cleric from Skutari (Skodra) who wrote two works: *De obsidione Scodrensi* (Venice, 1504); and *Historia de Vita et Gestis Scanderbegi Epirotarum Principis* (1st edn, Rome 1509 or 1510). The latter was a great success and was translated into several European languages. See Gegaj, *L'Albanie*, pp. xiii–ix.

93 Mehmed invaded Albania in 1474. His troops were led by Hadim (= Eunuch) Suleiman Pasha, whom Spandounes calls 'Ali Eunucho', then *Beylerbey* of Rumelia, one of the Sultan's favourites. Angiolello (ed. Ursu, p. 71) calls him 'Soliman Bassa Eunucho'. Skodra ('Scutari') was stoutly defended by Antonio Loredano on behalf of the interests of Venice. It was besieged from 15 July to 28 August 1474 until the Turks were obliged to desist and to withdraw. Angiolello, ed. Ursu, pp. 71–3, 103. Babinger, *Mehmed*, pp. 334–7. Mehmed's last attempt to take Kroia by siege was in 1478. It was, however, ceded to the Turks by terms of their treaty with Venice in the following year (see below, n. 98).

94 The attack on Lepanto was led by the same Suleiman Pasha ('Ali Eunucho') in May 1477. Omar Bey ('Amarbei') is not otherwise on record as having participated. Lepanto was saved by Antonio Loredano, then Venetian

captain-general of the sea. Sphrantzes, ed. Grecu, p. 146; *Chron. brev.*, II, pp. 518–19; Angiolello, ed. Ursu, pp. 107–8. Babinger, *Mehmed*, p. 353 (who dates the event to 1476). This is the last event recorded in the Memoirs of George Sphrantzes.

95 Sphrantzes introduces this Florentine incident into his narrative largely to explain one of the causes of the friendship between the Medici family and the Sultan Mehmed II. The attempt to murder Lorenzo and his brother Giuliano ('Juliano') was made during Mass in the Duomo (San Reparata) in Florence in April 1478. Giuliano was killed. The only one of the assassins who escaped was Bernardo Bandini (de' Baroncelli). He got away on a Neapolitan ship to Constantinople; and there Mehmed kept him under arrest until a Florentine ambassador arrived to take him back to his execution in Italy in December 1479. It was in gratitude for Mehmed's co-operation in this affair that Lorenzo commissioned the medal of him made by Bertoldo di Giovani. Babinger, *Mehmed*, pp. 384–7; Setton, *Papacy and Levant*, II, pp. 336–7.

96 Friuli had become a Venetian possession in 1420. The devastating attack on it by fire and sword came in September 1477. It was led by Iskender Bey, then *Sanjak Bey* of Bosnia; and the Venetian defence was undertaken by Girolamo Novella and his son. Babinger, *Mehmed*, pp. 357–8. The Spandounes family owned properties in Friuli. Nicol, *Byzantine Family*, pp. 217–18.

97 Maria-Mara Branković, great-aunt of Theodore Spandounes and step-mother of Mehmed II, who was then living at Ježevo in eastern Macedonia, was regarded by the Venetians as a useful and influential intermediary with the Sultan. Nicol, *Byzantine Lady*, pp. 110–19.

98 This is a reasonably accurate, if incomplete, account of the peace treaty between Venetians and Ottomans concluded in January 1479 by Giovanni Dario, secretary of the Senate, in Constantinople. Its terms were: Venice ceded to the Turks Skodra (Shkodër) in Albania, as Spandounes says, but also Mani in the south of Greece and all claims to Kroia (Krujë) in Albania and to the island of Negroponte (Euboia) and all the places taken by the Venetians during sixteen years of warfare (since 1463). Spandounes adds the cession by Venice of the islands of Lemnos and of 'Tridognia' off Lepanto, which had once belonged to his family (see above, text p. 166). The Venetians were also obliged to pay 100,000 ducats in compensation for debts still owed by Bartolommaio Zorzi and his colleagues as lessees of the Turkish alum mines, and 10,000 ducats a year for their duty-free franchise in Constantinople and the Ottoman Empire. *Chron. brev.*, II, pp. 519–20; Angiolello, ed. Ursu, p. 108. The Greek text of the treaty is in F. Miklosich and J. Müller, *Acta et Diplomata Graeca medii aevi sacra et profana*, 6 vols. (Vienna, 1860–90), III, pp. 293–8. The Latin version is in R. Predelli, ed., *I Libri Commemoriali della Republica di Venezia, Regesti*, 6 vols. (Venice,

1876–8), V, pp. 228–30, 238–9. Babinger, *Mehmed*, pp. 360–72; Setton, *Papacy and Levant*, II, p. 328; Miller, *Latins in the Levant*, pp. 479–81.

99 Leonardo III Tocco and his island County of Cephalonia were not included in the Venetian-Turkish treaty of 1479; but he was already a vassal of the Sultan. His first wife had been Milica (see above, text p. 159) and she is said to have been buried in the church of Santa Mavra on Leukas which her mother Helena had built. His second wife was Francesca Marzano, a niece of Ferdinand I (Ferrante) of Naples, and so an enemy of Venice. Nicol, *Despotate of Epiros*, II, p. 212; Babinger, *Mehmed*, pp. 383–4.

100 Ferdinand I of Aragon, King of Naples and (II) of Sicily (1458 and 1479–84) and his son Federigo, King of Naples (1496–1501). His skirmishes with the Venetians at Korčula ('Curzola') and at Gallipoli (near Otranto) seem to be otherwise unrecorded; though see Angiolello, ed. Ursu, pp. 110–11.

101 Gedik Ahmed Pasha was at the time *Bey* of Valona on the Albanian coast. The operation took place in August–September 1479. Spandounes seems to be the only authority for Mehmed's biological experiment with his prisoners. Leonardo III Tocco died in 1494. Angiolello, ed. Ursu, pp. 108–9; *Chron. brev.*, II, pp. 520–1; Stefano Magno, *Estratti degli Annali Veneti*, ed. Hopf, *Chroniques*, p. 208. Nicol, *Despotate of Epiros*, II, pp. 213–14; Babinger, *Mehmed*, pp. 383–4; Setton, *Papacy and Levant*, II, pp. 514–15.

102 The Ottoman capture of and massacre at Otranto occurred in the summer of 1480. It was conducted by Gedik Ahmed Pasha who sailed across from Valona. The affair is well documented by other sources. Angiolello, ed. Ursu, pp. 170–2; *Chron. brev.*, II, p. 522; *Chron. Turc.*, p. 121. Babinger, *Mehmed*, pp. 390–6; Setton, *Papacy and Levant*, II, pp. 343–5; *EI*, I, pp. 292–3 (Ahmad Pasha Gedik).

103 Mehmed II died at Gebze (Dakibyze) near Nikomedia on 3 May 1481. The date is confirmed by the Greek sources: *Ecthesis Chronica*, p. 39; *Historia Politica et Patriarchica Constantinopoleos*, ed. I. Bekker (Bonn, 1849), pp. 50–1, as amended by Schreiner, *Chron. brev.*, II, p. 523. Babinger, *Mehmed*, pp. 403–5.

104 George Gennadios Scholarios, whom Mehmed had appointed as Patriarch of Constantinople after the conquest, composed for him an exposition of the Christian faith, the text of which is printed in the *Historia Patriarchica* (*CSHB*), pp. 83–94; and in L. Petit, X. A. Siderides and M. Jugie, *Oeuvres complètes de Gennade Scholarios*, 8 vols. (Paris, 1928–36), III, pp. 453–8. The author of the *Chron. Turc.* (p. 121) says that Mehmed knew five languages – Turkish, Romaic (Greek), Frankish, Arabic, Chaldaic and Persian (which is in fact six!), and also that he liked to read of the deeds and wars of Alexander the Great and Julius Caesar. Babinger, *Mehmed*, pp. 410–11, 436–7, 499–502.

105 The cruelties perpetrated by Mehmed are emphasised by other writers. The

tale about the missing melon is told, albeit in less gruesome form, by
Angiolello, ed. Ursu, p. 122, and by the Genoese merchant Jacopo de
Promontorio-de-Campis, whose account of the inhumanity of Mehmed far
outclasses that of Spandounes; he too compares the Sultan to Nero. See
Babinger, *Mehmed*, pp. 429–31.

106 Mehmed II was forty-nine years of age when he died in the thirtieth year of
his reign (1451–81). Babinger, *Mehmed*, pp. 403–4. He was buried at the
mosque which he himself had built in Constantinople on 19 May 1481. He
was the first Ottoman Sultan not to be buried in Bursa. *Chron. brev.*, II,
p. 524. For a modern appraisal of the man and his character: Babinger,
Mehmed, pp. 409–32. The word 'Talasumani' (or 'Talismani') which
Spandounes employs to mean Muslim priests seems to be derived from the
word *Danishmend*. See below, part II, text p. 205 and n. 6.

107 Bayezid was governor of Amasya at the time of his father's death. The
Grand Vizier Karamani Mehmed Pasha intended that Bayezid's brother
Jem ('Cem') should succeed. The Pasha who intercepted his message to
Jem was that Sinan (Ahmed) Pasha Herzegoglou, a father-in-law of
Bayezid, who was then *Beylerbey* of Anatolia and also distantly related to
Spandounes as a son of the Duke of St Saba in Bosnia (see above, text p. 162
and n. 86). He was to be defeated and captured by the Mamluks of Egypt in
1486. *Chron. brev.*, III, pp. 162, 169. *EI*, III, pp. 340–2 (Ahmed Pasha Hersek
Zade).

108 The Grand Vizier was murdered by the Janissaries; but order was maintained by Bayezid's young son Kurkud ('Curchut') until his father reached
Constantinople. He entered the city on 19 May 1481 to celebrate his father's
funeral. Angiolello, ed. Ursu, pp. 112–19, gives a more circumstantial
account of these events. See especially: L. Thuasne, *Djem-Sultan, fils de
Mohammed II, frère de Bayezid II (1459–1495)* (Paris, 1892), pp. 26–8;
Babinger, *Mehmed*, pp. 404–8.

109 Jem's defeat by Bayezid at Yeni-Shehir (? 'Sultan Humi') in June 1481 and
his subsequent escape to Rhodes and then to Italy and France are events
well documented in other sources. *Chron. brev.*, II, pp. 524, 525, 526;
Historia Politica, pp. 52–4; *Chron. Turc.*, pp. 123–4; Angiolello, ed. Ursu,
pp. 172–83. Jem died in the Castel Capuano in Naples on 25 February 1495.
Thuasne, *Djem-Sultan*, pp. 35–9, 363–87; Setton, *Papacy and Levant*, II,
pp. 381–416, 425, 427–30, 482. His remains were eventually sent to
Constantinople and buried at Bursa. On his pervasive influence on Ottoman
policy after his escape to the west, see S. N. Fisher, *The Foreign Relations of
Turkey 1481–1512* (Urbana, Ill., 1948), pp. 21–50. The relics which the
Sultan sent to the Pope, Innocent VIII, were taken to Ancona and on to
Rome by an ambassador in April 1492. Thuasne, *Djem-Sultan*, pp. 296–392.

110 In the summer of 1484 Bayezid II campaigned against Stephen the Great
('Carabogdan') in Moldavia and captured the fortresses of Kilia ('Cheli')

and Akkerman ('Moncastro') (or Asprokastro, Cetatea Alba), which
Mehmed II had failed to conquer. *Ecthesis Chronica*, p. 42; *Historia Politica*,
pp. 64–5; *Chron. Turc.*, p. 127; *Chron. brev.*, II, p. 527; Angiolello, ed. Ursu,
pp. 183–4; Constantine of Ostrovica, ed. Lachmann *et al.*, pp. 145, 174
(where Akkerman is called Belgrade or Belgorod). See N. Beldiceanu, 'La
conquête des cités marchandes de Kilia et de Cetatea Albă par Bayezid II',
Süd-ost Forschungen, 23 (1964), 36–90.

111 The Mamluk Sultan of Egypt was Kaitbey (1468–96), with whom Jem had
temporarily taken refuge, and who had captured Adana and Tarsus in 1486.
Bayezid's campaigns against him are outlined in *Chron. Turc.*, pp. 125–7.
Peace was made in 1491. Angiolello, ed. Ursu, pp. 185–7. Fisher, *Foreign
Relations*, pp. 36–42; *EI*, IV, pp. 462–3 (Kait Bey).

112 This passage is very confused. By 'Poland' Spandounes means Bogdania-
Moldavia, on the borders of Poland. 'Carabogdan' is Stephen IV the Great
of Moldavia (1457–1504). The King of Poland who made peace with
him must be John Albert (1492–1501), son and successor of Casimir IV
Jagiellon. The Turkish commander 'Marco Zogli' may be identified as
Malkochoglu Bali, Bey of Silistria. Fisher, *Foreign Relations*, p. 33. *Chron.
Turc.*, p. 127, gives an even more confused account of these events, naming
the Voivode of Vlachia and Bogdania as 'Marko Phonti'. On 'Vlatheo'
(= Vlad IV of Wallachia), son of Ladislas of St Saba, see above, text p. 162.

113 Chimara on the Albanian coast was a notorious staging-post for pirates.
Bayezid's attack on it is chronicled also in *Chron. Turc.*, p. 127, and
Angiolello, ed. Ursu, p. 191, who seems to identify it with Valona.
Spandounes's brother Alexander evidently owned property in the district.

114 The lord of Kotor ('Catharo') was George Črnojević, son of Ivan of
Montenegro. Angiolello, ed. Ursu, p. 219, calls him 'Zuan Zernovich'.
Hopf, *Chroniques*, Table 12, says that he died about 1514. His dispossession
is mentioned by *Chron. Turc.*, p. 127, and more extensively by Angiolello,
ed. Ursu, p. 219. Fisher, *Foreign Relations*, pp. 53, 65. Lodovico il Moro
Sforza was Duke of Milan from 1494 to 1500 and died in 1508. The Venetian
ambassador to the Sultan, Andrea Zanchani, was appointed in September
1498. Angiolello, ed. Ursu, pp. 219, 221. Setton, *Papacy and Levant*, II,
pp. 511–14. George Buzardo is known from other sources as ambassador,
interpreter and apostolic nuncio. Angiolello, ed. Ursu, pp. 196, 199, 201–2.
Thuasne, *Djem-Sultan*, pp. 301–2, 320, 334–9. For Iskender Bey Pasha, see
above, text p. 165 and n. 96. Fisher, *Foreign Relations*, pp. 70–1.

115 War between Venice and the Turks broke out again in April 1499. *Chron.
brev.*, II, p. 532. Setton, *Papacy and Levant*, II, pp. 517–22. See especially:
G. Cogo, 'La guerra di Venezia contro i Turchi (1499–1501)', *Nuovo Archivo
Veneto*, 18 (1899), 1–76, 348–421; 19 (1900), 97–138 (it should be noted,
however, that Cogo had no access to the accounts of Angiolello, nor to
Spandounes, nor to the Greek accounts of the war). The Venetian captain-

general of the sea was Antonio Grimani. He was to be cashiered and imprisoned for his incompetence in this campaign, though later he was to become Doge of Venice (1521–3). The Turkish commander, Davud ('Tauth') Bey was Daud Pasha. *EI*, I, pp. 928–9. One 'Taut Bassa' was captured by the Venetians off Zonchio in 1500 (Angiolello, ed. Ursu, pp. 251, 261). The course of the war from 1499 to 1503 is described by Fisher, *Foreign Relations*, pp. 67–89, though he seems to have been unaware of the study by Cogo.

116 The harbour of Porto Longo (or Zonchio) was on the south-west coast of the Peloponnese, between Modon and Navarino. The French fleet of eighteen ships (some say more) mainly provided by the Hospitallers, arrived at the Gulf of Patras in mid-August 1499. The Venetian captains are correctly named as Andrea Loredan(o) and Alban d'Armer. The Turkish captain Barak Reïs ('Barach Raisi') and his sea battle with Loredano, in which both were killed, is described by the *Ecthesis Chronica*, p. 43; *Historia Politica*, pp. 55–6; Angiolello, ed. Ursu, p. 241. The huge battleship 'Chiaranta' is called 'Giaranda' by Angiolello, ed. Ursu, p. 229. Lepanto was finally taken by the Turks on 29 August 1499. 'Verso il Papa' means that the Turks, on their way up to Patras, sailed round the promontory called Capo del Papa. *Chron. brev.*, II, pp. 533–5. Cogo, 'La guerra di Venezia', 51–4, 58–9; Setton, *Papacy and Levant*, II, pp. 517–19.

117 Melchior Trevisan(o) was appointed to replace Grimani in September 1499. Cogo, 'La guerra di Venezia', 56–63.

118 Bayezid's capture of Modon on 9 August 1500 is similarly narrated in the *Ecthesis Chronica*, pp. 43–4; *Historia Politica*, pp. 56–7; *Chron. Turc.*, pp. 132–3; *Chron. brev.*, II, pp. 537–8. The longest account, derived from an eye-witness, is that of Angiolello, ed. Ursu, pp. 241–61. Coron surrendered a week later and Navarino (Zonchio) shortly after. Miller, *Latins in the Levant*, pp. 495–7; Setton, *Papacy and Levant*, II, p. 522.

119 Benedetto Pesaro was appointed captain-general in July 1500 after Trevisano had fallen ill and died. Gonsalvo Fernando de Cordova, Spanish governor in southern Italy, came out to join him at Corfu; and from there they captured Cephalonia in December 1500. Pesaro also retrieved the fortress of Navarino, though not for long. *Chron. brev.*, II, p. 539. Cogo, 'La guerra di Venezia', pp. 368–70, 388–412; Setton, *Papacy and Levant*, II, pp. 522–3.

120 Manuel, the second son of the Despot Thomas Palaiologos, left Rome about 1476 and gave himself up to the Sultan Mehmed, who received him warmly and generously. Spandounes writes below (text pp. 223, 229) of the special and honourable treatment given to Manuel at the court and in camp. When he died he was buried as a Christian at 'Sirentzion' (? Sergentzion), which Babinger, *Mehmed*, p. 180, suggests was the modern Istranca near Constantinople. Of his two sons, John, the elder, died young and was

buried in the patriarchal church of the Pammakaristos in Constantinople. The younger, Andrew, was made a Muslim by the Sultan Selim I with the name of Mehmed and lived in the seraglio. *Ecthesis Chronica*, p. 23; *Historia Politica*, pp. 34–5. Nicol, *Immortal Emperor*, pp. 115–16.

121 The legendary origins of the family of Palaiologos and its alleged connections with Viterbo are well enough known. Michael (VIII) Palaiologos, the founder of the imperial dynasty, was the son of Andronikos Palaiologos, who served the Empire in exile at Nicaea before 1261. Giangiorgio, who died without heir before 1533, claimed descent from Theodore, son of the Emperor Andronikos II Palaiologos, who had come into the Marquisate of Montferrat in 1306. Nicol, *Immortal Emperor*, p. 118. Constantine of Ostrovica, ed. Lachmann *et al.*, p. 86, interprets the name Palaiologos to mean 'renowned of old'.

122 'Perama' signifies the channel between the island of Chios and the mainland of Anatolia.

123 'Zonchio' near Navarino was retaken by Benedetto Pesaro and his Venetian fleet early in December 1500 but retrieved by the Turks in May 1501. *Chron. brev.*, II, p. 529; Angiolello, ed. Ursu, pp. 262, 264. Miller, *Latins in the Levant*, pp. 497–8. Miller identifies the Turkish sailor 'Camali' as Kemal Reis. A. E. Vakalopoulos, Ἱστορία τοῦ Νεοελληνισμοῦ, 4 vols. (Thessaloniki, 1968–74), III, pp. 77–8, correctly calls him 'Kamali', a Turkish pirate. See H. A. von Burski, *Kemal Re'is* (Bonn, 1928), pp. 26–32; *EI*, IV, pp. 881–2. On Ali Pasha the Eunuch, *Sanjak bey* of the Morea, see below, n. 129.

124 The Turks entered Durazzo in August 1501. *Chron. brev.*, II, p. 540; Angiolello, ed. Ursu, p. 264 (a very brief note). The commander of the French fleet was Philippe de Cleves et la Marck, lord of Ravenstein, governor of Genoa and admiral of the (French) Kingdom of Naples. Setton, *Papacy and Levant*, II, p. 538 n. 154; Fisher, *Foreign Relations*, pp. 79–80.

125 The combined attack on Mytilene (Lesbos) is mentioned by Angiolello (ed. Ursu, p. 265). On Mesih ('Mesit') Pasha, whom Theodore Spandounes claimed as a forebear, see above, text p. 164 and n. 91. The Bishop of Paphos ('Baffo') was Jacopo Pesaro, a cousin of the Venetian captain Benedetto Pesaro. Santa Maura (Leukas) was captured on 30 August 1502. Angiolello, ed. Ursu, pp. 266–7. Miller, *Latins in the Levant*, pp. 499–500; Setton, *Papacy and Levant*, II, p. 533; Fisher, *Foreign Relations*, pp. 82–3.

126 Some of the commercial interests and property of the Spandounes family, notably of Theodore's brother Alexander, were evidently in the area of Dalmatia.

127 The treaty between Venice and the Sultan was confirmed in May 1503. Its terms had been agreed in December 1502. They were ratified in a letter of Bayezid to the Doge in August 1503. Texts in Miklosich and Müller, *Acta et Diplomata*, III, pp. 344–50, 353–4; Predelli, ed., *Libri Commemoriali, Regesti*,

VI, no. 12, p. 65; cf. nos. 9, 16. *Chron. brev.*, II, pp. 541–2; Angiolello, ed. Ursu, pp. 267–8 (dating the treaty to 1502); *Chron. Turc.*, p. 135. Fisher, *Foreign Relations*, pp. 82–9.

128 The earthquakes in Constantinople and Didymoteichon happened on 10–11 September 1509. *Chron. brev.*, II, p. 544; *Ecthesis Chronica*, p. 48; *Historia Politica*, p. 61. It is the last event recorded in the two first drafts of the treatise of Spandounes.

129 This invasion of Anatolia by the armies of Ismail I Safavi, Shah of Persia (1502–24), was led by his officer Shah Kulu ('Sach Koules'). Bayezid sent Ali ('Halil') Pasha the Eunuch against it, but he was defeated and killed in 1511. The matter is described at greater length in the *Ecthesis Chronica*, pp. 48–9; *Historia Politica*, pp. 61–2. Inalcik, *Ottoman Empire*, p. 195. Ali Pasha the Eunuch had been *Sanjak bey* of the Morea (see above, text p. 175).

130 The circumstances of Bayezid II's illness and abdication on 24 April 1512 (he died on 26 May of that year) and the struggle for power between his sons Selim, Ahmed and Korkud are attested by many other sources. Selim emerged victorious in the winter of 1513. *Chron. brev.*, II, pp. 546–9; *Ecthesis Chronica*, pp. 55, 57–8; *Historia Politica*, pp. 68–71; Angiolello, ed. Ursu, pp. 270–5. On the Pasha Mustafa who had presented relics to the Pope, see above, text p. 171. The other Pashas (Viziers) executed by Selim were: 'Taut bei' and 'Zaiusbassi'. The first may be Daud, Bey of Gallipoli under Bayezid II. Another (?) 'Thauth Bassa', whom Spandounes claimed to have known, died of shame when dismissed from office. See below, text p. 208. The names 'Ducaginogli' and 'Zaiusbassi' are rendered as 'Douka Kenogli' and 'Gionouz basha' by the *Ecthesis Chronica*, pp. 51, 59. Gionouz or Yunus had been Aga of the Janissaries. Moravcsik, *Byzantinoturcica*, II, p. 119 (Duqakin-oglou), p. 139.

131 Selim I is generally reported as having been aggressively anti-Christian. Yet his tolerance of if not partiality towards Christians is noted by other Greek sources. The *Historia Politica*, p. 72, and the *Ecthesis Chronica*, p. 59, tell how he reopened Christian churches which had been closed by his father; and some of the Short Chronicles observe that he permitted the building of many churches during his reign. *Chron. brev.*, I, no. 33/79, p. 258, and no. 58/33, p. 425.

132 Selim's campaign against Ismail I of Persia is dated to the years 1514–15. Spandounes's account of the capture of Tabriz ('Thauris') is very similar to that given in the *Ecthesis Chronica*, p. 63; *Historia Politica*, pp. 73–4; *Chron. brev.*, II, pp. 550–2. Spandounes later (text pp. 257–8) repeats his account and goes on to relate how Ismail ('Sophi') recovered Tabriz.

133 The Mamluk Sultan of Cairo at the time, whom Spandounes calls 'Camsoingani', was Kanshawh Al-Ghawri (or Kansuh al-Ghuri). Inalcik, *Ottoman Empire*, p. 33; Setton, *Papacy and Levant*, III, p. 165. Later (text p. 257) Spandounes calls him 'Capson Gauri'. The date of his defeat by

Selim I is correctly given as 24 August 1516. *Chron. brev.*, II, p. 553; *Ecthesis Chronica*, p. 65.

134 The new Mamluk Sultan was Tuman Bey ('Tomobei'). He was defeated by Selim near Cairo and hanged there a few months later in January 1517. *Chron. brev.*, II, p. 553; *Ecthesis Chronica*, p. 66; *Historia Politica*, p. 76. Inalcik, *Ottoman Empire*, pp. 33–4; Setton, *Papacy and Levant*, III, p. 165. 'Aliduli' must be Ala-ad-Dawlah, ruler of the principality of Dulkadir, who was conquered and killed by Selim in 1515. Babinger, *Mehmed*, p. 402.

135 Selim I died on 21 September 1520. *Chron. brev.*, II, p. 554; *Ecthesis Chronica*, p. 68. The Mosque and Imaret of Suleimaniye was built by Sinan between 1550 and 1557 and was therefore hardly begun when Spandounes was finishing the last draft of his work in 1538.

136 The Annals of Angiolello came to an end at the year 1514. So also does the *Historia Politica*. The *Chron. Turc.* ends at 1512. Suleiman I became Sultan on 30 September 1520. Ghazali ('Gazeli'), who led the revolt in Egypt, is called 'Kazalis' in the *Ecthesis Chronica*, p. 77. The commander of the Ottoman forces against him was Ferhad Pasha, who had married Suleiman's sister. Merriman, *Suleiman*, pp. 34–5.

137 Suleiman's first campaign in Hungary was in May 1521. Belgrade surrendered to him in August of that year. *Chron. brev.*, II, pp. 557–8; *Ecthesis Chronica*, pp. 69–70. Merriman, *Suleiman*, pp. 57–9; Setton, *Papacy and Levant*, III, p. 199. The *Ecthesis Chronica* lists the relics taken from Belgrade as those of St Paraskevi and St Theophano, the alleged wife of the Emperor Leo the Wise.

138 Hadrian VI was elected Pope on 9 January 1522. He had been Cardinal Bishop of Tortosa and was in Spain when his appointment was announced. He was there as the viceroy of Charles V. Setton, *Papacy and Levant*, III, pp. 200–1.

139 This seems to be Andrea Matteo Palmieri, Archbishop of Acerenza and Matera in southern Italy (1518–38). Setton, *Papacy and Levant*, III, p. 403.

140 The long siege of Rhodes, which lasted for most of December 1522, is well documented and Spandounes has nothing to add. The Grand Master of the Knights was Philippe de Villiers de l'Isle Adam, Grand Prior of France. *Chron. brev.*, II, pp. 560–1; *Ecthesis Chronica*, pp. 71–3. Merriman, *Suleiman*, pp. 60–75; Setton, *Papacy and Levant*, III, pp. 208–16; Vakalopoulos, Ἱστορία τοῦ Νεοελληνισμοῦ, III, pp. 102–18.

141 For all his claim to inside knowledge of the affair of Jem ('Cem') Sultan, Spandounes here confuses the names of father and son, for they were not both called Jem. Jem Sultan, the brother of Bayezid II, had escaped to Rhodes and died in Italy in 1495 (see above, text p. 171). His son, who remained in Rhodes with his wife and family, was called Murad Bey. Thuasne, *Djem Sultan*, pp. 389–90; Vakalopoulos, Ἱστορία τοῦ Νεοελληνισμοῦ, III, p. 115.

142 Pope Leo X died on 1 December 1521. On his great plans for a crusade against Selim I, see Setton, *Papacy and Levant*, III, pp. 172–97. Spandounes, who clearly admired Leo X, claims to have been his confidant and adviser. His dislike of the next Pope, Hadrian VI, is evident. But he approved of Clement VII and of Paul III, each of whom made him a papal commissioner, partly to investigate the scandalous business of certain entrepreneurs in northern Italy in selling arms to the Turks. Clement VII referred to Spandounes as 'dilecto filio, patritio Constantinopolitano, familiari et commissario nostro'. Setton, *Papacy and Levant*, III, p. 411 n. 57 (citing document of January 1537).

143 Suleiman's treatment of Christians is described and condemned in an anonymous account of the condition of Greece in 1533 written by a Greek of Constantinople, printed in Sathas, *Documents inédits*, VI (Paris, 1885), pp. 313–17.

144 In July 1523 Pope Hadrian VI sent Cardinal Tommaso de Vio, Bishop of Gaeta ('Gaetano', Cajetan) (1519–34) to Hungary to help finance the defence of Skradin ('Scardona') which was under attack by the Sultan's troops. Kliš ('Clissa'), on the Dalmatian coast above Split, was in similar danger in 1523. It finally fell to the Turks in 1537 (see below, text p. 197 and n. 156). Papal concern for its safety was expressed in a number of documents. Setton, *Papacy and Levant*, III, pp. 219, 236 n. 28, 247 n. 69, 343 n. 131, 378 n. 112. I have failed to identify 'Thomasi Nigro' and 'Zuan Francesco Brancha'.

145 These events in Egypt occurred in 1523–4. On Mustafa Pasha, said to have been married to a sister of Suleiman, see Merriman, *Suleiman*, pp. 64, 68. 'Acmat bassa' is Ahmed Pasha, who played a large part in the siege of Rhodes. *Chron. brev.*, II, pp. 559–61; *Ecthesis Chronica*, pp. 75–6. Merriman, *Suleiman*, pp. 76–7. Ibrahim Pasha, the great favourite of Suleiman, who suppressed the revolt in Cairo and decapitated Ahmed, came from Riniasa ('Regnassa') on the coast of Epiros, south of Parga. See Nicol, *Despotate of Epiros*, II, pp. 172–3. Spandounes elsewhere (below, text pp. 210–11) has other tales to tell about the wealth and influence of Ibrahim Pasha. *EI*, III, pp. 998–9.

146 Suleiman's campaign across the Danube lasted from April to November 1526. The battle of Mohacs was fought on 26 August (not 28 or 29) 1526. *Chron. brev.*, II, p. 566; *Ecthesis Chronica*, pp. 73–4. Merriman, *Suleiman*, pp. 84–96; Setton, *Papacy and Levant*, III, pp. 348–9. Louis II Jagiellon had been King of Hungary from 1516 before meeting his death in 1526. His widow Mary escaped to 'Cossonia' (? Carniola) and later became regent of the Netherlands; she died in 1558. The Count Palatine Stephen Batori had been prevented by illness from taking command at Mohacs.

147 'Zuane' is John Zápolya, son of the Palatine Count Stephen Zápolya. John was Voivode of Transylvania in 1511 and King of Hungary from 1526 to

1540, being crowned as such on 11 November 1625. His election was disputed by Ferdinand I, Archduke of Austria (1521), who was the brother of Louis II's wife Mary and of the Emperor Charles V. These events took place between May and October 1529. *Chron. brev.*, II, pp. 566–7; *Ecthesis Chronica*, p. 77. Setton, *Papacy and Levant*, III, pp. 249–53, 300–3, 312–26. Spandounes repeats (text, p. 233 below) his observation about Suleiman's adoption of the 'Christian' custom of using tables and chairs.

148 The circumcision feast began on 27 June 1530 and lasted for three weeks. *Chron. brev.*, II, p. 567.

149 Inalcik, *Ottoman Empire*, pp. 35–6; Setton, *Papacy and Levant*, III, pp. 354–66. The passage about the fate of Kliš ('Clissa') is far out of context and refers to the year 1537. See below, text p. 197 and n. 158.

150 This adventure (dated to 3 September 1531) is narrated at length by the historian of the Knights Hospitallers, Iacomo Bosio, *Dell' Istoria della sacra religione et Illustrissima Militia di San Giovanni Gierosolimitano*, II (Rome, 1594), pp. 76–7, 80, 103–8. *Chron. brev.*, II, p. 568. Vakalopoulos, Ἱστορία τοῦ Νεοελληνισμοῦ, III, pp. 132–5. 'Isidoro Scandali' was really Nicholas Skandalis and his son John; and the Rhodian Greek was John Maria Strategopoulos. *Chron. brev.*, II, p. 568.

151 Suleiman's abortive campaign into Hungary came between April and November 1532. *Chron. brev.*, II, p. 569. Merriman, *Suleiman*, pp. 115–19; Setton, *Papacy and Levant*, III, pp. 365–6. Sathas, in Spandounes, ed. Sathas, p. xxiii, believes that Spandounes was present at the Turkish siege of Vienna in 1532.

152 The temporarily successful operations of the Genoese Andrea Doria, sent to the Peloponnese by the Emperor Charles V, are well documented by other sources. Coron was retaken from the Turks on 19 September 1532; Patras and its fortresses of Rion and Antirrion in October. But it was a very short Christian victory. Patras was lost again within a month, Coron on 1 April 1534. Especially valuable here is the account of Nikandros Noukios of Corfu, ed. J.-A. de Foucault, *Nicandre de Corcyre, Voyages* (Paris, 1962), pp. 158–61 (reproduced in *Chron. brev.*, II, pp. 637–9); *Chron. brev.*, II, pp. 569–72. Vakalopoulos, Ἱστορία τοῦ Νεοελληνισμοῦ, III, pp. 135–8; Setton, *Papacy and Levant*, III, p. 392.

153 The peace settlement between Suleiman and the Christian powers in 1533 was partly engineered by Ibrahim Pasha and Lodovico Gritti, the Venetian representative in Constantinople. Setton, *Papacy and Levant*, III, pp. 370–84.

154 'Caradin Bey' is Haireddin Barbarossa. He left Constantinople with his fleet in May 1537. Suleiman's Persian campaigns lasted from June 1534 to June 1536. *Chron. brev.*, II, pp. 573–6; *Ecthesis Chronica*, pp. 78–81. The activities of Lodovico Gritti and his murder at Medgyes in September 1534 are described by Setton, *Papacy and Levant*, III, pp. 289–91;

Merriman, *Suleiman*, pp. 257–9. 'Zuane' is again John Zápolya of Hungary.

155 Suleiman's Persian campaigns lasted from June 1534 to June 1536. *Chron. brev.*, II, pp. 573–6.

156 The two Christian captains defending Sardinia were Andrea Doria and 'Don Albarea', who might be Fernando Alvarez de Toledo, third Duke of Alva (1508–82). Setton, *Papacy and Levant*, III, p. 413.

157 A slightly different version of the murder of Ibrahim Pasha is given in the *Ecthesis Chronica*, pp. 78–9. Ayas Pasha is known as one of Barbarossa's naval commanders. Vakalopoulos, Ἱστορία τοῦ Νεοελληνισμοῦ, III, pp. 144, 146, 148; Merriman, *Suleiman*, p. 185; *EI*, I, 2, pp. 779–80, where his part in the murder of Ibrahim is not recorded.

158 Kliš ('Clissa') in Dalmatia was frequently under Turkish assault from 1534. Pope Paul III was keen to strengthen the fortifications of its castle on the coast which was held by Count Peter Kružić. The papal commissioner's name seems to be otherwise unrecorded, though Niccolo dalla Torre, who went with him as King Ferdinand's man, is known. Their expedition, in March 1537, was defeated. Count Peter was captured and beheaded. 'Amurat Vaivoda' is hard to identify. Setton, *Papacy and Levant*, III, pp. 378, 421–2.

159 Lutfi Bey, Grand Vizier, probably of Albanian origin, was Suleiman's brother-in-law; and as the Bey of Gallipoli he was the supreme naval commander. His depredations in Otranto and Apulia are briefly mentioned in the *Ecthesis Chronica*, p. 79. The *Historia Patriarchica*, pp. 160, 162, calls him 'Touphlipasias'. *EI*, V, pp. 837–8; Moravcsik, *Byzantinoturcica*, II, p. 178.

160 Girolamo Pesaro was Venetian captain-general of the sea in 1537–8. One Giovanni Vetturi is known to have been a provveditore of Corfu in 1524. 'Ionus' was Yunus Bey, earlier known as a Turkish envoy to Venice and a dragoman (interpreter). Setton, *Papacy and Levant*, III, pp. 233n, 424–5.

161 The Turkish siege of Corfu, from 27 August to 14 September 1537, is recorded at greater length in various sources. An eye-witness account is given by Nikandros Noukios, ed. Foucault, pp. 162–74. See also: *Chron. brev.*, II, p. 576; *Ecthesis Chronica*, ed. Lambros, pp. 80–1. Miller, *Latins in the Levant*, pp. 559–62; Vakalopoulos, Ἱστορία τοῦ Νεοελληνισμοῦ, III, pp. 143–50; Merriman, *Suleiman*, pp. 220–1.

162 Barbarossa's attacks on the islands of the Archipelago took place between spring and autumn 1537. The Duke of Naxos who was allowed to remain on payment of tribute was Giovanni IV Crispi. Aigina ('Lezena') was captured in October 1537. *Chron. brev.*, II, pp. 575–7; *Ecthesis Chronica*, pp. 80–1. Miller, *Latins in the Levant*, pp. 624–7; Vakalopoulos, Ἱστορία τοῦ Νεοελληνισμοῦ, III, pp. 150–6.

163 Girolamo Pesaro had orders to attack Butrinto and Parga. He was replaced

as captain-general in March 1538 by Vincenzo Capello. Setton, *Papacy and Levant*, III, pp. 427, 429n.

164 Barbarossa captured the islands of Skiathos and Skopelos and also attacked Crete in the spring–summer of 1538. *Chron. brev.*, II, pp. 577–8. Miller, *Latins in the Levant*, pp. 628–30; Vakalopoulos, Ἱστορία τοῦ Νεοελληνισμοῦ, III, p. 157. On Vincenzo Capello and the papal commissioner Marco Grimani: Setton, *Papacy and Levant*, III, p. 446.

165 Grimani's unauthorised venture to Preveza in the summer of 1538 is known from other sources. *Chron. brev.*, II, p. 579; Nikandros Noukios, ed. Foucault, p. 175. Miller, *Latins in the Levant*, p. 509; Setton, *Papacy and Levant*, III, p. 446.

166 One Alvise Badoer was Venetian ambassador to Constantinople in 1540. One Camillo Orsini was governor of Parma in 1547. Setton, *Papacy and Levant*, III, pp. 449n, 504n, 506. Suleiman's campaign in Moldavia (Wallachia) was in July–October 1538. 'Carabogdan' is Stephen whom Suleiman set up as Voivode. *Chron. brev.*, II, p. 578; *Ecthesis Chronica*, pp. 81–2. 'Zuane' is again John Zápolya, who was King of Hungary until 1540.

167 Pope Paul III finally negotiated a treaty of peace for ten years between Charles V, King of Spain, Naples and Sicily and Emperor (1510–56) and Francis I King of France (1515–47). It was signed at Nice in July 1538. Setton, *Papacy and Levant*, III, pp. 441–2. Peace between Venice and the Turks came two years later, on 2 October 1540, and resulted in the Turkish occupation of Nauplion and Monemvasia. These are events which Spandounes would surely have recorded if he had continued his story. But, for reasons which he does not make entirely clear, he left Venice for Rome in the summer of 1538 and wrote no more thereafter. *Chron. brev.*, II, pp. 579–80; *Ecthesis Chronica*, p. 82. Miller, *Latins in the Levant*, p. 509.

168 The last event recorded by Spandounes should probably be dated to August–September 1538. Barbarossa, coming from Crete rather than 'Chios', made for Preveza by way of Leukas rather than Cephalonia, and sailed into the Gulf of Arta. There he encountered and dispersed the allied Christian fleet commanded by Andrea Doria and 'don Ferrante', or Ferrante Gonzaga, viceroy of Sicily from 1535. *Chron. brev.*, II, p. 579. Setton, *Papacy and Levant*, III, pp. 445–8; Merriman, *Suleiman*, pp. 222–4.

II

Having now described in brief the origins of the house of Ottoman and the deeds of their Emperors, I shall go on to describe the offices of their court, their revenues, the form of their military strength, their style of living and of government, and the many ways in which they differ from the principalities of Christendom.[1]

First about their currency: they have ducats ('ducati') which they call *sultani* ('Soltanini') and which have the weight and value of Venetian ducats; and they have what they call aspers ('aspri' [= *akçe*]), four to a dram ('drammo' [= *dirhem*]), which is their manner of weight. Fifty-four of these make one Venetian ducat or Soltanino, for the two have equal value. They also have certain coins called *mangir* ('Manguri'), a copper currency which in my experience is in great circulation, at eight to the asper, though sometimes at twelve, sixteen, twenty-four, thirty-two, forty or forty-eight, for these coins have no stable rate. Most transactions are done in aspers. But it has been the custom that each new Sultan strikes his own issue; the old aspers are then invalidated and withdrawn and have to be exchanged at the mint, which gives ten new aspers for twelve of the old ones. This practice brought in 800,000 ducats and proved to be so lucrative that Mehmed II took to minting new aspers every ten years. The officials responsible for changing the coins were called *gümüs sarraflari* ('Gumis Sarazi'). Bayezid discontinued this practice. / Selim did not reign for ten years, though he minted three sorts of aspers. Suleiman also has not changed the rate.[2]

Now since the law of Mahomet forbids pictures or images, the Sultans do not put their own portraits on their coins as

Christian princes do, only inscriptions giving their titles and religious texts.

First let me say that the Sultans keep in their quarters 300 boys who sleep in various rooms in what they call the Oda or Chamber. The present Sultan [Suleiman] has increased this number to 400. Each Oda is managed and served by eunuchs. There are also resident teachers of Turkish letters for the boys, all of whom are sons of Christian parents and brought captive from Christian territory. Some of them belong to the Sultan, some have been given to him and live in his private household. These are called the *Içoglani* ('Icioglanlar'), which in Italian signifies intimate pages. Four of them are specially privileged by the Sultan and are supervised by the *Odaoglanlar*. Two of these sleep in the palace and keep guard while the Sultan sleeps; and they carry torches, two at his head and two at his feet, and daggers which they call 'Canzar' and also swords embellished in gold; and the two take turns in keeping constant guard over the Sultan's person. And when the Sultan goes out, one of them carries his cloak; he is called the *Çuhadar* ('Zochadar'). The other, called the *Sharabdar* ('Chipter'), bears a jug of water called 'Matara', for the Turks wash very frequently. Another of the boys has charge of the Sultan's sword and hands it to him when commanded; another carries his bow and quiver; / and the rest of the up to 400 boys follow behind. Some of these pages are often presented by the Sultan, at his own whim or convenience, to officials and dignitaries of his court. But the four specially privileged ones are made what they called the *Mütteferrika* ('Mutafaracha') [or elite palace guards] and get paid 100 aspers a day; and some rise to become Agas or *Sanjak* [*beys*]. 300 other such pages are kept in other centres such as Pera or Adrianople, with their own eunuchs and teachers.

Other eunuchs in the palace, once 80 but now 100 in number, serve the Sultan as his guards under the command of the *Kapici başi* ('Capigassi') or head-gatekeeper who guards the gate nearest to the

Sultan's person. He is a very important man, being closest to the Sultan and privileged to converse with him whenever he wants. He has to sleep alone in the chamber next to the Sultan, along with thirty other eunuchs and pages to guard the Sultan.

The other grandee among the eunuchs holds the office of *Haẓinedarbaşi* ('Casnatarbasi').[3] He is the head of the Sultan's inner Treasury, as distinct from the external Treasurer. He looks after the pay of the boys, their teachers, the musicians, and the maintenance of the women in the other seraglio, as well as the Sultan's personal requirements.

The third grandee among the eunuchs is the *Isaga* whom some call the *Kilerẓi başi* ('Chelarzibassi').[4] He looks after the Sultan's personal and private affairs, the confection of his food and other sensual pleasures. If the Sultan wants sexual gratification ('atto venereo'), it is the *Isaga* who fetches the lady from the seraglio, prepares her and lays her down on the Sultan's bed. He is a man held in the highest esteem and reverence. / Before the time of Mehmed II castration of the eunuchs had been performed simply by cutting the testicles. He, however, insisted on it being done more thoroughly, for he had once seen a gelded horse mounting a mule. To prevent such a possibility, he decreed that castration must be done root and branch. All those who were condemned to this vile treatment – and one out of every ten died under the operation – were sons of Christians. The Sultan keeps 100 eunuchs for his own service. The rest guard and serve the women. Some are kept at Pera and Adrianople; and some eventually rise to high office at court and state, such as Pashas or *Sanjak* [*beys*].

The Sultan is also served by thirty masters of their theology, who read to him and to the pages. They are well remunerated from the Eunuch's Treasury; and so are the doctors who minister to the imperial person.

There are also sixty foodtasters ('Chisnairi') who are supervised by the *Casnigir başi* ('Cisnairbasi'),[5] and these too are paid by the

205

111

Theodore Spandounes

Eunuch's Treasurer at the rate of eighty and thirty-three aspers a day respectively. The Sultan's food is brought to him by the boy pages called *Içoglani* ('Izoglani') and his drink by one of the *Odaoglanlar*, the supervisors of the boys.

There are also thirty 'Talissimani', their priests.[6] These too are paid by the Eunuch Treasurer, and they chant the offices at stated hours.

The man in charge of the Sultan's garden is the *Bostançi-başi* ('Bostanzibassi') with 300 workers; and he is held in high esteem, for he is allowed to talk to the Sultan, who frequently visits his garden. /

The kitchen staff are controlled by one called the *Mutbakh-emini* ('Mutpatemin'). He too is much respected, for he can approach the Sultan when he likes; and he has 260 kinds of cooks, 200 of them being 'Chismechiari'. The keeper of the kitchen accounts is the 'Mutpatiasixi'. They eat three times a day and on court days, Saturday, Sunday, Monday and Tuesday, they have up to 600 grand dishes called 'Signi', piled with rice and mince and other items. There are also twenty-five cellarmen ('Chelerzi') who keep the butter, cheese, olives, honey etc.'; and ten *Helvaçi* who make the much-favoured Turkish delicacy called *Halva* ('Calva').

There are fifty 'Baltaggi' [*Acem-oglans*] who cut wood for the palace, and others called *Sakkas* ('Saccha') who fetch water on horseback. The master butcher is the 'Casapbassi' with twenty assistants and some boys; and much of the meat that is spare is distributed in charity outside the building.

The master of the horse is the *Mirahur* ('Muracorbassi'). /

Such are the ministers and officials of the palace of the Turks. Outside the court and palace of the Sultan and in a walled enclosure live the women collected for him from many places wherever he found them to be fair and comely and had them given to him; there are also slaves – all to the number of 300. They have 100 eunuchs to look after them, and all are paid by the Eunuch Treasurer. The Sultan is wont to visit this seraglio of his ladies every morning when he rises, they being always enclosed and forbidden to speak to any other man, not even to their fathers. The eunuchs lead them out into a great salon and array them in ranks on either side of the room; and they lift their veils with which Turkish women cover their faces. The Sultan walks along the line of them and throws a kerchief which he carries to whichever of them pleases him best. The chosen one picks it up, bows, and kisses the hem of his robe at his feet. Her eunuch (for every ten ladies have three eunuchs to look after them) then takes her to be perfumed and leads her to the Sultan's bed. Those of the ladies who are thus chosen and impregnated are held in much greater respect by their servants. But when one of them has been used by the Sultan for forty days he no longer frequents her; and it is rare for a Sultan to have more than one son by the same lady, although Bayezid had two sons by the same mother; and the present Suleiman had four by a Circassian woman, his first having been borne by another. For in general the Sultans always sleep with virgins. Those whom he has not impregnated stay for some time in the seraglio and are then married off by him to one or other of his courtiers. Those with child stay inside and look after their sons . . . under the care of the Treasurer and the *Harem agasi* ('Isaga'), the [black eunuch]. / These are in the line of succession to the Empire. 208

[*Their form of government*]

They have three or at the most four 'Bassas' [= Viziers].[7] I have never known the numbers to be more or less. To these [Viziers] is committed all the management of the state. Everything passes through their hands, including the provision of the *Sipahis* ('Spachi' [cavalrymen]) and the Timariots ('Timarati' [holders of fiefs in return for military service]). Ambassadors coming to the Porte are directed to these Bassas, who then confer with their lord. Each one receives 25,000 ducats a year and they enjoy extensive privileges and honours and accumulate inestimable treasure. I recall having known an Albanian who was made a Bassa; he was called Davud ('Thauth Bassa') and he died of despair when he was relieved of his office. He was found to have left 1,000,000 gold ducats apart from his property in mills, slaves, horses and other movables which he had amassed. /

Up until the time of Selim the Sultans had only two *Beylerbeys* [or governors in charge of provinces, *beylerbeyliks*], that of Greece which is Europe and that of Natalia which is Asia.[8] The governor of Greece has to attend the Porte every day when the court is in session. The governor of Natalia stays always in his province. These officials are the equivalent of our captains-general and they are superior to all *Sanjak beys*, officers and lords. But Selim, after he had conquered the district of 'Azammia' [Amasya] in Persia and defeated the lord of 'Anadula' [Cilicia] commonly called 'Aliduli', and conquered 'Soria' [Syria] and 'Anchora' [Angora] and the whole of Egypt ruled by the 'Soldano' [Mamluk Sultan], changed his administration. He greatly increased the numbers of *Beylerbeys*, of *Sanjaks*, of *Subaşi* ('Subbassi') and of *Sipahis* ('Spachi').

The *Beylerbey* of Greece–Europe was answerable to the Sultan; he received 25,000 ducats per year; and he had 40 *Sanjak* [*beys*] under him, each one getting between 5,000 and 16,000 ducats. He also had 150 *Subaşi* getting 1,000 to 3,000 ducats; and 15,000 *Sipahis* ('Spachi') paid between 1,500 and 15,000 aspers. The *Beylerbey* of Natalia or Asia up to Kütahya ('Ciottei') received 20,000 ducats, and had under him 30 Sanjak [*beys*] and 8,000 *Subaşi* and *Sipahis*. The *Bey* of Karamania ('Archarmania') received 15,000 ducats, and had a total of 15,000 *Subaşi* and *Sipahis*. The *Bey* of Amasia had 15,000 ducats, 7 *Sanjaks*, and a total of 10,000 cavalry. The *Bey* of Diarbakir ('Diarbach') in Mesopotamia received more than the others, for he held the frontiers against Sophi, King of Persia. His provision was 30,000 ducats, with 20 *Sanjaks* and 15,000 cavalry. In ('Anadolu') Egypt the Sultan maintained a viceroy and its affairs were conducted in Constantinople. In Syria too there was a viceroy over all that the Sultan of Cairo had ruled; and he was responsible for paying all officials and had to send 1,000 ducats a year to Constantinople.

The privileges of the *Beys* in camp and in battle order are here outlined. The *Bey* of Greece takes precedence. And when the Sultan's son is in camp he is under the command of the *Bey*, 'which seems quite right to me, for military discipline must have its ranks'. / None of the *Beys* resides in Constantinople, except that of Greece–Europe. The others stay in their provinces and are authorised to pay up to 6,000 aspers to whomever they like.

[A note on the seating and pecking order of 'Bassas'.]

I have now said enough about 'Bassas' and *Beylerbeys*. But it is worth noting that if the Sultan wanted to upgrade a *Beylerbey* he could make him a 'Bassa', even though in common usage the two names and titles went together. The present Sultan Suleiman wanted Ibrahim Pasha [who was already Grand Vizier] to have the title also of *Beylerbey* and to have seniority over all; he gave Ibrahim so much power to appoint and dismiss that he was like a universal patron of all government officials. One day when the Sultan was in one of the towers where he kept his treasure in sacks of gold, Ibrahim tried to move one of the sacks; but it was far too heavy, for it had, so they say, 500,000 ducats in it; and the Grand Turk said to him: 'If you can carry it you can have it.' Ibrahim replied: 'I cannot lift it, though it would relieve me of many cares.' The Sultan at once gave it to him and sent him on his way. This I record to show how great was the esteem which he had for Ibrahim.

Then there is the great office of *Kadiasker* ('Cadilescher') of which there are two [supreme judges], / one of Greece–Europe one of Natalia–Asia.[9] They reside in Constantinople or wherever the court happens to be. They constitute something like a great patriarchate, for they are the most learned in theology and the law. The *Kadiasker* is supreme over all the *kadi* [or judges] and over the 'priests' whom they call 'Talismani', each one in his own European or Asiatic province. The latter has assumed much greater responsibility in recent years as a result of Selim's territorial acquisitions in Mesopotamia and in Egypt. The system seems to work well and to be commendable. The *Kadiaskers* preside over the court of appeal for all civil and criminal cases and they supervise all the *kadiliki* or judicial courts in the provinces. When a judge is appointed [usually for three years] the *Kadiaskers* report the fact to the Sultan; and, if he approves, the elected judge is taken to kiss the hand first of the Bassa, then of the Sultan, and is given an appropriate salary fixed by the *Kadiasker*. They have pride of place in audiences with the Sultan – and the Sultan issues no death penalties without consulting them.

The two heads of the Treasury are the *Defterdari* ('Tefterderi'), one in Europe and one in Asia.[10] They control all the books and accounts of the Sultan. In Italian the name is 'Quadernieri'. They are the accountants of all the imperial dominions and supervise taxation, meting out severe penalties, of torture or life / imprisonment, to defaulters or cheats. Mehmed used to have such people hanged. Bayezid instead had them gaoled in great numbers. Selim and Suleiman have been more lenient in this matter. The *Defterdari* sit in the same chamber as the Bassas, report regularly to the Sultan on the affairs of their provinces, and are highly esteemed. They hold court in great pomp, and they have 100 scribes and 25 clerks. Then there is the *Niçançi* ('Nizanzibassi'), the imperial chancellor, who signs all letters, decrees or privileges of the Sultan.[11] He too is much honoured and rides in great style. There is another official in charge of money and the weighing of weights and measures (*Veznedar*) who also sits with the Bassas and is highly respected.[12] Here follows the order of seating of all these dignitaries when in session. The 'Dragomanni' [interpreters] are not seated but remain standing at meetings.

The most honoured and most powerful of the Agas is the Aga of the Janissaries, who at present number 10,000 in Constantinople.[13] All of these are the sons of Christians recruited in the following manner: every five years or sometimes more often, as in Selim's reign, and according to the need or the whim of the Sultan, one out of every five boys in each province is selected and brought to the Sultan, except in some privileged places. He then singles out some for his seraglio; the rest are usually dispersed to stay with families of note in Anatolia for a while to be brought up in the Turkish faith, customs and laws. Then they are toughened up / by being made to carry stones and mortar on building projects as labourers for the Sultans and the nobles before being sent to various masters and captains to learn the arts of war; and some are directed to learn about naval warfare; for every Turkish fleet has some novices as well as experienced veteran Janissaries. They are the *Acemi oglanlar* ('Azamoglani'); and when they have been trained enough they are enrolled in the Janissaries.[14] At first they get three to five aspers a day; though Selim increased their pay with a bonus when he became Sultan, and so did Suleiman. But still they have but five aspers a day. Once a year they get a bow, two shirts and some cloth for inner and outer garments. They are under the command of the Grand Aga who gets 500 aspers a day, and so also are the Grand 'Protoghero' who gets 2,000 aspers a month, and the other 'Protogheri' [lieutenants], the *Yaya* ('Iaia' [infantry]) and the *Boluk başi* ('Billubassi' [sergeants]), all under the Grand Aga of the Janissaries.[15]

The Janissaries have their own clerk who once a month hands out to them one [extra] day's pay; and I have seen this official riding with great ceremony. He had his own *Subaşilik* ('Subaslich' [fief]) of 150,000 aspers per month.[16] The Janissaries are paid from the Treasury chief, the *Haẕinedarbaşi* ('Casnarbassi'). The *Kiaya* leader ('Iaiabassi'), gets twenty-five to fifty aspers a day. He carries the banner for the 100 men following him. The 'Protoghero' has to settle or punish any differences in the ranks, with the support of the *Boluk başi*. Out of every 100 Janissaries three go on horseback. All the rest go on foot; and anyone seen on a horse, unless he is wounded or has some other good reason, has his pay docked. All of them have their barracks, ten to a room, in Constantinople. Their commander there is the 'Odabassi', whose responsibility it is to provide horses to transport equipment and provisions. The final arbiter in any differences between their leaders is the Grand Aga. On their heads the Janissaries wear white caps ('zarchula') shaped like socks and somewhat similar to the headgear of the Jesuit friars ('frati Jesuati') except that they are made of felt not cloth and well starched so that they stand erect. No one else in Turkey wears such white caps. / Their three leaders wear red and white with a gold band. Disobedient troops are immured in a fortress outside the city and, very rarely, put to death as an example. The Janissaries are not allowed to marry; and they carry the following weapons: bow, sword, dagger, cuirass and musket, which they handle very well. They also act as the Sultan's personal bodyguards when he is out; and he has more faith in them than in anyone else. There are 3,000 *Acemi oglan* ('Azomogliani') or Janizerotti in Constantinople daily waiting to be enrolled in the ranks under the Aga of the Janissaries.

Another officer called the *Alem mehterleri* ('Emiralem')[17] has charge of the flags or standards. He is a man of great dignity and wealth and wears a unique white and green sash indicating his high honour and proximity to the Sultan. [His method of appointment and special privileges.] He heads the 'Flamburari' or rather *Sanjak beys* who wear special and distinctive hats with six horsehair plumes with gold tassels on top. /

The official who commands the greatest honour of all is the *Mufti*, the supreme doctor and expounder of [Islamic] law, to whom the Sultan pays great deference. His scribe ('Tiphte') records the laws as pronounced by the *Mufti* and none of the Kadis can question it.

The *Mütteferika* ('Mutafaracha') are the elite.[18] They are the sons of noblemen and number about 100 at present, since Suleiman has reduced their number by about a half. They receive payment from the inner Treasury of between 80 and 120–50 aspers a day and their main duties are to follow the Sultan when he goes to camp.

The Sultan's footmen ('staffieri'), made up of Janissaries, are called *Solak* ('Solachi').[19] Once they were 150 in number, but Selim increased them to 200 and Suleiman to 216. Half of them are left-handed and go to the left; half are right-handed and keep to the right. They have two Agas, two *Kiaya* ('Chiechaia') and four *Boluk-başis* ('Bulubassi' [sergeants]).

The gatekeepers [external] are 300 Janissaries under the command of the *Kapici başi*.[20] / The *Hazinedarbaşi* ('Casnatharbassi') of external affairs is the Grand Treasurer, with forty subordinates, responsible for collecting and managing all the Sultan's revenues. He is obliged to deposit 100,000 aspers every day in the *Hazine* ('Casana'), a turreted building which houses the imperial Treasury; if he fails to do so he loses his head.

The Aga of *Sipahis* ('Spacogliani') . . . now commands 3,000 horsemen . . . [21] The *Silahdar* ('Silictarii'), now increased to 3,000, are keepers of the Sultan's armoury commanded by the 'Silictarbassi'.[22] The *Ulufaji* ('Allophanzi [special cavalry]) / have been increased to 3,000 by Suleiman, commanded by an 'Allophangibassa'. The *Ghureba-oglans* ('Cariboglani') are about 1,000 in number.[23] The *Mirahur bassa* is the master of horse.[24] He commands 1,000 Janissaries and slaves, 300 of which serve at the court, the other 700 being distributed in Adrianople, Serres, Salonichi and other places in Greece and Natalia. The *Çavuş* ('Zausi' [led by their 'Zausbassi']), are now 200 in number and are state messengers who carry messages to and from the provinces.[25]

The *Topçubaşi* ('Topizibassi') is the chief gunner, whose numbers were raised to 100 by Selim and still higher by Suleiman for the conquest of Rhodes. He has established a munitions factory at Valona for the furtherance of the huge and marvellous projects that he has in mind for an offensive against the Christians, which may God forbid! /

218   The *Cepecibaşi* is the chief armourer ('Zebezibassi').[26]

The *Segmen başi* is the master of the hunt ('Seimembassi').[27]

The 'Doganzibassi' or chief hawker comes under the Grand Falconer [*Çakirki başi*].[28] There are about 6,000 Christian households who pay nothing to the Sultan each year except for a falcon or a hawk, which he makes over to his noblemen as it pleases him.

The 'Zagarizbassi' is the master of hounds, with about 1,000 Janissaries.[29]

The Sultan's camel corps is now larger than ever, up to 130,000 in number. Suleiman employed them in his campaigns against Belgrade and Hungary, for he transported great quantities of baggage. They are commanded by the 'Saravansibassi', under whom serves also the 'Cathirbassi' or chief muleteer.[30]

The *Arpa-emini* is a very important official, for he controls the grain supply to Constantinople and the court ('Arpahemim').[31]

The 'Calvasibassi' is in charge of the confection known as Halva for the Sultan's table.

The *Terziler* ('Terzibassi') is the master tailor who instructs Janissaries and servants in his art.[32] /

219   The *Shehir-emini* ('Meimeri') is the master mason in charge of buildings and walls; he too has a large staff of Janissaries and slaves.[33]

[Other workers and artisans who do various tasks about
the court.]

The *Mulazim* ('Masuli') are officials temporarily retired or who have been transferred and are waiting for other postings from their superiors.[34] They are usually about 8,000–9,000 in number.

The *Peiks* ('Beichi'), about thirty in number, are the Sultan's couriers who go on foot at the trot and are trained to do so.[35] The Sultans use them for urgent messages to go 100 to 120 miles, because they move faster than the 'Vlachi', the messengers who go on horseback. One August in Adrianople I found one of these 'Beichi' boasting that he had got from Constantinople before sunset, a journey that takes four days by horse riding only twenty to twenty-two miles a day. He had done it within twenty-four hours. The 'Vlachi' are the horseback messengers. But they do not ride at night and they change their horses along the way. Our own Christian couriers who ride night and day are thus much quicker.

The 'Bechlevani', of whom there are about eighty and of great stature are wrestlers who go about naked but for a loincloth and a short cloak which they discard when challenged to a bout.

The 'Machaiazi' are archers in the pay of the Sultan. /

There are others who hang about the court, some paid for such 220 services as the extraction of teeth, some simply scroungers, far more of them than we have in Christendom.

The total complement of the Sultan's court at present, on foot and on horse, is 35,000 salaried persons.

The number of Christians: in the time of Bayezid it was found that they numbered 1,112,000 Christian vassals paying the *haraç* ('Carazo') or tribute, apart from others who, though vassals, were exempt or privileged. A census taken in Selim's time counted 1,328,000, apart from those Christians in Egypt, Persia, Mesopotamia, Cilicia ('Alliduli') and other places that Selim conquered, who are computed separately. /

[*The revenue of the Sultan*]

The details here given have been carefully and truthfully recorded 221 and are demonstrably correct in case anyone should doubt them. [All figures are given in ducats.] First, from the poor Christians, the *haraç* ('caraz') brings in 1,500,000 a year; the silver mines – 1,000,000; the tax on cattle – at least 1,000,000; tolls and tariffs – 700,000; salt duties – 500,000; stamp duties on every state document – more than 100,000; defaulters who fail to pay their taxes to the court – more than 500,000; duties payable by resident foreigners who die without heir ('Beltamazi') or deriving from properties which have no owner – 400,000; from 'Passaggi' or travellers in transit [?] – 500,000; from exchange – 100,000; from presents – 300,000; the noblemen, all of whom are servants and stipendiaries of the Sultan, pay part of their estate when they die, for all that they may have sons, and this brings in about 700,000 a year. The tributes payable by vassal states are as follows: Cyprus – 8,000 as well as other presents; the principality of Wallachia – 12,000, now increased to 16,000, with certain gifts; Ragusa – 12,500 and half of their salt production; Chios ('Scyo') – 10,000; Zakynthos – 500; Cephalonia ('Cypro') – 8,000; the former Soldano's dominion [Egypt] pays through the viceroy in Cairo 15,000. In addition there are taxes payable by all towns and people, and the *Ispence* ('Spense' [*pençik*]) payable at thirty aspers per person for Christians and twenty-five for Muslims. The grand total is 11 to 12,000,000. Enough of revenues.

A good and commendable form of justice is available to a poor man who has been wronged. They call it 'Rocha'. The injured man can put his supplication on the end of a stick and wait for the Sultan to come by in the street. / The Sultan will then take the message with his own hand and put it in his turban. In the morning of the next day he will send for the man and hear his complaint. Suleiman, for all that he is a harsh persecutor of the Christians, follows something of the example of his forebears in this furtherance of justice; for he wants no one in his Empire to be tyrannised or unjustly treated.

[On the Turkish court and audience chamber in Constantinople]

A grand portal fashioned and decorated in marble and adorned with Moorish letters stands at the entrance, and behind it is a great courtyard. Beside this gate stands a very old church adjoining St Sophia, which, I am told, they made into a kitchen covered, like all the Sultan's buildings, with lead; and on the right side of this piazza is the Grand Signor's garden. One then comes to an equally decorative gate, at which one has to dismount unless of the rank of Bassa or *Beylerbey* . . . This second gate is guarded by the *Kapici* with staffs in their hands; and they are very strict especially with Christians and Turks of humble rank. / Beyond this second gate stands another, 223 smaller courtyard, on the right of which are the kitchens and on the left the stables. In this piazza are stationed the palace guards ('Capizi, Janissaries, Azamogliani, Spacogliani, Silictarii, Alophanzi, Mazuli') and all kinds of men waiting to be granted audience with the Bassas – and a splendid sight it is with their decorated turbans and colourful clothes. The chamber of the Bassas [Viziers] stands beyond this square; and here sit the Bassa with the *Kadiaskers*, *Defterderis* and the *Nişançi*. The only ones allowed to sit down during audience are the Aga of the Janissaries and the captain of the fleet at Gallipoli. The Bassa consults with the Signor about each request and gives the response. An ambassador may go to kiss the Sultan's hand and present his letter of credence. But it is the Bassa who deals with his request after consultation with the Signor . . .

Next to this chamber is the room of the secretaries and next to that the hall of the *Defterdari* [or head of the Treasury]; and beside these rooms there is a great loggia made of marble. It was here, as I recall, that the Despot of Greece, Manuel Palaiologos of blessed memory, used to sit when he was still alive – a privilege enjoyed by no other lord in Turkey; and next to this loggia is the gate leading into the Sultan's private quarters. Here Suleiman has built for himself a room with a ceiling of gold and precious stones. Near here the *Kapici* stand at its door; and its protection and security rest with the eunuchs and their 'Capizi Bassa Eunucho' who stands at the ante-chamber of the Sultan. / [Outside here in the loggia the Sultan would appear in 224 the morning to inspect the Janissaries and then to eat – the rest of his officials eating some paces away – and to give audience and receive obeisance and prayers for his well-being. Records were kept by the 'Divanjazizi',[36] and the officials would leave in due order of their seniority. Some of the officials are paid by the internal Eunuch Treasurer, some by the external Treasurer . . .]

Throughout the Empire everyone pays one tenth in tax; and there is no hereditary tenure of towns, castles or fiefs. When a *Sanjak bey* ('Sanzachi') or holder of a *timar* ('Timaratti') gets more than / 15,000 aspers from his holding he becomes a *subaşi* ('Subassi'), or holder of a *subaşilik* within a *Sanjak*.

All Christians over fourteen or sometimes more are registered for the *haraç* ('charazo'), the poorest paying 50 aspers per year, the richest 120; though some are privileged to pay less, or even nothing at all. The tax is collected by the 'Charazari' in each province, and with great severity. Everyone pays the *Ispence* ('Spenza') or land tax, Christians at thirty aspers per annum, the Turks at twenty-five aspers. The miserable Christians in Turkey often marry off their sons in childhood, as a means of evading the five-yearly round-up of boys for the Janissaries, since marriage made them exempt; though Selim sometimes broke this rule. All of them pay still more taxes and impositions on food, wine, animals and so forth; and it is a wonder that they manage to survive. /

Every Timariot, since the reform of the system by Selim, is obliged to go on campaign with a man and a horse when called to do so – except for those who are exempted by age or retirement, who are called the 'O[b]turach'.

. . . The duties and privileges of the *Sanjak beys* ('Sanzacchi') or provincial governors, who have power in civil and criminal matters, for all the authority of the *Kadi*. . . . The most honoured and important of such governors are those of Smederevo ('Semendria'), which was founded by 'prince Giorgio Cantacusino', and of other /

frontier districts, such as the Morea and Bosn[i]a, which have up to   227
1,000 Timarotti, all obliged to follow their *Sanjak bey*.

Some other kinds of servants of the Sultan are: the *Akinji*
('Achinzi') or auxiliary cavalry, especially committed to the slaughter
of Christians as a passage to Paradise. The *Azabs* ('Azapi') are native
Turkish footsoldiers, mainly from Natalia, and distinct from the
Janissaries. / The *Deli* are a small group of mounted men and every   228
lord and captain has some of them to lend pomp and colour to his
company. Their name means 'madmen', for they too yearn to die for
their faith.

The style of encampment, pavilions, tents etc. of the Sultan and
his troops is now described, notably the *Sipahis* ('Spacogliani') to
the number of 2,500 to 3,000. No one presumed to encamp close to the
imperial pavilion with the single exception, as I have observed, of
the Despot Manuel who, for all that he was a Christian, was given
unusual privileges by the Sultan Bayezid. / [There follows an account   229
of the pecking order of the *Beylerbeys* on the field of battle.]

The role of the Kadis, and the *Çavuş* in the camps. / The *Çavuş*   230
('Zausi') are responsible for maintaining discipline in the ranks.
Their methods of guarding the camp at night are similar to our
own. In former times they had no carriages or waggons for their
artillery guns and used to transport them with the utmost fatigue
and difficulty by dismembering them and carrying them in pieces
which they then had to reassemble for siege operations. Such was the
case until the 'Marrani', who had been expelled from Spain, brought
with them to Constantinople their method of using carts and waggons
for transporting cannons, as demonstrated by Charles in Italy.[37]
Many of the gunners are Christians and their number was greatly
increased by Selim. / [The success of the Ottoman army is due to
the energetic, tireless, vigilant and simple life of its soldiers, and
to the limitless expenditure provided by the Sultan and his administration.]

[The fleet]

231   In the time of Bayezid there were in Pera and Gallipoli about 120
galleys which I saw dragged ashore and left without any protection,
most of them in poor shape. Bayezid did not much care for the sea, as
witness the affair at Modon. Selim, who increased the numbers of his
artillery, also wanted to enlarge his fleet; and on the shore at Pera he
had a fine arsenal constructed, with walls and towers and a roof to
shelter his galleys, like that in Venice. He also began a restoration of
the arsenal of the Christian Emperors; though he died before this
work was finished. None the less, he greatly augmented the fleet and
tripled the number of paid sailors. Now there are 300 *Reïs* ('Rhaysi')
or captains of galleys, each paid forty to fifty aspers a day. Selim also
enlisted 3,000 oarsmen, who get five to eight aspers a days, as well as
3,000 others as novices ('Azamogliani', 'Janizzerotti'), making up a
standing naval force.

The supreme naval commander, their captain-general of the sea, is
the *Sanjak bey* of Gallipoli, who is also commander of Pera. There are
now three main naval bases besides Constantinople – Gallipoli,
Sinope ('Sinapo') and Nikomedia; and from these stations the
Sultan summons his fleet when needed for battle to assemble at
Constantinople. Most of the sailors are Christians. All of them, as well
as their captains, are well paid and well trained. Sometimes, though
rarely, a Pasha joins the fleet at Gallipoli to take supreme command
as captain-general of the sea. They also have horse transports and
232   provisions vessels. / When Suleiman invaded Rhodes he armed a
huge fleet [here numbered and itemised] . . . The Turkish Sultans have
increased their power at sea as a consequence of the squabbles and
pettiness of the Christian princes, as I have already remarked many
times. /

[The financing of the fleet, construction of ships,
provisioning, etc.]

[The social customs and religious observances of the Turks]

They generally eat three times a day, as noted above. They use a   233
lot of butter in their cooking and they eat a lot of rice with meat finely
minced and rolled into balls, with many other forms of pasta different
from ours. They regard it as wrong to use silver cutlery, though many
of the noblemen do; even the Sultan eats with wooden utensils as their
law prescribes. The nobles also prefer porcelain plates. They drink
water with sugar, honey and a kind of syrup, for their law forbids
them to drink wine, though many who are the sons of Christians
do so, often more than they should. At social gatherings they drink a
lot of sherbet ('Sopet') and so never bear the shame of appearing
drunk. Their wines are cultivated by Christians. The Turks, who are
forbidden to drink it, steep their grapes in a concoction which keeps
them fresh all year. Some of the wine comes from Candia and they
spend much money on it, for almost all the courtiers who are of
Christian parentage drink it. The women and children usually drink
water. The tables that they have are called 'Suffra' and are made of
leather ('corio'). On these they put their food and drink, their sliced
bread and napkins, and when they have eaten they clear it all away
and fold up the table. The native Turks rarely if ever drink wine for
they observe the law of Mahomet, as also do many Christian converts
to Islam even if they partook of wine in their youth.

As has already been noted, it was Suleiman who introduced the
Christian style of using tables and stools, and of making great
ceremony out of meals. Normally they sit on carpets on the ground,
cross-legged like tailors, with cushions of silk or other stuff. The lords
and gentry sit on what they call a 'Soffa'. The upper classes sleep on
mattresses; only the Sultan has feather beds. In the reign of Bayezid,
when there was a long era of peace, people took to less austere ways
of life. But Selim brought back the old ways, reminiscent of the more
military style of the days of Mehmed. Now, under Suleiman, a more

luxurious and indulgent way of life has come back, and people sleep in silken sheets and velvet blankets. The men's clothing consists of a long overshirt called a Kaftan, the Latin cassock ('Casacca'), and under it what they call a Dolman ('Duliman'). On their heads / the men wear the Turban, in various forms and colours, here described, according to their office or status. They shave their heads, leaving only a little hair on top, and also their beards, leaving only the moustache. This is the practice for all except the *Kadis* and the priests called 'Thalassumani'. The *Seids* ('Seiti') have their heads totally shaved and wear very thick beards; so also the *Hadji* ('Chazi') who have made the pilgrimage to Mecca to the tomb of their prophet Mahomet.[38] Older men of the upper class also tend to wear beards. Their boots and shoes are shod with iron and studs. They wear wide breeches with socks, except for the 'Thalassumani' and religious who go mostly bare-legged, though with a kind of shoes on their feet.

Their women wear the long Kaftan and the Dolman like the men, though more delicately fashioned. They too wear breeches and iron soled shoes, which make them sound like horses or mules on the stones of the streets. / They wear a form of headgear called 'Geber' shaped like a sugar loaf, tall and pyramidal. They wear some of their hair loose as ornament to the face, the rest in a plait which hangs down loose in the fashion of the ladies of Spain; and they wear scarves on their heads called in Turkish 'Macrama', in Greek 'Prosopsi' with veils richly worked in gold thread. They have wide belts like their men; and they wear gold and bejewelled ear-rings and similar necklaces and chokers.

Since the time of Bayezid they have taken to pomp and splendour. Selim brought from Cairo and Persia a vast treasury of jewels and other riches; and now the Turks are decked out in greater luxury than any other people, in cloth of gold, furs, jewellery and so forth, here described; and their women in like luxurious and opulent fashion. Their men are a jealous lot and maintain large numbers of women, as their religion allows them to do. One of the women is acknowledged to be the principal wife / and when made pregnant she has the right to secure the inheritance for her sons. Their ladies are very lascivious and voluptuous and for this reason they are kept indoors with eunuchs to guard them. When they go out they wear a veil of black silk so that no one can see their faces. They are not allowed to talk or communicate with anyone, not even with the male children born of another woman. Their boys stay with the women in the seraglio until they are of an age to go to school or to be apprenticed to a profession. They are all very subservient; and if they fall on hard times they are prepared to undertake any humble form of servitude. I recall the case of Ishak Pasha ('Isach') who was chief Pasha in the time of Bayezid and a great favourite of the Sultan. It was he who had advised Bayezid not to come to terms with his brother Jem ('Zen'); and in his declining years the Sultan granted him the retirement living ('Obturach') of Salonicchi; and there Ishak held court in great style with more than 500 servants, at least 200 of whom wore caps and hats fringed with gold; and in his audience chamber he had hanging from the ceiling a boot made of rough wood ('Carbattina') such as peasants wear instead of the shoe with soles and laces – this being to indicate to his slaves and friends that it was no shame to have risen to such heights from such lowly origins, entirely thanks to the mercy and favour of the Sultan. /

These Turks pay respect to a man according to his rank, dignity and condition. When they go to kiss the Sultan's hand, they have to leave their shoes ('Pasmacchi') outside the ante-chamber. Two of the guards then take them by the hands and they then humbly kiss the carpet. The Sultan gives the signal for the man to be brought forward to kiss either his hand or his foot or whatever; and all these niceties are determined by the rank and status of the suppliant. It is not their custom to take off their turban or hat as a mark of deference or respect as we do, as one gentleman to another or a youth to an old man. They

236

237

bow with their hats on; and they may or may not be allowed to sit down. If you go to kiss the Sultan's hand, you should take gifts; and on leaving you will be presented with a garment ('casacca') or a horse or some other favour. Someone will then approach you and say: 'My friend, the Sultan has given you a present worth 100 ducats more or less'; and he will then offer to buy it from you to the last asper. I have known this happen to foreign ambassadors; and to put it briefly, men are as much after money here as the Devil is after souls; and if you approach any Turkish lord with any request, however small, you will get nothing without a present. If you go to kiss the hand of such a nobleman, you will be permitted either to kiss the outside of it or, if you are more honoured, to kiss its palm. Usually you will be allowed to sit down; and if it seems that you are of no more than equal rank with the gentleman, sit with your legs crossed like a tailor. If your host is a grand prince and you wish to honour him, then sit on the heels and soles of your feet, for such is the customary style of honouring a lord of higher rank than yourself.

They are the most self-indulgent men in the world. They keep many women because their law encourages the propagation of children. / But they also cohabit with quantities of men. For all that Mahomet explicitly forbade sodomy and recommended the stoning of those guilty of it, this vice is commonly and openly practised without fear of God or man.

In matters relating to matrimony the *Naib* ('Naip', 'Naiplic') is an important magistrate. The *Kadi* grants the marriage licence, but then both parties have to give a certain amount of money to the *Naib*; if they do not, he has the power to punish either or both for adultery. If a Christian is caught in a sexual act with a Turkish woman, he can either be lashed or be forced to become a Muslim. I have known of men who have paid 500, 1,000 or even 2,000 ducats to avoid this penalty. If a Christian or a Turk is found in bed with a woman not his wife, he is paraded around the town sitting backwards on an ass with entrails on his head and the animal's tail in his hand. A man of status in these circumstances escapes the penalty and the shame by paying 1,500 ducats. But if the *Naib* finds a man with a boy, the man is fined only five aspers. Thus is the vile sin of sodomy made prevalent throughout Turkey. The women make themselves very provocative and attractive to men by using many perfumes; and men make themselves more sexually active by eating various hot confections that come from India and Syria; and they make many children. I recall seeing a tailor who had forty boys and girls; and if it had not been for the plague he would have had many more. The plague is very common in these parts; but the Turks take no precautions against contagion because they firmly believe in the inescapability of destiny, for good or ill. In the summer they are accustomed to take to the mountains called 'Iaila' with their families, where they can live more freely in the fresh air. / There they drink refreshing beverages called 239 Yogurt ('Iugurth') and Kaimaki ('Caimac') in which they put mountain ice.

[About their religion]

They build their churches more or less square in shape but with no altars like ours. They worship on the ground. Their buildings face not to the east but to the south; and they do not have so many chapels or oratories. Their priests ('Thalassumano')[39] go into the ceremonies washed and barefooted on to a specially decorated carpet called a prayer mat, and they bend down to pray and kiss the carpet. They all wash before praying, thus they believe purifying themselves of sin so that God hears their prayers, which they recite after the priests. They have no images, icons or sculptures. The walls of their churches are bare white; though they do have lamps. The campanile of their churches are round but with no bells. Nor do they allow Christians to ring bells, except in some privileged churches in the countryside. The campanile is topped not with a cross like ours but with a moon; and five times a day and night a priest declaims a prayer which can be heard from far away. And always they pray for division among the Christians; and in this respect their prayers appear to be sadly effective.

The Turks are very observant in their faith. They keep two Lents or Quadragesimos ('Rusi') every year and each one lasts a month. / During these periods they fast most sedulously, eating and drinking nothing from dawn to dusk, patiently enduring hunger and thirst until the appearance of the first star in the evening, when they break their fast and partake of meat and other food in their normal fashion. Not only do they not drink wine, they avoid the places where it is sold; and anyone found drunk during the 'Rusi' is severely punished. Their Easter ('Pascha') is celebrated with great joy and solemnity. The first of their Lents, which is called *Bairam* ('Barian') is generally observed by all for it is an obligation of their law. The second which comes later is called the Little Bairam ('Chazilarbarian') and is observed by all the religious, the *Seids* ('Seiti' [descendants of Mahomet]) as well as the *Hadji* ('Chazi'), or those who have made the pilgrimage to the tomb of Mahomet and gained plenary indulgence therefrom. The *Hadji* are supposed to fast during the Little Bairam ('Churzuchu Barian') for the rest of their lives. They are the equivalent of our pilgrims to Jerusalem. At Mecca, where the prophet's tomb is situated, there is an enclosed market or *bedestan* ('Bazestan') where precious goods such as gold, jewels, silk and slaves can be bought and wealthy Turks can deposit there goods for safe keeping; for most of the *Hadjis* are honest men. They are much respected, for not only have they earned redemption, they have also suffered great hardships on their pilgrimage, not least from thirst. They ride camels in those deserts because of the camels' tolerance of thirst. Their pilgrimage is not really complete unless it takes in also the Temple of Solomon in Jerusalem and Bethlehem where Christ was born. When they get home they are received with great honour and ceremony and almost all the shops are shut; / and they often wear white caps ('fazuoli') such as only the *Seids* wear. There are great numbers of *Hadjis*, for many go out of zeal for their faith and many others simply for show. They are frequently and fervently at their devotions, praying seven times a day and night, five times in church, two at home. They pray much more than Christians do. Their law expressly forbids a Jew or a Christian to talk about anything relating to the Mahometan religion. But they are always keen to bring over a Christian to their faith; and they use various methods, including false testimony to a *Kadi* which results in the Christian being punished and forcibly converted or martyred. Yet they forbid a Jew to become a Muslim; and they rate Christianity to be the next best and truest faith after their own.

They have 124,000 prophets, among them many of the Christian saints like St Peter, St Paul and all the other Apostles, and all the warrior saints like St George etc. They say that there is not one of the Christian saints who has not eaten or drunk with Mahomet; and that our Lord and Redeemer Jesus Christ was not the son or God but made by God; for God has no sons. They believe that Mary was a Virgin. I once saw a Jew in Salonika being beaten for blasphemy; / for they say that it was not Christ that the Jews crucified but another man in his place; and they say that Jesus Christ will come to judge the world with Mahomet beside him and that all devout Muslims will be put among the blessed. A blasphemer against Almighty God is punished with 100 lashes; a blasphemer against Mahomet or one of the prophets is put to death. For their law says that God has a long arm and can easily punish the blasphemer by Himself; but a poor prophet offended or blasphemed against must be protected by the death of the offender. If he is a Christian and repents of his crime he may be spared. But if he is a Turk there is no remedy but death. They do not accept that any woman goes to Paradise, only that the souls of women who have led a holy life go to a certain place where they suffer neither

241

242

good nor evil, while those who have led wicked lives go to eternal fire. They describe their Paradise as a place full of inconceivable delights and pleasures; according to his deserts each man there will have as many virgins as he likes assigned to him every day by God. They hold that Christian monks and nuns flout the divine law to go forth and multiply. All Turks go and marry for this purpose and they take as many wives as they can afford. They can always divorce one and take another; though the rejected wife has a legal claim on her dowry.

The Turks are devoted to washing their hands, their feet, their necks and all the body, including parts which I am ashamed to mention. When they are in Christian lands they like, wherever possible, to liberate birds which they find in cages and to perform other small acts of mercy different from ours. For they are very charitable. They maintain numerous hostelries called *karavansarai* ('Charvassara') where travellers can stay free of charge; they build many bridges over rivers; and hospitals where even those who are not sick can stay and eat free for three days whether they are poor, rich, Christian, Hebrew or Turk. /

243   Among the churches and hospitals in Europe ('Grecia') is that of Mehmed in Constantinople, a superb building, with his tomb nearby. The hospital is open to all, Christians, Jews and Turks; and its doctors give free treatment and food three times a day. I have seen men of the upper class and other grand persons lodging here, their horses being cared for. It has fourteen medical students and they attend lectures from their masters, who are well paid. The official in charge of this great Imaret ('Marath') is called the *Müteveli* ('Mutevoli'). Another great Imaret was begun by Bayezid and completed by Selim. The grandest of them all is [or will be] that begun by Suleiman. These Turks, large and small, are constantly engaged on such pious and charitable works — far more so than we Christians. /

They treat their servants better than we do – for Mahomet decreed   244
that no one should keep a slave for more than seven years, and
few break this commandment; and if someone has a son by a slave
girl, the girl is set free and her son comes into his inheritance like the
rest.

There are those called the *Seids* ('Seiti') who claim direct descent
from Mahomet and are held to be particularly holy. Anyone who
happens to strike a *Seid* has his hand cut off; though if the offender is
a Christian he is put to the flames without hope of pardon. If a *Seid*
commits an offence, he cannot be beaten or put to death. Usually he is
banished from the country or sent to die in prison if his crime is great.
In Turkey the testimony of a woman is held to be invalid, unless she
is the daughter of a *Seid*, in which case her word will be accepted and
believed even against the testimony of a male Christian. These *Seids*
wear turbans of green or white cloth to distinguish them from others;
and they are a perfidious and criminal lot and always looking for a
chance to provoke and antagonise the Christians, of whom they are
great persecutors. In Selim's day things were not so bad and many of
the *Seids* were in fact banished. But since Suleiman came to power, he
being very hostile to the Christians, the situation has changed for the
worse.

The *Kadi* are the judges and great powers in the land. They are
like priests ('Thalasumani') and may be promoted to the dignity of
Kadiasker ('Cadilescher'), as reported above.[39] Each has a magistrate
to assist him called a 'Parachadi', meaning a minor judge. The Kadi
are the Sultan's men and highly revered as representatives of
Mahomet on earth, vested in the robe of God and with supreme
judicial authority. / No *Sanjak bey*, for all the exalted nature of his   245
office, can condemn anyone to death without the permission of the
Kadi. There is one in each of the imperial provinces, and also a *Subaşi*
('Subasci'), who arrests the malefactor, submits him to torture and
elicits a confession of his crime, before taking him to stand trial before

the *Kadi*; and if he is condemned the *Subaşi* puts him to death.[40] The *Kadi* decides in cases of civil discord and administers summary justice, so that a case can be judged and decided in less than three hours. In cases of homicide he can rule that the murderer be handed over to his victim's next-of-kin, who can decide whether he be set free on payment of a fine or put to death in whatever manner they choose. I saw a case in which a woman who had seized the murderer of her son was not content merely with the culprit's death under torture, but tore the heart out of the man's chest and ate it. The *Kadi* forbids the carrying of weapons; but if someone unsheathes a sword against another, they cause him to be stabbed through his flesh and body with daggers and to be led around with these weapons sticking out of him. If one man strikes another and causes blood to flow, or if they injure each other's nose or eyes in fighting, they do not draw swords, not because they are cowards but because they are terrified of the Sultan. If one man gets killed in a fight, which rarely if ever occurs unless they are drunk, those in the neighbourhood are all obliged to hand over the murderer as a prisoner or, if they do not catch him, to pay to the nearest relative of the victim 24,000 aspers as blood money. The *Kadi* also has authority to condemn those who sell goods at more than the market price; and subordinate to him in this respect is an official called *Muhtesib* ('Murthasup') who with his boys patrols the markets checking on weights and measures of bread, meat and other commodities and granting licences to sell goods at correct prices. Offenders are reported to the *Kadi*; and the *Muhtesib* carries out the punishment of beating or slitting the nose of the offender. Another subordinate magistrate is the *Naib* ('Naip') whom we have already mentioned. He metes out punishment to the man or woman taken in adultery.[41] Yet another is the 'Casasso' who arrests persons found without a lamp at night; though the *Subaşi* can punish them only on the authority of the *Kadi*. /

246   To put it briefly, these *Kadi* have complete control, and their status

is very exalted. In the time of Mehmed it was even more so. But in the fourth year of the reign of Bayezid there was an incident that led to some diminution of their authority. As a result they were deprived of their jurisdiction over courtiers and those on the payroll of the Sultan's palace. In Constantinople there are always numbers of *Sanjak Beys* known as *Mulaẓim* ('Manzul'). These are provincial governors who have been transferred and have come to court pending new appointments elsewhere. They have a complement of slaves and servants; and while waiting for their next posting they used to be allotted the office of *Muhtesib* ('Murthasup'), to supervise prices, weights and measures. One such was a *Sanjak Bey* called Ahmed Bey. During his tenure as *Muhtesib* a ship laden with corn came in and he licensed it to sell its cargo on terms which were not satisfactory to a *Kadi*, whose name was 'Chiermastogli'. He was indignant, summoned Ahmed and sentenced him to be beaten for his insubordination. But those assigned to do the beating refused to obey the order, out of respect for the high dignity of Ahmed. The *Kadi* was furious, took off his shoe and made to hit Ahmed in the face with it. Ahmed shouted: 'You stupid Thalassuman, I am a captain of honour with many years of service!' He took the *Kadi* by the beard and shook it so hard that most of it came off in his hand. Had there not been some Pashas present who were friends of Ahmed things might have been worse. The *Kadi* went to the Sultan to complain. But the Pashas saw to it that no witnesses of the incident would testify. The Sultan relieved the *Kadi* of his office and issued a decree, which is still in force, that no *Kadi* thenceforth would have jurisdiction over the stipendiaries of the 'Porte', that is the court. Only the Pashas had that right.

In the provinces the *Sanjak bey* judges over disputes among the Timaratti and *Subaşi*. / In Constantinople judgment rests with their 247 Aga. The most honoured of the *Kadiliks* are those of Constantinople, Bursa, Adrianople and Gallipoli.

137

[Religion]

The four principal religious orders among the Turks are: *Kalenderi* ('Chalenderi' [itinerant dervishes]), 'Divani', 'Isechi', 'Torlacchi'.[42]

The *Kalenderi* let their beards and their hair grow long and they go about dressed in sackcloth or some form of cloak, and some of them in sheepskin with the wool on the outside. They eschew sexual pleasures ('lussuria') and wear iron rings in their ears, which are pierced, and also on their genital organs to prohibit sex, and they wear iron chains on their necks and arms. These are the most honoured and esteemed and are held to be more holy than all the other religious.

The 'Divani' are attired in similar fashion, though without the iron rings in their genitals; and they go about singing their chants and psalms and asking everyone for alms.

Most of the dervishes or religious men are of the lower class of people. Another kind are the 'Seichi'. They are close-shaven and wear woollen turbans and go about with banners demanding alms; and some wear silver rings in their ears; and these too are held in high esteem.

The most numerous of the dervishes are those called the 'Torlacchi'. Their order is comparatively new, having been founded about 120 years ago by one 'Misithorlac' who was flayed alive for having preached that Jesus Christ our Redeemer was God. These go about naked with only a skin to cover their pudenda, though some cover their shoulders with a skin and most carry a cloak of white felt. In the winter they suffer much from colds as a result of going naked; and they heat themselves with hot irons to their temples; their heads and beards are shaven. They live in sorts of communities or convents like our friars; but they are a vicious and wicked lot, given to murder and sodomy; and they are for ever killing people on the streets. Once one of them tried to murder the Sultan. It happened at the time when Bayezid was on his way to attack C[h]imara. His horse was stabbed on a street by a dervish with a knife. A Pasha struck him down with a cudgel. / Bayezid then decreed that all these dervishes must be 248 banned throughout his Empire. Selim, however, judged that by his time they had been punished enough. Some of them wear white caps with brims; most of them wear no hats; some wear a little sort of beret. They demand alms from Christians, Jews and Turks with the greatest impertinence, often thrusting a looking glass at their victims and exhorting them to examine themselves and their souls. They are wont to give you a tomato or a melon and demand an asper in exchange. In the street they carry hatchets in their belts; and some ride asses all day and then commit sex with the beasts in the evening. The Turks do not find this distasteful, for their law allows them to do what they like with anything that they have bought with their own money; and that includes the right to kill slaves that they have bought. They seem to regard their dervishes as more holy the more bestial they are. One of the dervishes found an ass that was not his own, led it to a corner of the street and committed a sexual act with it; he then tied two aspers to its tail as if he were paying a whore; and if anyone objected, his defence was that he had paid for his pleasure at his own expense. Some of these religious men will put a price on the years of service that they have rendered to God and find a buyer who will happily pay up without counting the cost or thinking of reimbursement.

[Marriage]

When a Turk takes a wife, agreement has to be reached with the parents about the amount of money that he offers as dowry to his wife, this being the other way round from our custom. If they are rich they will offer 2,000, 3,000, or 6,000 ducats if poor 25, 50 or 100 ducats. This has to be delivered to the wife's father, as well as beds, blankets, clothing for the wife and furniture for the house; and if she is to be the wife of some nobleman, jewellery, rings, necklaces and so forth. /

249   The wife is not obliged to present any dowry to her husband, though she generally does, and this is taken to her husband's house on the wedding day. The wedding takes place in this manner, though not in a church. The husband chooses a best man ('compar') called the 'Sagdiz', whose job it is to take the ring and to provide the torches and pay the musicians ('Zangistre') or women who dance and sing with various instruments to make the occasion festive and joyful. Preparations begin eight days before the wedding. The betrothed keep their faces covered so that no one can see them; and three or four days before the event the husband and his 'Sagdiz' invite guests who bring their presents. On the day before, the wife's mother anoints her daughter's hair and applies a certain red dye to it as well as to her hands nails and feet. On the day appointed, in agreement with the *Naib*, the magistrate who has been paid his fee, they send suitable presents to the *Kadi*, who prepares the necessary document after the promises have been exchanged. The document is called the 'Cozetto'. The 'Sagdiz' then goes to the bride's house with pipes and drums and, after a reception, her parents hand her over and he takes her off

250   hidden under a baldacchino in a horseback procession. / There is then a feast with dancing and entertainments; and when the guests have gone, the 'Sagdiz' leads the wife to the door of the bedchamber. There the husband asks her to remove the veil that hides her face. She declines; and the wretched man then has to uncover her forcibly which he does quite willingly, for they are a voluptuous lot. She makes to refuse him until he agrees to pay her a sum of money, in addition to the dowry. This fact is announced in the morning by the best man. Then, the marriage being consummated, the guests are assembled and they proceed, led by the bridegroom and his best man to a square ('Meidam') where horse racing takes place. The Turks have such feasts and ceremonies usually only for weddings, for the circumcision of their sons, and for the two easters ('Bariam') which they celebrate. /

A Turk is at liberty to repudiate his wife, though she may keep 251
the dowry and the counter-dowry which he promised her or take the
value in cash . . . A man is also free to take to wife the younger sister
of his previous wife whether she be alive or dead. But he cannot marry
the elder sister if he married the younger one first . . . Turkish men can
have as many wives as they like, as we already remarked; and their
sons, even if born of slaves, succeed to the inheritance and have
their share with the rest.

[Funerals and exequies]

They prepare their sepulchres well in advance of death. They
prefer to be buried in virgin soil and separately from one another.
Like us, they have consecrated ground where you can see cemeteries
and graves alongside each other. The corpse is accompanied to the
grave by many priests ('Thalassumani') and it is carried headfirst as
with the Jews but contrary to Christian usage. The priests chant as
they go: 'God is God and true God and Mahomet is his Prophet.' The
next of kin follow the corpse and, instead of wearing mourning
clothes or veils they wear hats with white stripes like the Armenians
wear; and sometimes they cover their horses with a kind of mantle
called a 'Saisma'. If the deceased was a great lord they parade his
insignia and weapons and standards and put something in the nostrils
of the horses so that they go neighing along the street, indicating that
the animals are mourning his passing; and for a great man they plant
plane trees and flowers at his tomb. The poorer people are buried in
the cemeteries as mentioned above and their graves are marked by a
slab of marble nearby inscribed with Turkish letters. Some tombs are
covered over with pediments. Those of Pashas, Sultans and other
important persons such as those who build mosques and hospitals
are housed in shrines or chapels alongside their charitable buildings;
and every day their vestments and turbans are changed as though

141

they were still alive and flowers of various kinds are placed on them according to the season of the year. They do not wear weeds for long, usually about eight days for parents and friends or three days for great men, although / relatives and especially the mother, sisters and wife of the deceased, accompanied by other friends and relations, will continue to visit the grave and make their own lamentations.

252

— FINIS —

Notes and commentary

1 Angiolello, ed. Ursu, pp. 123–52, gives an account of the Ottoman court, its officials and dignitaries, and of the army which is comparable to though less detailed than that of Spandounes; and, eager though he is to record the stipend or salary paid to each official, he fails to supply a description of the Ottoman coinage and currency. Where relevant, however, I have recorded in the notes the equivalent transliterations of Turkish titles as given by Angiolello. These are added with the letter A. and the page numbers. A. H. Lybyer in his book on *The Government of the Ottoman Empire in the Time of Suleiman the Magnificent* (Cambridge, Mass., 1913) supplies texts of two other similar lists of civil and military officials dating from 1534 and 1537 (Appendix I: pp. 239–61, Appendix II: pp. 262–75). For purposes of comparison, I have inserted references to this work in the notes with the letter L. and the page numbers.

2 See Babinger, *Mehmed*, pp. 456–7.

3 'Chasendarbassi': A. p. 124. L. pp. 127, 244.

4 'Chielerbassi': A. p. 124. L. pp. 125, 127, 244. Spandounes seems to confuse the *Kilerẓi başi* with the *Kiẓlar agasi* (or *Harem agasi*), whom he calls the 'Isaga', who was the black eunuch in charge of the Harem. See below, text p. 208.

5 'Ciesnigiri': A. p. 136.

6 This curious word, also presented by Spandounes in the forms 'Talassumani' and 'Thalassumani', and interpreted to mean 'priests', seems to be a distortion of the word *Danishmend*, signifying a graduate of a *medrese* or seat of learning. Angiolello offers no equivalent. But the term 'Talismani' is offered by L. pp. 205, 244.

7 '4 Viziri': A. p. 130.

8 'Beglierbei': A. pp. 147–8.

9 'Cadilascher': A. p. 131. 'Kaziasker Danishmends': L. pp. 189–91, 217–20, 247.

10 'Defterderi': A.pp. 131–2. L. pp. 167–75, 247.

11 'Nisanzi', 'Lizonsibasi': A. pp. 123–7. L. pp. 182–4, 248.

12 'Vexender': A. p. 133. L. pp. 132, 248.

13 'Gianizzeri': A. pp. 144–5. L. pp. 91–7, 249.

14 *Acemi oglanlar* = foreign youths as novices or recruits. L. pp. 79–82, 254–5.

15 L. pp. 105, 249–50.

16 L. p. 103.

17 'Imiralen': A. pp. 139–40. L. p. 252.

18 'Mutaferica': A. p. 133. L. pp. 129, 250.

19 'Solachi': A. p. 145. L. pp. 129–30.

20 'Capigi': A. pp. 134–6.

21 'Spachiolani': A. p. 137. L. pp. 98–100, 250.

22 'Silicharii', 'Silictari': A. pp. 137–8. L. pp. 98, 127, 250–1.

23 'Olofazi': A. p. 151. L. pp. 98, 105–6, 251. The *Gurebas* or Foreign Legion – 'Carpigit': A. p. 139.

24 'Inichaor': A. p. 142. L. p. 251.

25 *Çavuş*: L. pp. 130, 248.

26 'Ziebezi': A. p. 140.

27 'Sechmenbasi', 'segmen': A. p. 140 n. 2, p. 146. *Segban-basi* = 'master of hounds': L. pp. 96, 132.

28 'Ganzi overo falconieri': A. p. 140. *Chakirji-basi* and *Shahinji-basi*: L. p. 252.

29 'Zagarzi': A. p. 146.

30 'Servanbassi': A. p. 143. 'Carmandari', muleteers: L. p. 251.

31 'Arpaimi' or 'Corptmin': A. p. 143. The *Arpa-emini* were really in charge of forage for the stables. L. p. 132.

32 'Terzi overo sartori': A. p. 142.

33 L. pp. 132, 252.

34 'Musalemi': A. p. 150. L. p. 205.

35 'Prichi'(Peych)': A. p. 147. L. p. 130.

36 'Divaniaversisi': A. p. 132. This passage of the text has been summarised.

37 'Marrani': Jews and Moors from Spain: L. p. 241. The following passage has been summarised.

38 *Seids*: L. pp. 206–7.

39 'Thalasumani' (*Danishmends*): see above n. 6.

40 *Subaşi*: L. pp. 103, 219–20.

41 *Muhtesib* and *Naib*: L. pp. 218, 219.

42 The *Kalenderi* were wandering dervishes. The 'Isachi' or 'Seichi' may mean followers of Şeyh Bedreddin. The 'Torlacchi' were devotees of Torlak Kemal ('Misithorlac'). 'Divani' may be a misinterpretation of 'Mevlevi'. Inalcik, *Ottoman Empire*, pp. 190ff.

III

─────

252–60 [This is a short account of the customs and warfare of the two (Safavid) Kings of Persia Ismail I ('Sac Ismael') and his son Tahmasp ('Sac Tamas') commonly known as 'Sophi'. It is a confused and confusing piece, much of which Spandounes claims to have gleaned from a Mulla ('Mola') in Venice who had been with Ibrahim Pasha in Aleppo in 1533. It confirms that he was finishing writing his work in 'the present year 1538', that being the twenty-seventh year of the

258 life of Tahmasp (who succeeded his father Ismail in 1524). He also comments on the 'feudal' composition of the Persian army and society, which is more like the Christian than the Turkish, for the Turks have no feudal system. 'A unique case was that of Ahmed

259 Pasha ("Acmat bassa"), who held Argos in feudum from Selim. After Ahmed's revolt, Suleiman transferred the property to Ibrahim Pasha as a hereditary holding; although after Ibrahim's death it was bestowed on none else'. But in Persia there are many lords who own hereditary feudal holdings, and they are called 'Turcomani'.

This section concludes with a brief account of Suleiman's capture of Tabriz and Baghdad, and of the temporary Persian recovery of Tabriz. This is merely a repetition of pp. 196–7 of the earlier text.]

IV
_____

[In conclusion and in defence of the accuracy of his information, Spandounes makes much of the fact that it is based on the Turkish sources ('annali di Turchi') in contrast to the works of other writers who have relied on accounts emanating from Germany, Poland and other sources. These exaggerate the number of successive Sultans (up to and including Suleiman), whereas the Turkish annalists list only ten. They also say that Murad (I) ('Amurath') was the first Turkish Emperor to cross over to Greece, whereas it was in fact his father Orhan. He mentions an eye-witness account by Laonikos Chalkokondyles 'the Athenian' of the battle at Varna (in 1444), which is surely a fabrication; nor can one believe his statement that Chalkokondyles was a 'secretary' of Murad II; and he counters the criticism made by some that he does not mention the defeat of Sigismond. His reason for not doing so was because the 'annali di Turchi' make no mention of such an event. He accuses other writers of misrepresenting the amount of revenue of the Turkish state.

Finally, he apologises for his simple and illiterate style of writing, for he was never a writer by profession. He has merely done his best to record the essential facts in general terms.]

Bibliography

I SOURCES

A GREEK

[Gy. Moravsik, *Byzantinoturcica*, 3rd edn, 2 vols., I: *Die Byzantinischen Quellen der Geschichte der Türkvölker*, II: *Sprachreste der Türkvölker in den Byzantinischen Quellen* (Berlin and Leiden, 1983).]

Chalkokondyles, Laonikos, *Histories*, ed. E. Darkó, *Laonici Chalcocondylae Historiarum Demonstrationes*, 2 vols. (Budapest, 1922–7); ed. I. Bekker (*CSHB*, 1843). English translation and commentary (Books I–III) by N. Nicoloudis (Historical Monographs 16: Athens, 1996).

Chronica Byzantina breviora: Die byzantinischen Kleinchroniken, ed. P. Schreiner, 3 vols. (*CFHB*, XII/1–3: Vienna, 1975–9).

[The Short Chronicles provide valuable chronological notes and information about many of the events and Turkish conquests of the fourteenth to sixteenth centuries.]

Chronicle of the Turkish Sultans. Χρονικὸν περὶ τῶν Τούρκων Σουλτάνων, ed. G. T. Zoras (Athens, 1958); Elizabeth A. Zachariadou, 'Τὸ Χρονικὸ τῶν Τούρκων Σουλτάνων (τοῦ Βαρβερινοῦ Ἑλληνικοῦ κώδικα III) καὶ τὸ Ἰταλικό του πρότυπο', *Hellenika*, suppl. 14 (Athens, 1960).

Hellenika, suppl. 14 (Athens, 1960).

[An anonymous Greek chronicle of the sixteenth century, covering the years from 1371 to 1512, although in its original form it went from 1288 (Osman) to 1519 (Selim I). Moravcsik, *Byzantinoturcica*, I, pp. 296–7.]

Doukas (Ducas), *Istoria Turco-Bizantină (1341–1462)*, ed. V. Grecu (Bucharest, 1958).

[Moravcsik, *Byzantinoturcica*, I, pp. 247–51.]

Ecthesis Chronica ("Εκθεσις Χρονική), ed. S. P. Lambros, *Ecthesis Chronica and Chronicon Athenarum* (London, 1902).

[An anonymous Greek Chronicle of the sixteenth century narrating political events from 1391 to 1517 (in some manuscripts) or to 1453 (in others). For the earlier part the author seems to have used the histories of Doukas and Sphrantzes. Written in demotic Greek, it is in effect a more popular version of the *Historia Politica*. Moravcsik, *Byzantinoturcica*, I, pp. 251–2.]

Bibliography

Hierax Megas Logothetes, *Chronicle concerning the Empire of the Turks*, ed. C. Sathas, Μεσαιωνικὴ Βιβλιοθήκη, I (Venice, 1872), pp. 243–68. [Hierax, Grand Logothete of the church, lived in Constantinople at the end of the sixteenth century. His Chronicle is in 743 lines of verse and covers the period from 1300 to the reign of the Sultan Mehmed II in 1461. It has no independent historical value. Moravcsik, *Byzantinoturcica*, I, p. 293.]

Historia Politica et Patriarchica Constantinopoleos, ed. I. Bekker (Bonn, 1849), pp. 3–77, 78–204. [An anonymous Greek Chronicle of the sixteenth century narrating political and ecclesiastical events in the Byzantine world from 1399 to 1520 with a continuation to 1570. The section about the Patriarchate was translated into 'the common tongue' by Manuel Malaxos for the scholar Martin Crusius in 1577; the political section was translated for the same Crusius by Theodosios Zygomalas in 1578. Moravcsik, *Byzantinoturcica*, I, pp. 296, 412–13.]

Kritoboulos of Imbros, *Critobuli Imbriotae Historiae*, ed. V. Grecu (Bucharest, 1963); ed. D. R. Reinsch (*CFHB*, XXII: Berlin and New York, 1983). [Kritoboulos dedicated his *Histories* of the years from 1451 to 1467 to the Sultan Mehmed II, whom he much admired. Moravcsik, *Byzantinoturcica*, I, pp. 432–5.]

Miklosich, F., and Müller, J., *Acta et Diplomata Graeca medii aevi sacra et profana*, 6 vols. (Vienna, 1860–90).

Nikandros Noukios (Nicander Nucius) of Corfu, ed. J.-A. de Foucault, *Nicandre de Corcyre, Voyages* (Paris, 1962).

Pachymeres, George, *Histories*, ed. I. Bekker, 2 vols. (*CSHB*, 1835).

Sphrantzes, George, *Chronicon minus*, ed. V. Grecu, *Georgios Sphrantzes, Memorii 1401–1477. In anexă Pseudo-Phrantzes: Macarie Melissenos, Chronica 1258–1481* (Bucharest, 1966). [George Sphrantzes served the Emperors Manuel II and Constantine XI as a statesman and diplomat and his memoirs are thus based on much personal knowledge and experience. They were recycled, expanded and continued in a less reliable manner in the 1570s (the *Chronicon maius*) by Makarios Melissenos of Monemvasia. Moravcsik, *Byzantinoturcica*, I, pp. 282–8.]

B   ITALIAN

[A. Pertusi, 'I primi studi in Occidente sull'origine e la potenza dei Turchi', *Studi Veneziani*, 12 (1970), 465–552; A. Pertusi, *La Caduta di Costantinopoli*, 2 vols. (Verona, 1976).]

Angiolello, Giovanni Maria, of Vicenza, *Historia turchesca, 1300–1514*, ed., under the name of Donado da Lezze, Ion Ursu (Bucharest, 1909). [Pertusi, 'I primi studi', 480–2.]

Barletius, Marinus, *Historia de Vita et Gestis Scanderbegi Epirotarum Principis*, 1st edn (Rome, 1509 or 1510).

Bibliography

Marini Barletii de obsidione Scodrensi ad Serenissimum Leonardum Laurentanum Aristocratiae Venetae principem (Venice, 1504).
[In Sansovino (1654), pp. 300–21. See F. Pall, 'Marino Barlezio', in *Mélanges d'histoire générale*, ed. C. Marinescu (Paris, 1938), pp. 146–9.]

Bosio, Iacomo, *Dell' Istoria della sacra religione et Illustrissima Militia di San Giovanni Gierosolomitano* (Rome, 1594).

Cambini, Andrea Fiorentino, *Della Origine de' Turchi et imperio delli Othomani* (Florence, 1529).
[In Sansovino (1654), pp. 141–81.]

Giovio, Paolo (Paulus Iovius), *Commentario de la cose de' Turchi di Paulo Iovio, Vescovo di Nocera, a Carlo Quinto Imperatore Augusto* (Rome, n.d., but between 1526 and 1531).
[Other editions of the same: Venice, 1540, 1541. In Sansovino (1654), pp. 226–45.]
Turcicarum rerum Commentarius Pauli Jovii episcopi Nucerini ad Carolum V. imperatorem Augustum, ex Italico Latinus factus, Francisco Nigro Bassianate interprete. Origo Turcici Imperii. Vitae omnium Turcicorum Imperatorum. Ordo et disciplina Turcicae militiae exactissime conscripta, eodem Paulo Iovio autore. Addita est praefatio Philippi Melan[chthon] (Wittenberg, 1537).
[Other editions of the same: Paris, 1538, 1540.]

Predelli, R., ed., *I Libri Commemoriali della Republica di Venezia, Regesti*, 6 vols. (Venice, 1876–8).

Sagundino, Nicola, *Othomanorum familia seu de Turcarum imperio Historia, N. Secundino autore* (Vienna, 1551).
[Pertusi, 'I primi studi', 471; Pertusi, *La Caduta*, II, pp. 126–41.]

Sansovino, Francesco, *Gl' Annali Turcheschi overo Vite de principi della casa Othomana* (Venice, 1573).
Historia Universale dell' origine, guerre, et imperio de Turchi (Venice, 1654): *Trattato di Theodoro Spandugino Cantacusino* (pp. 107–31); *Vita di Sach Ismail, et Tamas Re di Persia, chiamato Soffi, di Theodoro Spandugino* (pp. 132–40); *Discorso di Teodoro Spandugino Cantacusino Gentil'homo Costantinopolitano Dall' origine de' principi Turchi* (pp. 182–207).
[Sansovino's collection of the earliest *Annali turcheschi* was first printed in Venice in 1560 and thereafter in seven more editions up to 1654.]

Sanuto, Marino, *I Diarii*, ed. N. Barozzi, G. Berchet, R. Fulin, F. Stefano, 58 vols. (Venice, 1879–1903).

Spandounes, Theodore, *Theodoro Spandugnino, Patritio Constantinopolitano, De la origine deli Imperatori Ottomani, ordini dela corte, forma del guerregiare loro, religione, rito, et costumi de la natione*, ed. C. N. Sathas, Μνημεῖα Ἑλληνικῆς Ἱστορίας. *Documents inédits relatifs à l'histoire de la Grèce au moyen âge*, IX (Paris, 1890), pp. iii–l (Preface), pp. 133–261 (text).
[Earlier partial editions of the text: Lucca, 1550, Florence, 1551. The French translation of the first draft of the treatise (1519) was published by C. H. A. Schefer, *Petit traicté de l'origine des Turcqz par Théodore Spandouyn Cantacasin*

Bibliography

(Paris, 1896). Thirty-eight folios of its first Italian version are printed in Villain-Gandossi, 'La cronaca italiana di Teodoro Spandugino'.]

C   TURKISH

[F. Babinger, *Die Geschichtsschreiber der Osmanen und ihre Werke* (Leipzig, 1927); A. Bombaci, *Storia della letteratura turca* (Milan, 1956); V. L. Ménage, 'The Beginnings of Ottoman Historiography', in *Historians of the Middle East*, ed. B. Lewis and P. M. Holt (London, 1962), pp. 168–79.]

Ashik Pasha-zade, *Story of the House of Osman*, ed. F. Giese, *Die altosmanische Chronik des Ašikpašazade auf Grund mehrerer und neuentdeckter Handschriften von neueren herausgegeben* (Leipzig, 1929); German translation by R. F. Kreutel, *Vom Hirtenzeit zur Hohen Pforte* (Graz, 1959).

[An anecdotal and often fantastic account up to the death of Mehmed II in 1481.]

Ibn Kemal Pasha-zade, *Story of the Dynasty of Osman*, ed. S. Turan (Ankara, 1954–7).

[The *Story* originally ended at 1510–11 but, at the Sultan Suleiman's request, it was continued up to the battle of Mohacs in 1526. It was heavily indebted to the *History* of Tursun Beg. Babinger, *Geschichtsschreiber*, pp. 26–7; Bombaci, *Storia*, pp. 345–6, 360–98.]

Khodja (Efendi) Sa'd ed-Din, *The Diadem of History* (Constantinople, 1862).

[His dates (1536–7 to 1599) exclude the possibility of his work having been available to Spandounes.]

Mehmed Neshri, *History of the Ottomans* or *Book of the Description of the World*, ed. F. Taeschner, *Ĝihannüma. Die altosmanische Chronik des Mevlana Mehemmed Neschri*, 2 vols. (Leipzig, 1951–5).

[Neshri, who wrote his account in the early years of the reign of Bayezid II (1481–1512) and died in the reign of Selim I (1512–20), was the most influential of the early Ottoman historians. V. L. Ménage, *Neshri's History of the Ottomans. The Sources and Development of the Text* (London, 1964).]

Tursun Beg, *History of the Sultan Mehmed II the Conqueror. Tarich-i ebul'feth sultan Mehmed chan*, ed. M. Arif (Istanbul, 1330 (= 1914)), pp. 36–57.

[Tursun Beg presents a highly literary and rhetorical account of Mehmed II and of the first six years of the reign of Bayezid II, composed towards the end of the fifteenth century. He was present at the siege of Constantinople in 1453. Bombaci, *Storia*, pp. 354–6, 360–89.]

D   OTHER

Busac, Hugues, 'Informations sur la très illustre lignée des Cantacuzènes, de Carola Cantacuzène de Flory, fille de l'illustre Conte de Jaffa, et de ses enfants', ed. V. Laurent, in E. Brayer, P. Lemerle and V. Laurent, 'Le

150

Bibliography

Vaticanus Latinus 4789: histoire et alliances des Cantacuzènes au
XIVᵉ–XVᵉ siècles', *Revue des études byzantines*, 9 (1952), pp. 70–7.

Constantine of Ostrovica, *Memoirs of a Janissary*, trs. by B. Stolz, with historical
commentary and notes by S. Soucek (Michigan Slavic Translations, 2: Ann
Arbor, Mich., 1975); German trs. by Renate Lachmann as *Memoiren eines
Janitscharen oder Türkische Chronik*, with commentary by R. Lachmann,
C.-P. Haase, G. Prinzing (Slavische Geschichtsschreiber, VIII: Graz,
Vienna and Cologne, 1975).
[Pertusi, 'I primi studi', 482–4.]

Felix Ragusinus (Felix Petancić), *Historia turcica* (uned.); *De origine et militari
disciplina magni Turce domi forisque habitata libellus* (ed. 1530).
[Pertusi, 'I primi studi', 489–92.]

George of Hungary, *Tractatus de moribus condicionibus et nequicia Turcorum*
(1st edn, Rome, 1480; another edn, Paris, 1514; German translation, with
Preface by Martin Luther, published in Wittenberg, 1539).
[J. A. B. Palmer, in *Bulletin of the John Rylands Library*, 34 (1951–2), 44–68.]

Massarellus, Angelus, 'Dell'Imperadori Constantinopolitani' (uned.), in Codex
Vaticanus Latinus 12127, fols. 349ᵛ–353.

Musachi, Giovanni, *Historia e Genealogia della casa Musachi, scritta da D. Giovanni
Musachio Despoto dell'Epiro*, ed. C. Hopf, *Chroniques gréco-romanes inédites
ou peu connues* (Berlin, 1873).

II SECONDARY WORKS

Arnakis, G. G., Οἱ Πρῶτοι 'Οθωμανοί. Συμβολὴ εἰς τὸ πρόβλημα τῆς
πτώσεως τοῦ Ἑλληνισμοῦ τῆς Μικρᾶς 'Ασίας (1282–1337) (Texte und
Forschungen zur Byzantinisch-Neugriechischen Philologie, 41: Athens,
1947).

Babinger, F., *Die Geschichtsschreiber der Osmanen und ihre Werke* (Leipzig,
1927).
  Mehmed the Conqueror and his Time, trans. R. Manheim, ed. W. C. Hickman
  (Princeton, N.J., 1978).

Barker, J. W., *Manuel II Palaeologus (1391–1425). A Study in Late Byzantine
Statesmanship* (New Brunswick, N.J., 1968).

Beldiceanu, N., 'La conquête des cités marchandes de Kilia et de Cetatea Albă
par Bayezid II', *Süd-ost Forschungen*, 23 (1964), 36–90.

Beldiceanu, N., and Beldiceanu-Steinherr, I., 'Un Paléologue inconnu de la
région de Serrès', *Byzantion*, 41 (1971), pp. 7–17.

Bombaci, A., *Storia della letteratura turca* (Milan, 1956); French translation by
I. Mélikoff, *Histoire de la littérature turque* (Paris, 1968).

Bon, A., *La Morée franque*, 2 vols. (Paris, 1969).

Bouras, Ch., Τὸ ἐπιτύμβιο τοῦ Λουκᾶ Σπανδούνη στὴ βασιλικὴ του
'Αγίου Δημητρίου Θεσσαλονίκης, 'Επιστημονικὴ 'Επετηρὶς τῆς

Bibliography

Πολυτεχνικῆς Σχολῆς, VI: Τμῆμα 'Αρχιτεκτόνων (Thessaloniki, 1973), pp. 3–63.

Burski, H. A. von, *Kemal Reʾis. Ein Beitrag zur Geschichte der türkischen Flotte* (Bonn, 1928).

Buschausen, H. and H., *Die Marienkirche von Apollonia in Albanien* (Byzantina Vindobonensia, VIII: Vienna, 1976).

Cogo, G., 'La guerra di Venezia contro i Turchi (1499–1501)', *Nuovo Archivio Veneto*, 18 (1899), 1–76, 348–421; 19 (1900), 97–138.

Dölger, F., *Regesten der Kaiserurkunden des oströmischen Reiches*, V: *1341–1453* (Munich and Berlin, 1965).

Ducellier, A., *La façade maritime de l'Albanie au moyen âge: Durazzo et Valona du XIᵉ au XVᵉ siècle* (Thessaloniki, 1981).

Encyclopaedia of Islam, 4 vols., ed. T. W. Arnold *et al.* (Leiden, 1913–34); new edn, ed. H. A. R. Gibb *et al.* (Leiden, 1960–).

Fassoulakis, S., *The Byzantine Family of Raoul-Ral(l)es* (Athens, 1973).

Ferjančić, B., *Vizantijski i Srpski Ser u XIV stolecu* (*Byzantine and Serbian Serres in the Fourteenth Century*) (Posebna izdana Srpska Akademija nauka, DCXXIX, 21: Belgrade, 1994).

Fisher, S. N., *The Foreign Relations of Turkey 1481–1512* (Illinois Studies in the Social Sciences, XXX, 1: Urbana, Ill., 1948).

Geanakoplos, D. J., *Emperor Michael Palaeologus and the West, 1258–1282. A Study in Late Byzantine–Latin Relations* (Cambridge, Mass., 1959).

Gegaj, A., *L'Albanie et l'invasion turque au XVᵉ siècle* (Louvain, 1937).

Gibbons, H. A., *The Foundation of the Ottoman Empire. A History of the Osmanlis up to the Death of Bayezid I, 1300–1453* (Oxford, 1916).

Grey, C., trans., *A Narrative of Italian Travels in Persia in the Fifteenth and Sixteenth Centuries* (Hakluyt Society: London, 1873).

Guilland, R., *Titres et fonctions de l'Empire byzantin* (Collected Studies: London, 1976).

Harris, J. P., 'A Worthless Prince? Andreas Palaeologus in Rome – 1464–1502', *Orientalia Christiana Periodica*, 41 (1995), 537–54.

Imber, C., *The Ottoman Empire, 1300–1481* (Istanbul, 1990).

Inalcik, H., *The Ottoman Empire. The Classical Age 1300–1600* (London, 1973).
'The Policy of Mehmed II toward the Greek Population of Istanbul and the Byzantine Buildings in the City', *Dumbarton Oaks Papers*, 23–4 (1969–70), 231–49.

Jireček, C. J., *Istorija Srba*, ed. J. Radonić, I–II (Belgrade, 1952).

Jorga, N., *Byzance après Byzance* (Bucharest, 1935).

Laiou, Angeliki E., *Constantinople and the Latins. The Foreign Policy of Andronicus II, 1282–1328* (Cambridge, Mass., 1972).

Lybyer, A. H., *The Government of the Ottoman Empire in the Time of Suleiman the Magnificent* (Harvard Historical Studies, XVIII: Cambridge, Mass., 1913).

McLeod, W., 'Castles of the Morea in 1467', *Byzantinische Zeitschrift*, 65 (1972), 353–63.

Ménage, V. L., 'The Beginnings of Ottoman Historiography', in *Historians of the Middle East*, ed. B. Lewis and P. M. Holt (London, 1962), pp. 168–79.

Merriman, R. B. M., *Suleiman the Magnificent, 1520–1566* (Cambridge, Mass., 1944).

Miller, W., *The Latins in the Levant. A History of Frankish Greece (1204–1566)* (London, 1908).

Moravcsik, Gy., *Byzantinoturcica*, 3rd edn, 2 vols., I: *Die Byzantinischen Quellen der Geschichte der Türkvölker*; II: *Sprachreste der Türkvölker in den Byzantinischen Quellen* (Berlin and Leiden, 1983).

Nicol, D. M., *The Byzantine Family of Kantakouzenos (Cantacuzenus) ca. 1100–1460. A Genealogical and Prosopographical Study* (Dumbarton Oaks Studies, XI: Washington, DC, 1968).

  The Byzantine Lady. Ten Portraits 1250–1500 (Cambridge, 1994).

  The Despotate of Epiros, II: *1267–1479. A Contribution to the History of Greece in the Middle Ages* (Cambridge, 1984).

  The Immortal Emperor. The Life and Legend of Constantine Palaiologos, Last Emperor of the Romans (Cambridge, 1992).

  'The Last Byzantine Rulers of Monemvasia', in *Travellers and Officials in the Peloponnese*, ed. Haris A. Kalligas (Monemvasia, 1994), pp. 62–7.

  The Last Centuries of Byzantium, 1261–1453, 2nd edn (Cambridge, 1993).

  Meteora. The Rock Monasteries of Thessaly, 3nd edn (London, 1975).

  The Reluctant Emperor. A Biography of John Cantacuzene, Byzantine Emperor and Monk, c. 1295–1383 (Cambridge, 1996).

Nicoloudis, N., *Laonikos Chalkokondyles. A Translation and Commentary of the 'Demonstrations of Histories' (Books I–III)* (Athens, 1996).

  Ἐπιδράσεις τῶν "'Αποδείξεων 'Ιστορίων" τοῦ Λαονίκου Χαλκοκονδύλη στὸ ἔργο τοῦ Θ. Σπανδούνη, *Hellenic Historical Society: 14th Panhellenic Historical Conference* (Thessaloniki, 1994), 135–42.

Noli, F. S., *George Castrioti Scanderbeg 1403–1468* (New York, 1947).

Ostrogorsky, G., *Serska oblast posle Dušanove smrti (La principauté serbe de Serrès)* (Posebna izdana Vizontološkog Instituta, 9: Belgrade, 1965).

Papadopulos, A. Th., *Versuch einer Genealogie der Palaiologen, 1259–1453* (Munich, 1938).

Pertusi, A., *La Caduta di Constantinopoli*, 2 vols. (Verona, 1976).

  'I Primi studi in Occidente sull'origine e la potenza dei Turchi', *Studi Veneziani*, 12 (1970), 465–552.

Polemis, D. I., *The Doukai. A Contribution to Byzantine Prosopography* (London, 1968).

Prosopographisches Lexikon der Palaiologenzeit, ed. E. Trapp, H.-V. Beyer, R. Walther, *et al.* (Österreichische Akademie der Wissenschaften, Kommission für Byzantinistik: Vienna, 1976–).

Bibliography

Runciman, S., *The Fall of Constantinople 1453* (Cambridge, 1965).

The Great Church in Captivity. A Study of the Patriarchate of Constantinople from the Eve of the Turkish Conquest to the Greek War of Independence (Cambridge, 1968).

Schwoebel, R., *The Shadow of the Crescent. The Renaissance Image of the Turk* (Nieuwkoop, 1967).

Setton, K. M., *Catalan Domination of Athens, 1311–1388*, 2nd edn (London, 1975).

The Papacy and the Levant (1204–1571), 4 vols., I: *The Thirteenth and Fourteenth Centuries*; II: *The Fifteenth Century*; III: *The Sixteenth Century to the Reign of Julius III*; IV: *The Sixteenth Century from Julius III to Pius V* (The American Philosophical Society: Philadelphia, 1976–84).

Thuasne, L., *Djem-Sultan, fils de Mohammed II, frère de Bayezid II (1459–1495) . . . Etude sur la question d'Orient à la fin du XVᵉ siècle* (Paris, 1892).

Vakalopoulos, A. E., Ἱστορία τῆς Θεσσαλονίκης, *316 BC–1983* (Thessaloniki, 1983).

Ἱστορία τοῦ Νεοελληνισμοῦ, 4 vols. (Thessaloniki, 1968–74).

Villain-Gandossi, 'La cronaca italiana di Teodoro Spandugino', *Il Veltro. Rivista della civiltà italiana*, 2–4, anno XXIII (Rome, 1979), 151–71; reprinted in C. Villain-Gandossi, *La Méditerranée aux XIᵉ–XVIᵉ siècles* (Collected Studies: London, 1983), no. III.

Weiss, G., *Joannes Kantakuzenos – Aristokrat, Staatsmann, Kaiser und Mönch – in der Gesellschaftsentwicklung von Byzanz im 14. Jahrhundert* (Wiesbaden, 1969).

Woodhouse, C. M., *George Gemistos Plethon. The Last of the Hellenes* (Oxford, 1986).

Zachariadou, Elizabeth A., *Trade and Crusade. Venetian Crete and the Emirates of Menteshe and Aydin (1300–1415)* (Venice, 1983).

Zakythinos, D. A., *Le Despotat grec de Morée*, 2 vols., I: *Histoire politique*; II: *Vie et institutions*, édition revue et augmentée par Chryssa Maltézou (London, 1975).

Index

Index

Index

Ducaginogli 63
Durazzo 60

eating habits 127
Edirne (Adrianople) 22
Egypt 56, 69–70, 114, 122
Eirene Branković née Cantacuzene 29, 31, 39, 40
election of Popes 11–12
Epiros 26, 27–8
    see also Albania
eunuchs 110–13
Evrenes (lord of the Turks) 15

Fait bassa 49–50
fasting 132
Ferdinand I, Archduke of Austria 71, 72
Ferdinand I, King of Aragon and Naples 43, 49–51
Ferhad Pasha 65
Ferrante Gonzaga, viceroy of Sicily 79
fleet 21, 126
Flory, Carola Cantacuzène de xviii
food 127
foodtasters 111–12
footmen 119
Franco Acciajuoli, Duke of Athens 38
fratricide 17–18
Frederick (Federigo), King of Naples 49
Friuli 48, 57
funerals 141–2

Gaetano (Cardinal Tommaso de Vio, Bishop of Gaeta) 69
Gallipoli 19, 49
gatekeepers 119
Gedik Ahmed Pasha (Gidi Cadmath bassa) 50–1, 53
Gedik Mustafa 55
Genoa 19, 32
George Branković, Despot (son of Stephen) 39–40
George (Jurgo) Branković, Despot in Serbia 29, 31, 35, 38–9
George Črnojević, lord of Kotor 56
George Glava (Glabas), lord of Didymoteichon 20
George of Hungary (Brother George) xxv–xxvi
George Palaiologos Cantacuzene (Sachatai) xvi–xvii, 29, 35
Ghazali (Gazeli) 65

Giangiorgio, Marquis of Montferrat 60
Gin Cantacuzene see Manuel Cantacuzene
Gin Spata 26, 27
Giorgio Buzardo 57
Giovanni IV Crispi, Duke of Naxos 77
Giovio, Paolo xxiv
Girolamo Novella (Count Hieronymo di Verona) 48
Golemo Arianiti 47
Gonsalvo Fernando de Cordova, Duke 59, 60
government officials 113–21
governors
    Beylerbeys 114–15
    Sanjak beys 114, 124–5, 137
Grand Aga 117, 118
Grand Sachatai (Tamburlan Sachatai), Emperor of the Tartars 23–4
Greece 114
Gregory (Grgur/Curgur) Branković, Despot 31, 39, 40
Grimani, Antonio 57
Grimani, Marco 78
Gritti, Andrea 62
Gritti, Lodovico (Alvise) 73

Hadim Suleiman Pasha (Ali Eunucho) 48
Hadrian VI, Pope x, 34, 66, 67, 69
Hali Bassa Eunucho (Ali Pasha) 60, 63
harem 111, 112–13, 129
Hass Murad Pasha xviii
Helena Palaiologos 38
Helene Cantacuzene, Empress 41
Hexamilion wall 29, 42
Hieronymo di Verona, Count (Girolamo Novella) 48
Horestiade see Adrianople (Edirne)
hospitals 134
household officials 110–12
Hungary 21, 35, 45, 65–6, 70–1, 72, 120

Iancho Vaivoda (John Hunyadi) 45
Ibrahim Pasha 70, 73, 74–5, 115, 144
Innocent VIII, Pope 55
Ioannina see Janina
Ionusbei Dragomano (Yunus Bey) 76
Isaac (nephew of Alexios Komnenos) 11
Isechi 138
Ishak Pasha xvi, 129
Isidoro Scandali (Nicholas Skandalis) 72
Iskender Bey (Schender bassa) 48, 57

Index

Index

Index

Index

Made in the USA
Lexington, KY
18 October 2014